HEGEL, FREEDOM, AND MODERNITY

SUNY Series in
Hegelian Studies

William Desmond, Editor

HEGEL, FREEDOM, AND MODERNITY

Merold Westphal

STATE UNIVERSITY OF NEW YORK PRESS

Production by Ruth Fisher
Marketing by Dana E. Yanulavich

Published by
State University of New York Press, Albany

For information, address the State University of New York Press,
State University Plaza, Albany, NY 12246

Library of Congress Cataloging-in-Publication Data

Westphal, Merold.
    Hegel, freedom, and modernity / Merold Westphal.
        p.   cm. — (SUNY series in Hegelian studies)
    Includes bibliographical references and index.
    ISBN 0-7914-1015-3 (alk. paper). — ISBN 0-7914-1016-1 (pbk. :
alk. paper)
    1. Hegel, Georg Wilhelm Friedrich, 1770–1831—Views on freedom.
2. Hegel, Georg Wilhelm Friedrich, 1770–1831—Religion.
3. Modernism.   I. Title.   II. Series.
B2949.F7W47   1992
193—dc20   91-18876
                                                                         CIP

10 9 8 7 6 5 4 3 2 1

CONTENTS

PREFACE

Hegel is above all else a philosopher of freedom in the modern world. In the title of his splendid book on the culmination of Hegel's system, *Hegels Lehre vom absoluten Geist als theologisch-politischer Traktat,* Michael Theunissen points to the most important dialectical feature of Hegel's theory of freedom. It is a kind of political theology, a theory in which religion and society are always treated as inseparable. Having seen the two happily married in ancient Greece, only to be painfully divorced later on, Hegel believes he finds a happy reunion in the reconciliation of Christianity with modernity. The essays that make up this volume explore the political and religious dimensions of Hegel's theory of freedom in the modern world.

But the portrait he took to be a celebration of modernity now looks to us later moderns to be at least as much a critique of modernity. So perhaps it is not a coincidence that the time in which Hegel has exploded from oblivion (in the English-speaking world) to regain a major place in the philosophical canon has also been a time in which modernity has become increasingly problematic to us moderns, a time in which we have become less confident in our understanding of freedom and less complacent about our practice of freedom. The essays that make up this volume also explore the tension between celebration and critique in Hegel's theory of freedom in the modern world.

I speak of us moderns because I cannot deny my modernity any more than I can deny my Americanness. But these essays were written during years when my identity as a American became increasingly problematic and when I came to see modernity as the larger context of my ambivalence. I was (and am) proud to be an American. But I came to be (and remain) ashamed of much that America does and stands for. At times my country has been the embodiment of its lofty ideals of "liberty and justice for all"; but at other times it has been their betrayal. My suspicion is that this ambiguity of the American experiment has its roots in the liberal modernism that is its ideology.

I cannot say that Hegel was the catalyst of my discomfort. That role has been played by the events of our recent history and by my attempts to make biblical faith my own. But I can say that Hegel has been enormously helpful to me as I have worked through these issues, even where I find his own views problematic. For I invariably find insight in his thinking, even when it is accompanied by oversight.

"Hegel's Theory of the Concept" is a good place to begin. The astonishing interplay between the Logic (both versions) and *The Philosophy of Right* calls our attention both to the familiar fact that the *Realphilosophie* presupposes the Logic and to the astonishing fact that the converse is equally true. Not only is the Logic fundamental to the System as a whole, but already the Logic is a theory of freedom.

What is more, it is a theory of freedom diametrically opposed to the identification, so basic to modern, liberal sensibility, of freedom with independence. By making friendship and love the keys to understanding freedom, Hegel defines it not merely as a mode of intersubjectivity but more concretely as a mode of interdependence. Freedom is to be understood as the paradoxical identification with an Other whose otherness is not compromised thereby. Neither party is absorbed into the other; they remain two, and yet they are one.

"Hegel, Human Rights, and the Hungry" shows Hegel affirming both subsistence rights and property rights. For liberalism these two tend to fall apart, with property rights dramatically curtailing if not entirely abolishing subsistence rights. But for Hegel it is just the reverse. Property rights are *aufgehoben* in a larger context that includes subsistence rights, providing important substance to Hegel's refusal to identify freedom with independence.

The full theory of community presupposed by these moves is not developed until the next chapter, but here we find one of its most crucial elements, the primacy of spirit in Hegel's social theory. Among the major philosophers before Marx, perhaps only Aristotle and Locke make economic matters as central to their thought as does Hegel. And yet we find him here (like Aristotle and against Locke) decisively putting economic pursuits in their place. The consumerism into which liberal modernity has increasingly degenerated is subjected to compelling critique in an argument that puts the Hegelian method of working from abstract to concrete in the service of a humanistic vision that refuses to bow down and worship at the temple of Productivity. Neither use values nor exchange values are the highest values.

"Hegel's Radical Idealism: Family and State as Ethical Communities" pursues the critique of liberalism by contrasting its contractual model of intersubjectivity with a communitarian model. This is developed first in the context of the family, where marriage is presented as a contract to transcend the standpoint of contract. Here sex is given an almost sacramental significance and at the same time decisively put in its place, a subordinate place quite different from the place of primacy increasingly given to it by modern societies. The parallel between what happens to sex in this chapter and what happened to economic values in the previous one is striking.

But the main theme is the affirmation of community as a higher value. Here the crucial and central concept of *Sittlichkeit* is introduced and expounded. While a civil society in which economic needs and contractual relations is included under this heading, *Sittlichkeit* or ethical community finds its fulfillment in the state as the *Aufhebung* of civil society. Hegel makes it clear that by the state he does not mean the government or the party over against the people but a nonindividualist and noninstrumentalist way in which a people constitute themselves and establish their political and economic institutions.

If Hegel's view of the kind of institutions that would realize his alternative to liberal modernity—for example, constitutional monarchy unconstrained by legislative power—strikes us as naive, and if we see in his vision of community the basis for a critique of modernity that he did not explore very energetically, his alternative vision nevertheless retains the possibility of becoming the kind of critique that not only points out the flaws of the present reality but also points on to new possibilities.

"Donagan's Critique of *Sittlichkeit*" interrupts this cheerful (but not triumphalist) reading of Hegel by developing a Kantian critique of Hegelian ethico-political thought in the light of the horrors of National Socialism. Echoing earlier debates about "Hegel and Prussianism," Donagan suggests that Hegelian theory embeds its norms so deeply in historically contingent life and customs (*Sitten*, thus *Sittlichkeit*) as to leave it helpless before totalitarian movements that would put it to ideological use.

In exploring this critique we learn two things. First, no doubt the form of Hegelian social thought can be filled with a content we find repulsive, but this is no less true of the form of Kantian morality. Everything depends on the content. And just as the Bible has substantive content that can be appealed to against attempts to use it in defense of, say, slavery or apartheid, so Hegelian thought, as we have already seen in part, has resources that can be activated against the kind of statism represented by the Nazis.

Second, and perhaps more important, having learned that the Kantian strategy is not necessary, we discover that in any case it is not possible. The foundationalist claim to a timeless universality, to a knowledge unsituated within and thereby uncontaminated by historical contingency is as central to modernity as Enlightenment as contractual intersubjectivity is to modernity as liberalism. The claim to have the "view from nowhere" is central to Kantian ethical theory and to any critique of Hegel developed out of it. But without realizing it, Donagan embeds his own putative Kantianism in an actual Hegelianism by making it necessary to be a member of a particular society, ours, to get out of the empty formalism with which Kant has regularly been charged. The freedom from historical particularity that distinguishes Kantian *Moralität* from Hegelian *Sittlichkeit* turns out to be a pipe dream.

These first four essays provide a kind of minicommentary on *The Philosophy of Right*. The next three pick up the hint dropped above that there is more critique in this man's philosophy than he (and most others) have dreamt of. They explore what I view as a failure of nerve on Hegel's part, a reluctance to allow the vision of freedom set forth there and, in an earlier version, in the *Phenomenology*, to unfold into the critique of modernity they contain. At the same time the link between Hegel's politics and his methodological commitment to an antifoundationalist holism, comes to the fore. But even where epistemological issues emerge, the question of freedom never disappears from view.

"Dialectic and Intersubjectivity," "Hegel and Gadamer," and "Hegel and Husserl: Transcendental Phenomenology and the Revolution Yet Awaited" develop three theses I first presented in *History and Truth in Hegel's Phenomenology*. The first of these is that for Hegel the transcendentalism of Descartes and Kant is *aufgehoben* in a post-transcendental understanding of understanding. Transcendentalism is preserved in that the activity of the knowing subject is recognized; but it is transcended in that this condition for the possibility of experience is seen as itself conditioned, as situated in an historical-social context that it can never fully objectify and from which it can never fully extricate itself through reflection. In this "situation epistemology" it becomes both possible and necessary to ask, Who is the transcendental subject? This question is as natural to Gadamer as it is terrifying to Husserl because the answer will always be some historically specific We.

The second thesis is that while Hegel recognizes the relatedness of all acts of intentionality to the historically specific life-world in which they occur, he does not draw relativist conclusions from this. Just as John Hick was later to appeal to eschatology in an attempt to solve the problem of the verifiability of religious knowledge, Hegel appeals to eschatology to solve the problem of historical relativity. In keeping with his holism, he refuses even to attempt to uproot knowledge from the sociohistorical soil in which it grows. Instead, he argues that this is a defect only so long as that world is itself incomplete and thus penultimate. If knowledge is always the expression of its world, and if that world were the Kingdom of God, the perfection of freedom, then that knowledge, so far from being condemned to relativity, would by virtue of its very relatedness be the absolute knowledge Hegel wants.

The final thesis is that Hegel spoils this ingenious solution by adopting a realized eschatology. His argument calls for finding the realization of freedom only in a global community of reciprocal recognition free from war and propaganda (the media as we know them, including their economic and political uses). His failure of nerve is the failure to recognize that the modern state falls doubly short of being that community. In the first place, as a national state it is obviously not universal, and even under the best of circumstances relates to its international others only in the contractual terms that Hegel has so cogently criticized. In the second place, as a liberal state, it is not that kind of community in itself, even when considered as if it were a self-contained and self-sufficient entity. By Hegel's own criteria, modernity fails to be the realization of freedom and the historical condition for the possibility of absolute knowledge.

In short, Hegel is somehow unable fully to accept the challenge of his challenging understanding of human freedom. Against this background, our final group of essays concerns the religious dimension of Hegel's theory of freedom in the modern world. Hegel's vision of social community is one in which the legitimate claims of individual and society, of self and other are reconciled only where intersubjectivity is constituted through bonds stronger than those of liberal society. Those bonds can only be, in his view, religious. His social vision is, to a large degree, a more concretely developed version of the utopian visions of ethico-religious community to be found in Kant's *Religion Within the Limits of Reason Alone* and in Schleiermacher's *On Religion: Speeches to Its Cultured Despisers*. But it differs in at least three important ways.

First, it is more thoroughly worked out conceptually, even to the point of discussing the shape of the social institutions that would be the embodiment of freedom. Second, it is more specifically Christian than Kant's deism and Schleiermacher's pantheism. Indeed, as we shall see, it turns out to be overtly Protestant. Finally, and most importantly, it loses its utopian character and is presented as a realized eschatology. In this way it largely loses its critical form, but not, I want to insist, its critical content.

While Hegel supports the separation of church and state, he emphasizes the inextricability of religion and society. And, since he views freedom as the essence of religion not less than of society, it is not surprising that he evaluates religion by the criterion of freedom. Thus in "Hegel, Hinduism, and Freedom" we find him doing the kind of critical analysis that today is primarily associated with liberation theology. His evaluation of the metaphysical theory and the cultic and social practices of these traditions leads him to the conclusion that Hinduism is from start to finish a religion of unfreedom.

Here it would be strange to speak of Hegel's theory having lost its critical power. But perhaps it is just his ability to offer a critique of other religions and societies that hides from Hegel the degree to which his theory has lost its capacity for critique of its own here and now. For one can scarcely read his diatribes against Hinduism without wondering why he does not apply the same criterion as energetically to his own society and its Christian culture.

In "Hegel and the Reformation" we find Hegel again capable of critique only against "them." This time the critique extends to the Christian religion, but only to its Roman Catholic form. His affirmation of (Lutheran) Protestantism as the religion of worldly freedom has two main points. Although he tends to conflate a Reformation principle of subjectivity with an Enlightenment principle of autonomy, bringing Luther and Descartes together in a manner that neither would relish, his preference for the Lutheran interpretation of the Eucharist is clearly and solely dictated by the question of freedom. The other point concerns the worldliness of Protestant freedom. Hegel loves to contrast the monastic vows of chastity, poverty, and obedience with, respectively, the Protestant affirmation of what he calls family, civil society, and the state.

Two other features of this essay deserve mention. Here we find Hegel not only willing to acknowledge that the modern world is not the full realization of Lutheran-Hegelian freedom, but also willing to say that it ought to be. Had this overcoming of Hegel's usual *Angst vor dem Sollen* been more frequent, the critical content of his theory would not have been so largely disguised by its ideological form.

If Hegel makes it abundantly clear in his affirmation of Protestantism that he has no sympathy for the secularist tendencies of modernity, he makes it equally clear that politically he is no puritan. He has no interest in a theocratic polity. This is where the fun begins, or, to be more precise, this is where Hegel's real problem begins. If against theocracy he affirms the separation of church and state, how can he insist, against secularism, that freedom requires not merely a religious, but even a Protestant foundation to society?

We see this dilemma define itself sharply in "Hegel, the Old Secularism, and the New Theocracy." Due to the circumstances of its original presentation, this essay has more of a journalistic tone than the others. We see the nature of Hegel's dilemma by placing him in our own world. On the one hand we find him unable to side with the secularizing tendencies of modernity, and this for two reasons. First, the freedom he looks for is not found even in the liberal societies that are the glory of secular modernity. Second, because of his commitment to the primacy of ethical and religious values, he is hostile to the tendency in these societies to give autonomy and primacy to such pre-ethical values as sexual enjoyment and economic consumption.

On the other hand, Hegel is bound to be, if anything, even more critical of the theocratic revolt against "secular humanism." The tendency of the new theocracy to view religion as a kind of technology for producing morality runs entirely against Hegel's more nearly organic understanding of social development. Moreover, these movements are only selectively critical of the values of secularism. On questions of sexual morality there is a big difference, but it is hard to find any quarrel over the materialism (consumerism) of modernity.

But perhaps the most basic quarrel between Hegel and the new theocracy concerns the latter's epistemological sectarianism. Here Hegel's Enlightenment commitment to reason as distinct from authority means, as was clear in "Hegel and the Reformation," that the religious foundation of society must arise out of discourse that is public and open to all. The appeal to criteria that are not shared is a threat to the freedom of the community as a whole, for it lays the foundation for a social order founded on constraint rather than consent, on oversight rather than insight; and liberal society, for all its defects, is at least a legitimate victory over the power of pious parties.

Those who, like myself, are moved by the force of Hegel's critique of both the old secularism and the new theocracy, are bound to ask, What next? Is there a path between this Scylla and that Charybdis? If there is, we shall no doubt have to find it for ourselves. But we can continue to learn from Hegel, even if he can show us no more than what won't work.

It is clear that by proclaiming Protestantism to be the basis of freedom in the modern world and by repudiating any theocratic interpretation of the religious foundation of society Hegel has committed himself to what we are compelled to call a nonsectarian protestantism. What might this be? Will it have the substance required to found freedom in community beyond the limits of liberalism, or will it prove to be as impotent as the deistic religion of reason to which the Enlightenment and especially the French Revolution turned with somewhat similar hopes?

Suddenly we realize that Hegel's claim to be able to translate the content of religion from the religious form of *Vorstellungen* to the philosophical form of *Begriffe* is of the highest social importance. For this is the key to an epistemologically nonsectarian Protestantism.

"Hegel's Theory of Religious Knowledge" addresses this issue in two ways. First, it helps us to distinguish between the Protestantism Hegel affirms and that which he rejects. The latter is the Kantian version that denies the possibility of a conceptually articulated and rationally grounded knowledge of God and which seeks to derive religion from some immediate certainty of faith or feeling. Schleiermacher's theology, both in the *Reden* and in the later *Glaubenslehre,* is for Hegel the paradigm of a subjectivism in Protestantism that does not contribute to worldly freedom. The Kantian critique and its cousins in Hume, Jacobi, and Hamaan show the limits of the Understanding, but not the limits of Reason, which remains capable of knowing God. Protestantism's affirmation of worldly freedom cannot flourish in Kantian soil.

But if knowledge of God is to be rational it cannot be sectarian, and even in his discussion of the proofs of God's existence we see Hegel's strategy for purifying religious knowledge from the positivity that keeps it from being public. That strategy is to use the Logic as the hermeneutical guide for a reinterpretation of traditional materials, in this case the proofs. In the process Hegel seeks to close two gaps between the human and divine. Like Aquinas he would close the epistemological gap by showing that it is possible for human reason to know God. And like Spinoza he would close the ontological gap by showing that God is not to be conceived as the separate, transcendent being of traditional theism, but rather as a universal power that is, not our creator, but our very being.

In other words, Hegel suggests that Aquinas' proofs are infected by positivity, that his natural theology is dependent on his revealed theology, that when he concludes his proofs with the words, "And this we know to be God," he actually imports content from a specific historical tradition not established by the proof itself. The bold counterclaim is that Hegel's version is free of such historical contingency, since all its content comes from a Logic that is the articulation of pure thought.

The final two essays, "Hegel, Pannenberg, and Hermeneutics," and "Hegel, Tillich, and the Secular," explore the shape of Hegel's logically purified Protestantism by placing him in dialogue with two more recent Protestant theologians. Both essays explore what I have been calling his realized eschatology, what Fackenheim describes in the Tillich essay as his claim to ultimacy for "the modern bourgeois Protestant world." The different ways in which these three thinkers deal with the manifest defects of present reality constitute an important trialogue.

But in the present context the project of reinterpretation from *Vorstellungen* to *Begriffe* is perhaps more important, a project that joins Lessing in seeking to replace accidental truths of history with necessary truths of reason. Here instead of the proofs for the existence of God, the primary material is the doctrine of the incarnation. By reinterpreting this from a claim uniquely true of Jesus of Nazareth to a universal truth about the relation of the human to the divine as established by the rational ontology of the Logic, Hegel transforms Jesus from an ontologically unique event to an epistemologically unique event, historically important as the actual discoverer of the truth that the human and divine are one, a truth that is only accidentally related to the contingency of the historical Jesus.

Two results immediately emerge. By placing Protestantism in this hermeneutical and ontological context, Hegel has at the very least made dramatic progress toward his goal of making it nonsectarian. At the same time, he has at the very least made it highly questionable whether in any meaningful sense this Protestantism is any longer Christian. Of course, apart from his own claim to have reconciled Christianity and modernity, there is no reason why Hegel needs to be a Christian thinker. But if he is as far from being one as these analyses suggest, the possibility is strengthened that his religion is all too similar to the deism of the Enlightenment, namely that whatever its strengths it is too far from institutional religion to be able to sustain itself as the spiritual foundation of freedom in the modern world.

The verdict of history is, I believe, unambiguous. Hegel's project has failed. His philosophy has not been able to provide the spiritual foundation for freedom in the modern world. Even if we conclude that he succeeded in a high degree in being his own time comprehended in thought, the world he brought to conceptual articulation was not yet itself sufficiently rational when judged by his own standards. These essays seek to sort out, from a philosophical perspective, where his theory might remain fruitful for reflection, critique, and practice, and where it is most problematic. They leave us with the question posed by Barth and Fackenheim in the Tillich essay: If Hegel's project fails, where do we go next? Nothing in the limits of Hegel's project makes either secularism or theocracy look more attractive. The quest for a society that embodies a religiously inspired experience of community without succumbing to the tyrannies of theocracy remains our task.

Merold Westphal
Fordham University

ACKNOWLEDGMENTS

The essays collected in this volume were originally published during the nineteen seventies and eighties in a variety of places, as listed below. I want to thank the following for permission to republish them in the present volume: Cambridge University Press, Humanities Press, *Idealistic Studies, The Journal of Religion, Man and World,* Mercer University Press, Martinus Nijhoff, *The Owl of Minerva.*

1) "Hegel's Theory of the Concept," in *Art and Logic in Hegel's Philosophy,* ed. Warren Steinkraus and Kenneth Schmitz (New Jersey: Humanities Press, 1980), 103–19.

2) "Hegel, Human Rights, and the Hungry," in *Hegel on Economics and Freedom,* ed. William Maker (Macon, Ga.: Mercer University Press, 1987), 209–28. Reprinted by permission.

3) "Hegel's Radical Idealism: Family and State as Ethical Communities," in *The State and Civil Society: Studies in Hegel's Political Philosophy,* ed. Zbigniew Pelczynski (New York: Cambridge University Press, 1984), 77–92.

4) "Donagan's Critique of *Sittlichkeit,*" in *Idealistic Studies* XV, 1 (January 1985), 1–17.

5) "Dialectic and Intersubjectivity," *The Owl of Minerva* 16, no. 1 (Fall 1984): 39–54.

6) "Hegel and Gadamer," in *Hermeneutics and Modern Philosophy,* ed. Brice R. Wachterhauser (Albany: SUNY Press, 1986), 77–92.

7) "Hegel and Husserl: Transcendental Phenomenology and the Revolution Yet Awaited," in *Critical and Dialectical Phenomenology,* ed. Donn Welton and Hugh J. Silverman (Albany: SUNY Press, 1987), 103–35.

8) "Hegel, Hinduism, and Freedom," *The Owl of Minerva* 20, no. 2 (Spring 1989): 193–204.

9) "Hegel and the Reformation," in *History and System: Hegel's Philosophy of History,* ed. Robert L. Perkins (Albany: SUNY Press, 1984), 73–92.

10) "Hegel, the Old Secularism, and the New Theocracy," in *Hegel's Philosophy of Spirit,* ed. Peter Stillman (Albany: SUNY Press, 1987), 151–69.

11) "Hegel's Theory of Religious Knowledge," *Beyond Epistemology: New Studies in the Philosophy of Hegel,* ed. F. G. Weiss, 30–57. Copyright 1974 by Martinus Nijhoff, The Hague, Netherlands. All rights reserved, including the right to translate or to reproduce this book or parts thereof in any form. Reprinted by permission of Kluwer Academic Publishers.

12) "Hegel, Pannenberg, and Hermeneutics," *Man and World* 4 (August 1971): 276–93.

13) "Hegel, Tillich, and the Secular," *The Journal of Religion* 52 (July 1972): 223–39. Copyright 1972, The University of Chicago.

Sigla

Abbreviations used in the notes and in the text are to be found in the first part of the bibliography.

Thanks to Richie McCombs for help in preparing the manuscript.

THE BASIC THEORY OF FREEDOM

1 Hegel's Theory of the Concept

"The subject-matter of the philosophical science of right is the Idea of right, i.e., the concept of right together with the actualization of that concept." So begins the introduction to Hegel's *Philosophy of Right*. Since Hegel defines right in terms of freedom,[1] his account of the actualization of that concept is the story of how freedom is actual in the modern world. This occupies almost the entirety of Hegel's text. Thus the concept of freedom is developed for the most part not by itself but in the context of narrating its actualization. But if either the reader or the writer is to have any way of recognizing what counts in the modern world as the actuality of freedom, some prior understanding of the meaning of freedom seems to be required. It is this which the introduction seeks to provide, a purely conceptual analysis of freedom.

This analysis will of necessity be incomplete, just because of its a priori character. "The shapes which the concept assumes in the course of its actualization are indispensable for the knowledge of the concept itself." (PR, ¶1) To repeat, it is only when we grasp "the concept of right *together with* the actualization of that concept" (my italics) that we can adequately grasp that concept. The adequate conceptual grasp of any content can never be reached by conceptual analysis alone. Yet a prior understanding of the concept is needed to guide the discovery of that actualization of freedom which alone can provide us with an adequate conceptual grasp. It is tempting to think of this prior understanding in terms of hypothesis or conjecture, but we know from his discussions of Reinhold that Hegel rejects this suggestion out of hand.[2] Whence this preunderstanding of freedom, then? There can be only one Hegelian answer—from the Logic. For in Hegelian philosophy it is always the Logic which provides the conceptual wherewithal for any truly speculative understanding of nature or spirit.

The conceptual analysis of freedom presented in the introduction to the *Philosophy of Right* does not disappoint these expectations. It is indeed derived from the Logic, in particular from the analysis of the Concept as universal, particular (or specific), and individual. This triadic structure of the Concept thus becomes the basis for getting at the genuinely speculative element in Hegel's political philosophy. My purpose here, however, is just the opposite. It is to throw a little light on the logic of the Concept by reflecting on Hegel's employment of the categories Universality, Particularity, and Individuality in developing a preunderstanding of freedom.

This procedure will no doubt make some readers feel uncomfortable. The Logic, we will be told, is intelligible in its own right, and is first to be understood by itself as pure thought before any consideration of its employment can be legitimated. That there is something genuinely Hegelian about this response I shall not deny. But there is something equally Hegelian about my own procedure as well. After all, for Hegel the truth is the whole, and no part of philosophical science can be fully understood apart from its detailed relations to the others. I have just quoted Hegel's claim that the concept of right or freedom cannot adequately be understood apart from the shapes of its actualization in the world. I am taking this in the strong sense to mean that even the concepts from the Logic which go into spelling out that prevenient concept of freedom to which the introduction is devoted cannot be adequately understood in and by themselves but only when we see them at work in the *Philosophy of Right* and elsewhere.

It is in this sense that I understand Hegel's "knowing before you know" (or don't go into the water before you have learned how to swim) critique of critical philosophy. In a paper presented to the Hegel Society of America at Notre Dame in 1972, John Smith reminds us that Hegel praised the critical project of examining the categories and directed his criticism only toward the tendency to separate such criticism from "first order" knowing, thus examining the categories while they were "idling." "Hegel's fundamental complaint, then, is that Kant analyzed the categories as functions of thought, not when they were functioning in actual knowing, but only in their status as necessary conditions for knowing. . . . " In support of this suggestion Smith quotes from section 41, *Zusatz* of the *Encyclopedia,* where Hegel writes, "So that what we want is to combine in our process of inquiry the *action* of the forms of thought with a criticism of them."[3] This requirement seems to me at best to be only partially satisfied in the Logic itself. Thus it serves as another justification for seeking to understand the Logic in terms of its so-called "application." The activity of the categories of Universality, Particularity, and Individuality in Hegel's political theory belongs to the deduction, analysis, and criticism of them in his Logic.

Methodologically, then, I believe my project has ample Hegelian validation. But I claim no scientific status for my attempt at interpretation. This humility is strategically motivated, I hasten to confess, for it leaves me free to invoke hypotheses and test them out, which is what I intend to do. My initial hypothesis is that the following sentence from the *Zusatz* to section 7 of the *Philosophy of Right* is the key to the logic of the Concept: "Freedom in this sense, however, we already possess in the form of feeling—in friendship and love, for instance." The meaning of my hypothesis is both (a) that the structure of the Concept as Universality, Particularity, and Individuality is necessary to an adequate understanding of friendship and love, and (b) that if we think through the meaning of friendship and love adequately we will have developed the structure of the Concept as Universality, Particularity, and Individuality. Since I am trying to work toward the Logic and not from it, it is obviously the latter form of the hypothesis which I shall be exploring.

* * *

The suggestion that friendship and love are the true meaning of freedom follows a summary of sections 5 through 7, which define freedom in terms of the triadic structure of the Concept. While Hegel once suggests that Universality, Particularity, and Individuality are abstractly the same as Identity, Difference, and Ground (EL, ¶164), they here function as Indeterminacy, Determination, and Self-Determination. Since these categories have an obvious bearing on the question of freedom, the task is to see how the original triad can legitimately be translated into them.

The first equivalence is that of Universality with Indeterminacy. Hegel puts it this way:

> The will contains (α) the element of pure indeterminacy or that pure reflection of the ego into itself which involves the dissipation of every restriction and every content either immediately presented by nature, by needs, desires, and impulses, or given and determined by any means whatever. This is the unrestricted infinity of absolute abstraction or universality, the pure thought of oneself.

Freedom involves the ability to abstract from every dependence upon an other, and since it is always and only in relation to an other that anything is determinate and not the "indeterminate immediacy" of pure being, freedom involves "my flight from every content as from a restriction" (PR, ¶5).[4]

There is a freedom which takes this moment of independence as its whole meaning. Theoretically it is "the Hindu fanaticism of pure contemplation" in which the fundamental structures of the self's being-in-the-world are systematically undermined. Practically it is exhibited in the Terror of the French Revolution with its "irreconcilable hatred of everything particular" [*jedes Besondere*], i.e., everything determinate in the social order (PR, ¶5Z). "Only in destroying something does this negative will possess the feeling of itself as existent." This freedom professes to serve some new and better actuality but cannot do so, for any such actuality "leads at once to some sort of order, to a particularization [*Besonderung*] of organizations and individuals alike; while it is precisely out of the annihilation of particularity [*Besonderung*] and objective characterization that the self-consciousness of this negative freedom proceeds." Hegel indicates the one-sidedness of this freedom as absolute independence curtly by calling it "freedom as the Understanding conceives it" (PR, ¶5Z).[5]

The second equivalence is already before us, that of Particularity and Determination, for it matters little whether the content from which this negative freedom flees as from a restriction is called *Besonderheit* or *Bestimmtheit*. But freedom that would be actual cannot flee forever. For "my willing is not pure willing but the willing of something. A will which, like that expounded in section 5, wills only the abstract universal, wills nothing and is therefore no will at all" (PR, ¶6Z). To will something the will must include the moment of "the finitude or particularization [*Besonderung*] of the ego," which is described in this way:

> (β) At the same time, the ego is also the transition from un-differentiated indeterminacy to the differentiation, determination, and positing of a determinacy as a content and object. Now further, this content may either be given by nature or engendered by the concept of spirit. (PR, ¶6)

This latter qualification is important, for it indicates that the other which cannot be excluded from freedom is of two sorts, natural, that is, the impulses and inclinations *(Triebe und Neigungen)* of immediate selfhood in their otherness to rational self-determination, and spiritual, that is, both social institutions and concrete other selves in their otherness to the independence of the self who would be free. This second moment, Particularity or Determination, is no less essential to freedom than the first. For the self which can respond to its own natural immediacy and to the other selves around it only by withdrawal or destruction cannot be said to be free. On the other hand, this moment by itself is just as abstract and inadequate as the first. For the self which is only a function of its impulses and inclinations or of the other selves it encounters is no more free than the self which flees from every content as from a restriction. Indeed, it can scarcely be called a self at all.

Only a caricature of freedom arises, then, when either the moment of Universality = Indeterminacy or that of Particularity = Determination is asked by itself to provide a definition. But neither moment can be eliminated from the concept of freedom. What is needed is a genuine unity of the two, antithetical as they seem. We already know that the unity of Universality and Particularity will be called Individuality, and we might guess that the unity of Indeterminacy and Determination will be called Self-Determination, though in both cases, as in calling happiness the highest good, the task of comprehension lies ahead and not behind. Hegel writes:

> (γ) The will is the unity of both these moments. It is particularity reflected into itself and so brought back to universality, i.e., it is individuality. It is the *self*-determination of the ego, which means that at one and the same time the ego posits itself as its own negative, i.e., as restricted and determinate, and yet remains by itself, i.e., in its self-identity and universality. (PR, ¶7)

Three comments on this passage may help us get to the heart of the matter. First, it serves to validate the third equivalence, that of Individuality and Self-Determination. Self-determination is defined as the preservation of self-identity in the process of determination. Only that which is in some strong sense individual can endure determination without becoming simply a function of those others through whom this determination is mediated. Such endurance involves the retention of more than that logical self-identity which permits one to be an object of reference or the subject of predication. It requires that real self-identity which is here equated with the moment of universality, which, as we have seen, is the moment of independence.

Second, we are referred directly back to the Logic, where this unity of self-identity and determinateness is central. We can now understand why, when Hegel calls the Concept "the principle of freedom," he goes right on to say, "Thus in its *self-identity* it has original and complete determinateness," and, when defining the structure of the Concept in terms of its three moments, he describes Individuality as the unity of Universality and Particularity, "which negative self-unity has complete and original *determinatenooo*, without any loss to its *self-identity* or universality."[6]

Third, Hegel calls this unity of self-identity and determination which constitutes Self-Determination or Individuality "the innermost secret of speculation," though the Understanding disdains it as "inconceivable" (PR, ¶7). The passage before us indicates both why the synthesis is so easily dismissed as inconceivable and how we may begin to conceive it after all. Self-determination means determination, which means that the self stands in relation to its own negative, to another through whom its determination is mediated. The self is thus *dependent* upon the other for its determinateness. Yet, if this is to be self-determination, it must be a self-mediating activity, and the self must retain its self-identity and universality, i.e., its *independence*. Hegel here uses one of his favorite locutions, *bei sich bleiben*.[7] This means to keep control of oneself, to stay conscious and not pass out. The task, which Understanding finds impossible, is so to remain in control of oneself in giving oneself up to the mediating activity of the other that the whole operation can be called a self-mediating activity and not something which happens to me while unconscious, after which I come to again to learn about my new determinateness. It could then be said that "the ego determines itself insofar as it is the relating of negativity to itself" (PR, ¶7), or that the self is *Vermittlung* but not *ein Vermitteltes* (WL 2:241 = SL 602).

This is possible, on Hegel's account, because self-determination means "that at one and the same time *the ego posits itself* as its own negative, i.e., as restricted and determinate, and yet remains by itself . . . " (PR, ¶7).[8] We have already seen that the self cannot be determinate except in relation to another, and that it cannot be free if this relation is either withdrawal or destruction. But if this other is in some sense itself, the possibility of a more positive relation begins to lose its inconceivability. The only problem is that this solution sounds a bit too Fichtean.[9] The otherness of the other seems compromised.

At this point Hegel's earlier allusion to the categories of Identity, Difference, and Ground is helpful, for it reminds us that for Hegel identity always involves some difference. If the other through whom the self is determined must *in some sense* be identical with that self, we must inquire more carefully what that sense may be. A second formulation from section 7 calls for our attention.

Still, both these moments [self-consciousness as universal and as particular] are only abstractions: what is concrete and true (and everything true is concrete) is the universality which has the particular as its opposite: but [only] that particular which by its reflection into itself has been equalized with the universal.

Here otherness sounds less Fichtean. It has the status of an opposite *(Gegensatz)*. But it must have become equalized *(ausgeglichen)* with that to which it stands opposed. We are not told which way the scale must be tipped to bring about this balance. Whether the reflection into itself of the other which confronts the self is a scaling down of its power and activity so that it does not overwhelm the self or a scaling up of its dignity so that its activity is of the same sort as that of the self, the result is that the self and its other are somehow on a par. They are not the same in the sense of numerical identity but of qualitative similarity. This seems the opposite extreme from the Fichtean overtones of the previous formulation. If one thinks of the struggle for recognition in the *Phenomenology,* for example, it seems that neither way of looking at it will do. For if the other from whom the self seeks the determination of recognition is numerically identical with itself, there can be no acceptance of the claim to human dignity but only the repetition of that claim. While if the other is the same as the self in the weaker sense of being qualitatively similar, equal in being another full-blooded human self, we can see nothing in such equality to weaken the Understanding's suspicion that the self must either destroy the selfhood of the other by becoming its master or give up its own by becoming the slave, in neither case achieving freedom.

Turning to the *Zusatz* to section 7 for help we find a definition of freedom in terms of the three moments of the Concept. It repeats the familiar idea that the self posits itself as its other yet remains by itself in this other; but it provides us with no assistance in making sense out of these Hegelian clichés. Just at this point, however, occurs the sentence which my hypothesis makes central to interpreting Hegel here. "Freedom in this sense, however, we already possess in the form of feeling—in friendship and love, for instance." The explanation continues,

Here we are not inherently one-sided; we restrict ourselves gladly in relating ourselves to another, but in this restriction know ourselves as ourselves. In this determinacy a man should not feel himself determined, on the contrary, since he treats

the other as other, it is there that he first arrives at the feeling
of his own self-hood. Thus freedom lies neither in indeterminacy nor in determinacy; it is both of these at once.

Guided by these descriptions and reminded of whatever experiences of true friendship or love we may have had, we suddenly see
how the abstract antithesis between numerical identity and mere
qualitative sameness does not exhaust the possibilities. Genuine
otherness is preserved, since friendship and love require numerical
duality and not numerical identity. Yet we can speak of identity and
not mere qualitative sameness, for friends and lovers are not merely
different numerical units of the same sort—they constitute together a new reality which they express by saying "We," This whole
is more than the sum of its parts. As its constituents the parts are
identical with each other, for each of them simply is that We just as
much as each is also a distinct I.[10]

*   *   *

Such reflections on the way friends and lovers relate to their
counterparts illuminate the kind of identity with difference which
the Concept expresses. This confirms Hegel's own view that the theory of the Concept is a theory of freedom, of personality, and of that
sense of ego which the slave lacks (EL, ¶163Z). When loving intersubjectivity is taken as basic, two conspicuous features of the logical
exposition of the Concept appear in a new light, namely the ubiquity
of the concept of creativity and the transition from Essence to Concept, more specifically, the development of the triadic structure of
the Concept from the category of reciprocity.
    The creation motif is never far from sight. The concept is *un-
endlich, schöpferische Form, freie, schöpferische Tätigkeit,* or simply
schöpferische Macht. It is *das Formierende und Erschaffende;* and
one can speak of *das Schaffen des Begriffs,* or even of the Idea as
Schöpferin der Natur.[11]
    All this tells us that the concept is something active and not
inert. In its individuality the Concept is *das Wirkende* (EL, ¶ 163).
Frequently Hegel expresses this central theme in Aristotelian language, the concept being related to its objectivity as soul to body or
seed to plant.[12] We are given a theory of development which at first
appears to be but a restatement of the Aristotelian theory of substantial form as the merger of formal, final, and efficient causality.
But Aristotle's is a theory of life, not of spirit, and while Hegel recognizes the Concept to be "the principle of all life" (EL, ¶160Z) and

the organic level to be "the stage of nature at which the Concept emerges," (WL, 2:224 = SL 586), it is only at the level of spirit that its true meaning is manifest. This means that no Aristotelian interpretation of Hegel's creation talk will be adequate. As creative the Concept is *das Wirkende* indeed, but the organic-developmental models of soul-body and seed-plant give at best a partial account of this. For, as we have seen, the theory of the Concept is a theory of intersubjective selfhood and thus of spirit. Its task is to give an account of determinateness through an other such that this "is not a *limit,* as though it were related to another *beyond* it [*einem Jenseits*] . . . . " (WL 2:245 = SL 605) How does the concept of creation contribute to this central problematic?

The *Zusatz* to section 161 of the *Encyclopedia* is of special importance in this connection. For while both the original paragraph and the first long paragraph of the *Zusatz* are devoted to the Aristotelian-developmental aspects of the Concept, the final brief paragraph goes beyond this to the level of spirit.

> The movement of the concept is as it were to be looked upon merely as play: the other which it sets up is in reality not an other. Or, as it is expressed in the teaching of Christianity: not merely has God created a world which confronts Him as an other; He has also from all eternity begotten a Son in whom He, a Spirit, is at home with Himself [*bei sich selbst ist*].

Three models of the self in relation to its other are given here. In play the other is not really an other, but the figment of the self's active imagination. Remember Puff?

> One gray night it happened, Jackie Paper came no more
> So Puff the Magic Dragon ceased his fearsome roar.
>
> His head was bent in sorrow, green scales fell like rain
> Puff no longer went to play along the cherry lane
> Without his lifelong friend, Puff could not be brave
> So Puff that mighty dragon sadly slipped into his cave.

The strength of this model is that it completely removes the *Jenseits* character of the other for the self; its weakness is that the other is somewhat ephemeral. The freedom of the child at play is total, but not very real.

The second model is that of God as Creator in relation to the world. Since the world depends on God for its continued existence,

it is sometimes viewed as no more truly other to God than Puff
was to Jackie Paper. But creation is more often seen as an exercise
of omnipotence voluntarily limiting itself, giving genuine otherness to the world. This is the view Hegel has in mind, for while
the other of play is "in reality not an other," when god creates the
world it "confronts him as an other." The strength of this model is
obviously that otherness gains integrity; its weakness that otherness can all too easily emerge once again as a *Jenseits,* outside the
reconciliation of the Concept. This possible obstinate otherness is
not incorrigible. As Creator God could either destroy the world he
has made, or, alternatively, abandon it. But we have already seen
that destruction and withdrawal are anything but the freedom
Hegel is seeking to grasp; and nothing in the concept of Creator
suggests that God has any options but these in the face of a world
turned hostile.

The third model is that of the eternal love between the Father
and the Son. As eternal the Son is truly other, neither imaginary
like Puff nor contingent like the world. But while otherness is most
complete in this model there is no estrangement or hostility here.
For in place of the child's sovereignty over his imaginary playmates
and God's over the created world, the relation here is that of reciprocal love. Only in love is even God able to be *bei sich selbst* in his
other. Though Hegel doesn't mention it here, this holds for his relation to the world as well. For it is only as Redeemer, not simply as
Creator, that God can be at peace with the world. It is the God who
loved the world who sent his Son, not to be its Judge but its Savior
(John 3:16–17).

It is now possible to give Hegel's creation talk its proper place
in his theory of the Concept. By itself it is not an adequate model of
the conceptual structure being developed. But it helps to express
two essential elements of that structure. The first is the active, effective nature of the self as *das Wirkende.* The other is that aspect
of love which Hegel especially wishes to highlight, the non-
otherness of the most genuinely other (PR, ¶158Z). Taken together
the three models we have just examined are not just a progressive
series. The first two belong to the third as part of its meaning. In
love the threatening aspects of otherness are as thoroughly eliminated as in play and creation (but without having to eliminate otherness as such and with it the benefits which only real otherness
can confer). In love the other does not owe its existence to me, but we
are so related that I feel no need of that sort of power over the other
in order to be myself. I can live in the real world without resort to
the pathological phantasies in which I elevate myself to the role of

Creator and reduce the world to a collective Puff with whom I play in childish sovereignty.[13]

* * *

Lest we get carried away here we must remember that the Logic does not try to tell us how or where this freedom as loving reciprocity is to be realized. It only tells us what it is to be free. It does so, however, by calling our attention to the fact that love is only a special form of reciprocity and that there is another reciprocity which is not freedom at all. It is this contrast between two reciprocities which constitutes the transition from Essence to Concept in the Logic.

As a category of Essence Reciprocity expresses a world wholly subject to natural necessity. It is composed of substances, thus of independent and self-sufficient units. It is a world, however, not a chaotic multiplicity, solely because these units do have one mode of relation to one another, causal necessity. Since they are both active and passive, cause and effect in relation to one another, causal necessity has the form of Reciprocity.

In this world independence and identity are mutually exclusive. Causal necessity involves a special form of identity. The effect, being simply the expression or unfolding of the cause, loses its independence and becomes simply an aspect of the cause's career. As the distinction between them vanishes, they become identical. The attempt to see the world exclusively and consistently from this point of view leads to Spinozism, where the world has only one substance in it, or, alternatively, to the Laplacian way of saying the same thing in a different language. If, as the category of Reciprocity itself suggests, some plurality is to be preserved, it must be by viewing the units which make up the world in abstraction from their causal relations, as external and contingent in relation to one another. I have no difficulty, for example, viewing the misfortunes of my beloved and bumbling Chicago Cubs as wholly unrelated to the political climate in Washington. In Reciprocity as a category of Essence I alternate between two incompatible viewpoints, one which views the units of the world as mutually indifferent to one another, and one which views them as so tightly bound together by natural necessity as to lose their independent identity. Clearly neither of these represents freedom in Hegel's sense.

If there is to be a reciprocity which does constitute freedom, it must overcome the mutual exclusiveness of independence and identity. It is in just these terms that Hegel states the transition to the

Concept.[14] The truth of necessity is freedom, we are told, and that of substance the Concept. For reciprocity can be seen as infinite, negative self-relation; negative in that it involves the independence of actualities in relation to one another, but infinite self-relation because "their independence only lies in their identity" (EL, ¶157–58). This harmony of independence and identity is crucial to freedom. The old identity excludes independence.

> The identity [*Einheit*] of the things, which necessity presents as bound to each other and thus bereft of their independence, is at first [i.e. while Reciprocity is still a category of Essence] only inward, and therefore has no existence for those under the yoke of necessity. (EL, ¶158Z).[15]

Where identity has this character it not only leaves the so-called individuals "bereft of their independence" but also deprives them of any awareness or enjoyment of their identity. There is no experience of love or of community. But there is another kind of identity.

> It then appears that the members, linked to one another, are not really foreign to each other, being, as it were, at home, and combining with itself [*bei sich selbst ist und mit sich selbst zusammengeht*]. In this way necessity is transfigured into freedom.... (EL, ¶158Z).

Just as we have previously seen Hegel describe love as a contradiction and the unity of the concept as inconceivable to the Understanding, we now are reminded that it is not exactly easy to think this unity of identity and independence. "The passage from necessity to freedom, or from actuality into the concept, is the very hardest, because it proposes that independent actuality shall be thought as having all its substantiality in the passing over and identity with the other independent actuality." Once again, to help us get headed in the right direction, Hegel tells us that love is what he is talking about, love as the liberation which can also be called I, free spirit, and blessedness (EL, ¶159).[16]

* * *

I have been discussing the theory of the Concept as a theory of freedom rather than as a theory of knowledge, as a theory of the practical rather than the theoretical self. Of course, Hegel would not have called this part of the Logic by the name Concept if his theory were not also a theory of knowledge (and the object of knowledge as well). But in spite of saying "Concept" instead of "Freedom" when naming the final level of categorial development, Hegel himself seems to give the epistemological part of his theory a secondary place. "The Concept," he writes,

> when it has developed into a concrete existence that is itself free, is none other than the I or pure self-consciousness. True, I have concepts, that is to say, determinate concepts; but the I is the pure Concept itself which, as the Concept, has come into existence. (WL 2:220 = SL, 583)

However we interpret this contrast between the self's being the Concept and its having concepts, a complete analysis of Hegel's theory of the concept would have to develop its epistemological discussions which are constantly and overtly interspersed throughout the discussion of freedom to which I have limited myself up to this point. My first hypothesis, that love is the key to the structure of the Concept, would be enhanced both in strength and in philosophical interest if a second, corollary hypothesis could be established, namely that the theory of loving intersubjectivity which is the direct meaning of the Concept as a theory of the practical self is the guiding metaphor for the theory of knowledge which has reached the same level of philosophical insight. In other words, knowing, too, is to be understood in its highest form as the nonviolent unity of the self and its other. In the space and time remaining to me I can but outline such a reading of Hegel's text.

As a theory of knowledge Hegel regularly contrasts his view of the Concept with that of the Understanding, which views it as an abstract universal, devoid of particularity and individuality. It is thus without content of its own, the mere form of our subjective thought. Two features of this view are especially stressed, the independence of the object and the subjectivity of thinking.

The independence of the object consists in its being unconditioned in relation to the concepts through which it is thought. It is there first, standing ready made over against the concept, possessed of its being and truth prior to any rendezvous with the concept. The content thus falls on the side of the object. The concept is an empty and inert form which comes to it from without. This kind of thinking is subjective, for it is separated from its truth. The truth is supposed to reside in the content or object, while thinking is entirely the activity of the subject. The abstract universals employed in such thinking are generated, as their name suggests, through the activity of abstracting; and it is the knowing subject who must perform this operation of neglecting some features presented to consciousness while focusing attention on others. Since it is the contingent purpose of the knower which directs this process, it can also be said that an interest external to the subject matter presides over this whole domain of thinking.

On this view the truth of the object is not an intelligibility or meaning it can reveal to us but rather a brute otherness which we must forge weapons to overcome. Abstract universals are those weapons, by means of which we hope to deprive the object of its original independence and render it subject to our purposes and interests. Knowing is the desire to master and dominate. Without any specific reference to technological purposes and interests, Hegel has described the essence of calculative thinking.

Knowledge at the level of the Concept contrasts sharply. This highest kind of knowing, attested by both religion and philosophy (WL 2:225–26 = SL, 587–88), assumes that things have their being and truth by virtue of the Concept at work within them. The form by which they are known is identical with the form by which they are what they are. Since the form is already present in the content Hegel can say, *"dass wir die Begriffe gar nicht bilden"* (EL, ¶163Z). We do not need to impose our external purposes on the processes of thought. This is not to say that knowledge, any more than love itself, is entirely devoid of interest. It is to say that the subject no longer seeks to use the object. The guiding interest is no longer the subject's private purpose, but its openness to the object so that the object may reveal both itself and the subject for what they are. In thus giving itself up to the object, the subject does not discover that in ceasing to be the master it has become the slave. The impetus toward domination is undermined as a new identity takes shape. For the form which is the truth of the thing and the form which is the thought of the subject are one and the same.

Hegel, as is his wont, lapses into lyricism.

> The universal is therefore *free* power; it is itself and takes its other within its embrace [*greift über sein Anderes über*], but without doing violence to it; on the contrary, the universal is, in its other, in peaceful communion with itself. We have called it free power, but it could also be called *free love* and *boundless blessedness,* for it bears itself towards its other as towards *its own self;* in it, it has returned to itself. (WL 2:242 = SL, 603)[17]

We might call this the Golden Rule of the Concept. For Hegel it is the norm for philosophical knowledge as well as for life with our neighbor.

2 HEGEL, HUMAN RIGHTS, AND THE HUNGRY

The Question of Subsistence Rights

"It is wrong to say 'first bread, then liberty,' concludes theologian Michael Novak. Democratic capitalism delivers freedom *with* economic development." So reads the two-page headline of a recent Smith-Kline centerfold in *Time* magazine. In the accompanying essay, Novak recites a litany of the evils of Hitler and Stalin (as if they were the threats to human rights in the world today) and praises, among others, Aleksandr Solzhenitsyn and Adam Smith, without pausing to reflect on what each might have to say about the other. Then, in support of rejecting the "first bread, then liberty" slogan, he writes, "Systems which deny liberty in the name of bread usually produce neither bread nor liberty."[1]

The irony is that Novak's theology of corporate capitalism ends up giving aid and comfort, even divine sanction, to the unholy alliance at the heart of the contemporary human rights crisis in the Western Hemisphere. I refer, of course, to the alliance between right-wing military dictatorships that deny to major portions of their populations both bread and liberty, and the United States government and multinational corporations that are all too eager to cooperate with them for their own strategic or economic advantage.

Still, Novak may have highlighted one of the crucial issues of our time. His dichotomy of bread and liberty raises the question of the proper relation between economic rights and political and civil rights. The colonial powers who have dominated the inter-American context since the sixteenth century have given priority to the latter, at least in recent times. This is perhaps due to both ideological and practical reasons. The ideological reason, suggested by Henry Shue, is that Western liberalism has tended to assume a priori that scarcity is only moderate and has consequently had "a blind spot for severe economic need."[2] The practical reason may be even more important. It grows out of the decolonizing process. The colonial powers have discovered that granting political independence is relatively painless if economic dependence can be maintained.[3] In a context where it is a serious question whether the function of such agencies as the International Monetary Fund is to overcome or perpetuate the colonial heritage,[4] it becomes useful to make as much noise as possible about political rights (if rights are to be discussed at all), so as to distract attention from economic rights, which remain utopian.

But if Henry Shue is right, subsistence rights are absolutely fundamental or basic rights. This means that if they are denied, no rights whatever are secure. For basic rights are defined as those that are "essential to the enjoyment of all other rights."[5] Basic rights relate to basic vulnerability. If their enjoyment is an essential condition for the enjoyment of all other rights, then their denial, whether actual or only threatened, becomes the instrument by which all rights can be denied. The right to physical security, for example, is such a right, for no one can enjoy any right at all if there are those who can credibly threaten to murder, maim, torture, and so forth, a person for trying to exercise that right. But the right to at least a minimal satisfaction of such basic human needs as food, clothing, shelter, and medical care is equally basic; for whoever can credibly threaten to deprive me of these can deter me from the exercise of all other rights.[6]

But if this is true, there can be no genuine granting of political rights while economic rights (at least basic subsistence rights) are denied. Moreover, the neocolonial economic situation that dominates so much of our hemisphere would then be an institutional or systematic violation of human rights.[7] Though we do not need Hegel's help to reach these conclusions, it is precisely by taking seriously as a hermeneutical principle his maxim that "the truth is the whole"[8] that one is led to them; for it is by refusing to look at political rights in isolation from the larger context in which they are situated that one becomes deeply suspicious of the decolonizing process.

Hegel writes, of course, in a historical context quite different from our own. He thinks of colonization only as an antidote to poverty in the mother countries, rather than as an agent of poverty in the colonies (246–48).[9] He does not even mean the same thing by *Recht* that we mean by "right" in the phrase "human rights." But Hegel does link the concept of right intimately to that of freedom;[10] his theory has implications for the pressing contemporary question of the proper place and significance of economic rights; and his methodological holism may be an indispensable, intellectual tool for developing a critical and constructive social theory.

The Primacy of Spirit
in Hegel's Theory of Property Rights

At the outset we must take note of Hegel's historical idealism. By this I mean a theory of the same sort but diametrically opposed to the historical materialism of Marxism. According to the latter,

> the *ultimately* [*in letzter Instanz*] determining element in history is the production and reproduction of real life. . . . The economic situation is the basis, but the various elements of the superstructure . . . exercise their influence upon the course of the historical struggles and in many cases preponderate in determining their *form*. There is an interaction of all these elements in which . . . the economic movement finally asserts itself as necessary. . . . We make our history ourselves, but, in the first place, under very definite assumptions and conditions. Among these the economic ones are ultimately decisive.[11]

What I refer to as Hegel's historical idealism is the view that the material or economic factor is not what is ultimately decisive in human history. This is probably nowhere clearer than in the famous discussion of the master-slave relation in the *Phenomenology of Spirit.* Hegel is there unmistakably talking about real slavery, the exploitation of human labor for economic benefit. But he makes it clear that the driving factor is not economic need and desire, but a spiritual need for recognition—the acknowledgment of one's status as, in Kantian language, an end and not merely a means.[12] In the language of Hegel's own *Logic,* we can say that in the historical institutions of slavery, of which neocolonial agribusiness based on export cropping is but one of the latest forms, the economic factor is *Schein* (the manifest surface) and the noneconomic factor *Wesen* (the latent depth).

In his lectures on the philosophy of history, Hegel reaffirms and develops this position at considerable length. Though it is not nearly as explicit in the *Philosophy of Right,* a careful analysis of the text would confirm Hegel's consistency on this issue. The point of introducing the concept of historical idealism is not to get Hegel properly labeled and pigeonholed, but rather to bring to light an important suspicion. Does Hegel's theory, with its decentralizing of the economic factor, mean that his theory of right will be just another version of the "Western liberalism" that has "a blind spot for severe economic need," and that consequently talks a lot about political liberty and very little about economic justice, and thus

relegates subsistence rights to a secondary and optional status? In
short, does Hegel's idealism function as the ideological legitimation
of bourgeois complacency by diverting attention from the harsh realities of poverty?[13]

This seems, at first, to be the case. For, though Hegel begins
his discussion of right with a theory of property, he assiduously sep-
arates this from all considerations of need. "The rational aspect of
property is to be found not in the satisfaction of needs but in transcending the pure subjectivity of personality. In his property a person exists for the first time as reason." (41Z).[14] More specifically, "If
emphasis is placed on my needs, then the possession of property appears as a means to their satisfaction, but the true position is that,
from the standpoint of freedom, property is the first embodiment of
freedom and so is in itself a substantive end" (45). Everything that
relates to desire, need, impulse, interest, advantage, welfare, and so
forth—though obviously involved in the significance of property—
belongs to the "particular" aspect rather than to the "rational" aspect, and is thus a matter of "indifference" from the standpoint of
freedom's first embodiment (37, 37Z, 45, 49, 59).

Because human needs and their satisfaction are given such a
decisively subordinate role in Hegel's theory of property, he is able
to say, "What and how much I possess, therefore, is a matter of indifference so far as rights are concerned" (49). Though this statement is eventually qualified, as we shall see, it gives expression to a
central point that must not be over-looked—the primacy of spirit in
Hegel's social theory. His theory of right is a theory of rational freedom; and it is an essential thesis that, as bearers of this freedom,
we are distinguished as spirit from even the highest forms of nature, namely animals. It is because property is being considered as
the first embodiment of rational freedom[15] that everything must
be excluded as of secondary importance that pertains to life needs
and their satisfaction. As Shlomo Avineri writes, "Hegel views property within a context far wider than that of mere necessity and
physical need to which natural law theories have relegated it. For
him, the discussion of property is part of his general philosophical
anthropology."[16]

This break with the naturalism of earlier natural-law theory
is an essential distinction of Hegelian theory. He is very explicit
about it from the outset. In paragraph 4 of the introduction he
writes, "The basis of right is, in general, spirit *[das Geistige];* its
precise place and point of origin is the will . . . the system of right is
the realm of freedom made actual, the world of spirit brought forth
out of itself like a second nature." In the preface he complains that

while the world of nature is assumed by everyone to be inherently rational, the ethical world, this second nature, "is not allowed to enjoy the good fortune which springs from the fact that it is reason which . . . has its home there. The universe of spirit is supposed rather to be left to the mercy of chance and caprice, to be Godforsaken, so that according to this atheism of the ethical world the truth is only to be found elsewhere."

In a lengthy addition to this passage, Hegel distinguishes the laws that belong to these worlds respectively as the laws of nature and the laws of right. "In nature, the highest truth is that there is law; in the law of the land, the law is not valid simply because it exists." Instead, the distinction between what the law is and what it should be is all too possible. But "a schism and a conflict of this sort is to be found only in the territory of spirit. . . . "

This inseparability of right and spirit is a point to which Hegel constantly returns in his lectures. In H. G. Hotho's notes on the 1822–23 lectures, we read that "right proceeds solely from spirit, for nature has no laws of right." And in G. Homeyer's notes on the 1818–19 lectures we read,

> The principle of right does not reside in nature, at any rate not in external nature, nor indeed in the subjective nature of man insofar as his will is naturally determined, i.e., in the sphere of needs, impulses, and inclinations. The sphere of right is the sphere of freedom in which nature, insofar as freedom externalizes itself and gives itself existence, does indeed appear, but only as something dependent. . . . The unification of freedom and necessity has been brought about not by nature but by freedom. Natural things remain as they are and have not freed themselves from law in order to make laws for themselves. But spirit breaks away from nature and produces for itself its own laws. Thus nature is not the basis of rights.[17]

John Plamenatz has summarized this central motif nicely. With reference to Hegel's theory of property rights, he says, "To make a claim is not to give vent to an appetite; it is not to be demanding in a way that even an animal can be."[18]

Positively speaking, there are two equally important aspects to this distinctly human character of property. Both concern "transcending the pure subjectivity of personality" (41Z). My personhood remains pure *(blosse)* subjectivity as long as my claim to being an end in myself remains a mere claim that no part of the world external to me confirms. The *Aufhebung* of this condition is the first

embodiment *(Dasein)* of my freedom; or better, it is my transition
from potential to actual freedom.

One way this happens involves my relation to nature. In property some part of the natural (subhuman) world becomes mine.
"This is the absolute right of appropriation which man has over all
'things' " (44). This absolute right is an expression of the fact that
"matter for itself does not belong to itself" (52). Thus, property
"means at bottom only to manifest the preeminence of my will over
the thing and to prove that it is not absolute, is not an end in itself.
This is made manifest when I endow the thing with some purpose
not directly its own.... The free will, therefore, is the idealism
which does not take things as they are to be absolute, while realism
pronounces them to be absolute.... Even an animal has gone beyond this realist philosophy since it devours things and so proves
that they are not absolutely self-subsistent" (44Z, cf. 59, 61).[19] Ownership is the act by which "the natural is torn from its autonomy
and is placed at human disposal."[20] This *Versachlichung* (objectifying) of nature makes it clear that nature plays object to human subjectivity and is the means to human ends. As in the master-slave
struggle for recognition in the *Phenomenology,* economic benefit is
secondary to questions of status, rank, and ultimately, of worth,
though here the issue is our relation to nature rather than to
each other.

But nature is only one aspect of the external world. Other human beings are the other. The second way in which the external
world confirms my claims to personhood through property is
through the recognition by other human selves of my rights as a
property owner. Hegel's discussion of this occurs especially in the
section on contract, but it is anticipated by the regular assumption
that property rights are empty apart from their being recognized or
acknowledged (51, 51Z, 55).

There are two points at which it may seem at first glance that
Hegel compromises his thoroughgoing separation of property rights
from economic needs and their satisfaction. The first occurs in his
discussion of equality (49 and 49Z). In the course of rejecting the notion that everyone should have the same amount of property, he argues, "Of course men are equal, but only *qua* persons, that is, with
respect only to the source from which possession springs; the inference from this is that everyone must have property.... From this
point of view it is false to maintain that justice requires everyone's
property to be equal, since it requires only that everyone shall own
property."

This clearly implies that those who have been completely dispossessed, whether by the criminal acts of individuals, or by an economic system that produces and tolerates dispossession (a criminal system in Hegelian theory),[21] have had their rights violated. But this has nothing to do with the fact that their "basic human needs" may go unmet. It remains true that "what and how much I possess . . . is a matter of indifference as far as rights are concerned" (49). The property I own may be far from sufficient to provide for my subsistence needs; and my property rights will not have been violated as long as I own something. The society that refuses to bulldoze the shanty town in which I live so as to respect my rights as a "homeowner" will have done all that is required by Hegel's theory of property rights, even if it provides me with no work or with work at wages so low that I cannot feed and clothe my family. What is at stake here, as before, is what Hegel called legal status *(Rechtzustand)* in the *Phenomenology* (chap. 6). What property rights are to guarantee is not my survival as an organism, but my status as a person.[22] (It might be helpful in this context to remember that in Hegel's theory of punishment as well as here it is possible to preserve the latter without preserving the former.)

It also may seem on a superficial reading that under the heading "Use of the Thing," Hegel draws a much tighter bond between property and economic needs than his otherwise unmitigated idealism would allow. "Yet my need, as the particular aspect of a single will, is the positive element which finds satisfaction, and the thing, as something negative in itself, exists only for my need and is at its service. The use of the thing is my need being externally realized. The thing thereby stands revealed as naturally self-less and so fulfills its destiny" (59, cf. 63). But by identifying need as the "particular" aspects of the will, he reminds us that, as before, it is not the essential (rational) thing. This is why he is able to continue, "But the owner's will, in accordance with which the thing is his, is the primary substantive basis of property; use is a further modification of property, secondary to that universal basis, and is only its manifestation and particular mode." By holding to the position that use is for the sake of ownership and not ownership for the sake of use, Hegel remains faithful to his idealist interpretation of property, subordinating the importance of economic needs and their satisfaction.

Both of these apparent exceptions to the separation of property from need express Hegel's view that status must have an external manifestation, and not remain a mere claim. Thus, I must actually own some property and use it, not that my *needs* may be met, but that my *status* as bearer of rights may be expressed as an empirical fact. It is the world of spirit that is at stake, but for Hegel that world is the deepest truth about the empirical world rather than a kind of Platonic alternative to it. Spiritual realities must therefore have empirical embodiment.

Hegel's theory of rights and rational freedom begins, then, with a theory of property that deliberately and consistently cuts itself off from our contemporary concern about "basic human needs" and about subsistence rights as basic rights. It would appear that Hegel's *Philosophy of Right* belongs with Locke and Adam Smith among those classics of Western liberalism that have "a blind spot to severe economic need."

Hegel's Theory of Property as a Critique of Liberal Theory and Practice

The Purpose of Abstract Right.

Yet many of the careful interpreters of Hegel's thought have seen this text as a radical break from, and a penetrating critique of, precisely that liberal tradition.[23] It is important to ask whether this is true, and, if so, how it is possible. The point is not to see whether Hegel can be rescued from his critics, but to find out how his thinking can be of help to us as we face the crisis of human rights and "basic human needs" that defines our own situation.

To that end we need to remember what has already been said about the *purpose* of the theory of property we have been considering and then, more importantly, to inquire into its *limits*. The clue to both the purpose and limits of Hegel's theory can be found in the previously cited claim that "property is the first embodiment of freedom (45). Hegel is giving us a theory of rational freedom as a determination of (objective) spirit. The fundamental distinction between nature and spirit, and thus between animal life and human existence, means that any theory of property that gives primary importance to biological needs and the sustaining of life would in effect fail to acknowledge the fundamental difference between human society and a beehive or anthill. It would fail to be an analysis of the distinctive human situation to which Hegel is addressing himself.

Thus, Hegel's theory is incompatible with any practice whose principle is the slogan, "first bread, then liberty." It stands as a protest against any materialistically inspired politics, whether left-wing "totalitarian" or right-wing "authoritarian," which structures economic life, which obviously has to do with survival needs, so as to treat human beings only as mouths to feed, while ignoring their rights as free, self-determining human persons. On this point Hegel stands in agreement with Michael Novak, the conservative heir of classical liberalism.[24]

But Hegel's theory is also incompatible with any theoretical interpretation of rights and political association as means to biological ends,[25] and this puts him in tension with liberalism. For Locke takes civil society as a means to preserving property rights, which in turn are viewed as a means to the preservation of life, and this is already true in Hobbes.[26] This strand of liberal theory is also alive and well in Michael Novak; for he not only repudiates the "first bread, then liberty" philosophy. He affirms a "first liberty, then bread" philosophy, because he takes liberty (in the sense of political and civil rights, but not subsistence rights) to be the causal condition of bread. As he sees it, "human rights and liberty are not merely the goal for which wealth is to be created. They are the means for creating it. . . . The experiment with human rights . . . is also an experiment in economic development. If all humans are equal, each must be free to make significant economic decisions— and if they are so free, the greatest social energy within the universe will be released. . . . Free persons dream. Free persons invent. Free persons create. Freedom enriches, for wealth is not fixed but created."[27]

This tendency to envision liberty as a means to bread, political life and its rights as a means to survival and happiness, runs directly counter to the primacy of spirit in Hegel's social thought. One can almost feel him wincing in response to any praise of freedom on the ground that it enriches, a standard liberal move.

The purpose of Hegel's theory of property rights, then, is not to legitimate liberalism's insensitivity to severe poverty, but to keep the theory of a rational society from lapsing to the subhuman level. Yet the intention of a theory is no reliable index of its actual function.[28] Might not the Hegelian theory of property function in essentially the same way as Lockean theory? Yes, of course—all the more easily in light of its critiques of the naturalistic tendencies of liberalism, and what happens to the question of survival in that context. But this can happen only when we ignore not only the clearly stated purpose of the theory, but also self-imposed limitations that are stated with equal clarity. In other words, the theory itself overtly repudiates such use.

The Limits of Abstract Right.

The self-imposed limitations of the theory are also expressed in the statement, "property is the first embodiment of freedom" (45; cf. 41 and 41Z). This time the accent changes so that we read, "property is the *first* embodiment of freedom" [emphasis added]. What is the meaning of this priority? Joachim Ritter's reply to this question is as provocative as it is ambiguous. He speaks of "the decisive thesis of the *Philosophy of Right,* that all substantial, spiritual-ethical orders of freedom also come to existence with the civil right of property. Thus, the abstract, external sphere of property posited in civil law is understood by Hegel as the condition of the possibility of actualizing freedom in the whole range of its religious, political, and ethical substance."[29]

The ambiguity of this claim lies in the crucial term "condition." Is property a causal condition of freedom in the totality of its other expressions? This would be an awkward interpretation; for, as we have just noted in relation to Novak, Hegel is very reluctant to speak of political life and civil rights as means to any ends. Nor can we find any support in Hegel's thought for the idea that liberty is the causal condition for bread—to say nothing of the much more encompassing claim that property rights are the causal condition of all other manifestations of freedom.

But perhaps this is not how we should read Ritter. After all, when he writes that property is "the condition of the possibility of actualizing freedom" it sounds as if property is transcendentally, rather than causally, prior to the other dimensions of freedom. But this can only be a misleading suggestion of Ritter's Kantian terminology, for we are not dealing with a theory of a possible experience, but with a theory of social reality. It is not even clear what it would mean to speak of property as a transcendental condition of freedom in its other dimensions, for it is clearly not a form or category of consciousness but a social institution. Still, this reading is not an entirely blind alley; for in the Kantian context the transcendental is a special case of the logical. Though Ritter does not himself suggest it, the impossibility of giving a causal or transcendental meaning to the priority of property leads to asking whether we must speak instead of a logical priority. This turns out to be the authentically Hegelian sense in which property is the *first* embodiment of freedom. It is logically first.

The importance of Hegel's logic for his theory of objective spirit is considerably greater than the attention that has been given to it.[30] Beginning with the third paragraph of the preface, he stresses the dependence of the *Philosophy of Right* upon the *Science of Logic*, and in the introduction he develops this in considerable detail. One of the most explicit acknowledgments of the role of the logic in the *Philosophy of Right* concerns the very point before us. "The fact that when a thing or a content is posited first of all in accordance with its concept or as it is in itself, it then has the form of immediacy or pure being, is the doctrine of speculative logic, here presupposed" (33). This comes as a comment on the *Einteilung* or *Gliederung* (organization) of the entire book, according to which, for example, the family is the first moment of *Sittlichkeit* (ethical life), and Abstract Right—which we have been discussing—is the first moment of the entire theory of objective spirit.

Property is the *first* embodiment of freedom because it is freedom in its immediacy, and the logic that determines the proper form of philosophical thinking requires that we begin with the immediate. Philosophical thinking moves from immediacy to mediation, from abstract to concrete. Because these two expressions are virtually synonymous (33, 34, 41Z), it is time that careful notice be taken of Hegel's title for the section we have been exploring, namely, "Abstract Right." In the title, and from the opening sentence of this section, Hegel emphasizes the abstractness and immediacy of his subject matter. He also insists that he is dealing with what is formal, rather than substantial (37, 37Z, 40, 42).

All three contrasts signify the same thing. To call a subject matter or discussion abstract rather than concrete, immediate rather than mediated, or formal rather than substantial is to say that it is part of a complex whole that has been isolated from its proper context. In its isolation it can neither be, nor be seen to be, what it in truth is; for "the truth is the whole." Only in the totality of their relations to the whole can any of the parts (moments) either be, or be understood to be, what they truly are. This is one of the simplest, but most far-reaching and fundamental, of Hegel's methodological commitments.

In the present instance this methodological point is of substantial significance; for it involves a dramatic self-limitation to the theory of property that Hegel presents under the title Abstract Right. The property rights of legal persons are the *first* embodiment of freedom, not because they are the most important form of freedom, not because they are the causal condition of other modes of freedom,[31] but because they are the least developed, least adequate, least rational form that freedom can take without ceasing to be freedom. Hegel is very blunt about this. "In his property a person exists for the first time as reason. Even if my freedom is here realized first of all in an external thing, and so falsely realized, nevertheless abstract personality in its immediacy can have no other embodiment save one characterized by immediacy" (41Z). Of the individual who mistakes this part of freedom for its essence, he writes, "To have no interest except in one's formal right may be pure obstinacy, often a fitting accompaniment of a cold heart and restricted sympathies. It is uncultured people who insist most on their rights, while noble minds look on other aspects of the thing. Thus abstract right is nothing but a bare possibility and, at least in contrast with the whole range of the situation, something formal. On that account, to have a right gives one a warrant, but it is not absolutely necessary that one should insist on one's rights, because that is only one aspect of the whole situation" (47Z).

Just as the individual whose behavior and attitudes are defined entirely in terms of rights is pathetically less than a real person, so the society implicit in the meeting of legal persons is abstract, immediate, formal, and false, because it is "only as owners that these two persons exist for each other" (40; cf. 104).

The limited aspect of "Abstract Right" stems from the fact that "freedom is here the freedom of the abstract will in general, that is, the freedom of a single person related only to himself" (40). It is only as freedom becomes that of a person richly related to what is other than the self that freedom is properly understood, and that the true significance of property rights themselves can be grasped. The "other" to which the individual self needs to be related is first of all the Good (Morality), then the community based on love rather than self-interest (Family), then the community based on economic self-interest (Civil Society), and finally, the community based on the solidarity of a people sharing common laws and customs. (State).[32]

Already in the introduction, Hegel had laid the conceptual groundwork for recognizing the abstractness of abstract freedom as a serious defect. The concept of the free will contains "the element of pure indeterminacy or that pure reflection of the ego into itself [relation of the self only to itself] which involves the dissipation of every restriction and every content either immediately presented by nature, by needs, desires, and impulses, or given and determined by any means whatever. This is the unrestricted infinity of absolute abstraction or universality, the pure thought of oneself" (5). In this account, however, "it is only one side of the will which is described, namely this unrestricted possibility of abstraction from every determinate state of mind . . . my flight from every content as from a restriction. When the will's self-determination consists in this alone, or when representative thinking *[Vorstellung]* regards this side by itself as freedom and clings fast to it, then we have negative freedom, or freedom as the understanding *[Verstand]* conceives it."

Hegel knows that those familiar with this technical vocabulary will recognize in his reference to *Vorstellung* and *Verstand* a critique that can be succinctly summarized: this subject matter has not yet been adequately conceived. In the following paragraphs, he develops the further moments that are necessary for the whole concept of freedom to be expressed; but before he does so, he seeks to make more vivid and concrete the inadequacy of the first moment when taken by itself. He asks what it would look like as a mode of human being in the world and gives two examples. "While still remaining theoretical, it takes shape in religion as the Hindu fanaticism of pure contemplation, but when it turns to actual practice, it takes shape in religion and politics alike as the fanaticism of destruction—the destruction of the whole subsisting social order. . . . Only in destroying something does this negative will possess the feeling of itself as existent. . . . Consequently, what negative freedom intends to will can never be anything in itself but an abstract idea, and giving effect to this idea can only be the fury of destruction." In 5Z, where these two examples are developed a bit more fully, Hegel makes it explicit that his political reference is to the Terror of the French Revolution.[33] It is precisely this seriously defective concept of freedom, "freedom of the abstract will in general, that is, the freedom of a single person related only to himself" (40), in terms of which Hegel later defines Abstract Right.

Because property is the first embodiment of *freedom* for Hegel, his theory is a critique of liberalism's (naturalist) tendency to make biological survival and economic prosperity the end for which political and civil rights are the means. Now, because property is the *first* embodiment of freedom (in the Hegelian sense of logical priority), his theory is also a critique of liberalism's (formalist) tendency to define freedom without paying sufficient attention to questions of morality, the family, political community, and severe poverty. When Locke makes property rights first, it is because they are the end to which everything else is means. When Hegel puts them first it is because in their immediate form as the minimal mode of human freedom they are in radical need of correction and completion through contextualizing.[34]

The Limits of Civil Society

Each of the new moments or contexts is essential; and only the whole is the truth. But there is one of them that is of special importance for the present discussion, namely, Civil Society. For it is by placing Abstract Right in the context of Civil Society that the whole dimension of economic needs and their satisfaction, so deliberately excluded at first, is brought decisively back into the picture. Civil society is that dimension of public, human association that is based on the pursuit by individual persons of their own (economic) interests and welfare—defined in terms of their natural and culture-bound needs (157, 182–94). It is Hegel's insistence that his own theory of property rights be completed and corrected by incorporation into the theory of civil society, so defined, that makes it possible for him to overcome the paradox involved in liberalism's simultaneous overemphasis on the economic goals of life and blindness to severe poverty.[35]

By itself, of course, this move will shed little light on how Hegel's theory is a critique of liberalism, rather than its apology; for, however strong the tendency of much contemporary liberalism may be to talk about political and civil liberties in the face of staggering poverty, the mere mention of Locke and Adam Smith reminds us that no one has accused classical liberalism of ignoring the economic side of life. And we have already noted that Hegel's own theory involves a reaction to what can be viewed as an excessive materialism or naturalism in the natural law, liberal tradition. When Hegel's holism requires the theory of property rights to be placed in the context of civil society, he is putting back together what the early forms of liberalism never separated. What we need to see is how the treatment of economic needs in Hegel's theory of civil society is a critique of their treatment in classical liberal theory, and of the very uncivil society it seeks to legitimate.

For Hegel civil society is "an association of members as self-subsistent individuals in a universality which, because of their self-subsistence, is only formal" (157). Here universality signifies totality and refers to society as a whole in distinction from its parts. But by referring to this universality as formal, Hegel indicates that "here the Idea is present only as relative totality . . . "(184), one which still requires further contextualizing. Society is being viewed in abstraction from the total context in which it would be fully rational. Thus, Knox's translation of "formell" as "abstract" is fully justified (cf. 190–92).

Hegel proceeds immediately to specify wherein this defect consists. Referring to the independent individuals who are the building blocks of liberal theory and practice, he writes, "Their association is brought about by their needs, by the legal system,—the means to security of person and property—and by an external organization for attaining their particular and common interests" (157). In subsequent paragraphs Hegel hammers away at this fundamental tenet of liberalism, namely that society and its institutions have only an instrumental significance in relation to private self-interest. The individual is the end, society the means (182Z, 183, 187, 190, 192).[36]

Expressed in the language of Hegel's logic, this primacy of self-interest or "selfish ends" (183) and the corresponding instrumentalizing of the social order means that "in Civil Society universal and particular have fallen apart" and that "here ethical life is split into its extremes and lost" (184Z). There is a unity of particular and universal, because the individual is a member of society, but "this unity is not the identity which the ethical order requires, because at this level . . . both principles are self-subsistent. It follows that it is not as freedom but as necessity that the particular rises to the form of universality" (186). In other words, as Knox's expansive translation suggests, social participation is experienced as compulsion. Hegel himself has already translated all this into the language of experience with the simple reminder that "most people regard the paying of taxes as injurious to their particular interest" (184Z).

Whereas liberalism presents such a society as the triumph of rationality and modernity, Hegel says, "This system may be prima facie regarded as the external state, the state based on need, the state as the Understanding envisages it" (183, cf. 187, 189). In other words, liberalism has quit before its task was completed. It rightly views society as concerned with the satisfaction of human needs; but in so doing it lapses into a mode of thinking less than fully rational, and (quite naturally) legitimates a society less than fully rational.

Ritter describes this irrationality as the *"Versachlichung* of all relations between persons. . . ."[37] Grounded in the property relation and the fact that "it is only as owners that these two persons really exist for each other" (40), this depersonalizing of human relations is the highest principle of civil society. It is tempting to translate *Versachlichung* somewhat freely as "instrumentalizing," for reference is to the process that on the one hand is the making of society into a means to individual ends, and, on the other hand, simultaneously reduces persons themselves to their market value and thereby makes them into means instead of ends. As exchange value comes to dominate over use value,[38] human needs themselves become abstract (for example, the need for money rather than for food) and the means of meeting them equally abstract (for example, labor as earning power rather than labor as performing a necessary task). But "when needs and means become abstract in quality . . .

abstraction is also a character of the reciprocal relation of individuals to one another" (192).

It is easy to read in this critique of the nature of human interaction in civil society an idealistic critique of liberalism's *homo economicus*, a kind of modern day Esau willing to sell his spiritual birthright for a mess of economic pottage. Critiques of modern society by Heidegger and Jacques Ellul come to mind. But the affinity of this critique with that made by Marx in the 1844 manuscripts is perhaps the most striking of all.

Still, even if one were to go further and argue that Marx's critique grows right out of Hegelian analysis,[39] we have yet to make contact with the contemporary problem that has occasioned this look at Hegel—that of "basic human needs", and the question of subsistence rights. We must now note that Hegel's critique of civil society goes a further crucial step. Because its theory of society is individualist and instrumentalist, civil society creates inhuman modes of life and interaction. But in the process, it has not even achieved the end for which these sacrifices were to be the means. It miserably fails the test of economic practice. Liberalism may be a great recipe for increasing the wealth of nations, but (and here Hegel turns the individualism of liberalism against it) it means poverty and misery for many individuals. "Civil Society affords a spectacle of extravagance and want as well as of the physical and ethical degradation common to them both" (185). The discussion of poverty to which this statement is a kind of topic sentence is well known (241–46). Hegel sees clearly that it results not from a breakdown of civil society but from its normal functioning, and that it involves not a lack of wealth but a vastly disproportionate distribution of it. He sees that capitalist society is driven by its own internal impetus toward colonial empire building, but finds neither colonizing nor internal efforts to deal with the problem to be any really adequate solution.[40] In short, one of the reasons liberalism and liberal society are not to be accepted as fully rational is that they have not the resources, theoretical or practical, for solving the problem of poverty in a market economy. Though they disagree on the proper strategies for solving this problem, the liberal liberals of today (like Keynes and Galbraith) and the conservative liberals of today (like Friedman and Gilder) agree that the problem is one of properly managing and fine-tuning the basic mechanisms of civil society. Hegel's analysis suggests that the problem is much deeper. His lack of enthusiasm for collectivist alternatives—because the freedom of the individual is an important achievement of the modern world—does not blind him to the fact that the juxtaposition of wealth and poverty in liberal society gives the lie to its claim to be rational.

In the context of Hegel's entire argument, there seems to me little difference between saying that a society that has not solved the problem of poverty in the midst of extravagance is an irrational society, and saying that such a society has violated the rights of the citizens it has abandoned to poverty. In short, Hegel's hermeneutics of holism, which seeks to lay bare the abstractness not only of abstract right but of civil society as well, leads to affirming the integrity of subsistence rights.

Hegel himself is explicit about this. In the discussion of abstract right, he says, "That everyone ought to have subsistence enough for his needs is a moral wish and thus vaguely expressed is well enough meant, but like anything that is only well meant it lacks objectivity" (49). He rightly recognizes, that within the abstract framework of abstract right, whose abstractness he harps on endlessly, there is no basis for subsistence rights to be anything but pious wishes. But in the richer, more fully rational context of ethical life, what was once (logically speaking) a utopian dream becomes a legitimate demand. "Children have the right to be fed and educated at the expense of the family's common capital" (*ernährt und erzogen zu werden,* 174). Hegel's whole discussion of poverty makes it clear that parents in turn have a right to what is needed for fulfilling this obligation. Hegel's theory of a rational society posits subsistence rights as genuine human rights. Its logic leads to the conclusion that any theory or social order that treats them as optional or utopian is not advanced, but primitive, operating at a level of rationality so partial as to be pathetic or perhaps criminal.

3 Hegel's Radical Idealism:
Family and State as Ethical Communities

Hegel's theory of the family is important both for its own sake and for the light it throws on his understanding of the state. On its own account his systematic discussion of the family stands out both for the illuminating interpretation it presents and by its mere existence, since the major modern philosophers have not paid much attention to the family in its own right. On the relation of family to state Hegel's view calls attention to itself by flying in the face of the tendency, strong in his own time and even stronger in our own, to view civil society as both the model and the goal (essence, telos) of the state.

It is the way Hegel makes the family the model (but not the goal) of the state which I wish to explore in this essay, hoping that something of the intrinsic importance of what he says for the theory and practice of family life will come to light as well. In the light of this modeling relationship between family and state Hegel's social theory can be called radical idealism, just as his metaphysics is called absolute idealism.

In this context the term 'radical' has both its etymological and its popular senses. In etymological terms Hegel seeks to be radical by getting us to the very root of what family and state are. Deviations from the essences he exhibits would have to be interpreted as 'untrue' or unhealthy approximations of the real thing. In popular terms he is radical by being sharply and deliberately out of step with prevailing attitudes and behaviors. To take him seriously would require fundamental change, both in his own times and in ours.

Similarly the term 'idealism' has a double meaning in relation to naturalistic or materialistic alternatives. In the order of explanation radical idealism denies that family and state can be accounted for in terms of sexual or economic needs as their basis, while in the order of evaluation it denies that these needs are the definitive standards by which family and state should be judged.

This preliminary sketch of radical idealism is too negative to be very satisfying. But Hegel's dialectical thinking is negative thinking, and our point of departure will have to be what the family and state are not. Above all, they are not contractual relationships, and we will have understood most of what I am calling radical idealism when we fully understand why he writes: "To subsume marriage under the concept of contract is thus quite impossible; this subsumption—though shameful is the only word for it—is propounded in Kant's *Philosophy of Law*. It is equally far from the truth to ground the nature of the state on the contractual relation, whether the state is supposed to be a contract of all with all, or of all with the monarch and the government" (PR, ¶75)[1]

There are three reasons why Hegel thinks it shameful to think of family and state in terms of contract models. Contractual relationships are (1) abstract, (2) contingent, and (3) self-centered.

On the first point Hegel protests against the tendency in philosophy and legal theory to confuse "rights which presuppose substantial ties, e.g., those of family and political life, and rights which only concern abstract personality as such." In the notion that family and political life involve "substantial ties" there lies embedded Hegel's distinctive understanding of community as an essential feature of human experience and fulfillment. But the meaning of "substantial ties" comes to light through contrast with another kind of human bond, those "rights which only concern abstract personality as such." This type of relationship is exhibited above all in property ownership and contract. In such contexts "it is only as owners that these two persons really exist for each other" (PR, ¶40). In a sales contract, for example, the only relevant factor in the relationship between two persons is that each is the owner of property he is willing to exchange for the other's property. Reciprocal recognition, which is so central to Hegel's understanding of human existence as spirit, occurs here.[2] But since each person is much more than an owner of property and all these other dimensions of who each is get left out of the relationship as irrelevant, it is a very thin or incomplete form of recognition. Hegel calls it abstract because it is arrived at by abstracting from so much of what makes up the identity of each person. The beautiful woman who wants to be loved for who she is and not just for her good looks, and the wealthy man who wants to be appreciated for more than the benefits he can bestow know just what Hegel means by "abstract personality," even if neither understands his terminology immediately. Whatever else defines the "substantial ties" which Hegel finds essential to family and political life, they will have to be relationships of whole or concrete persons to each other.

In addition to being abstract, contractual relationships are contingent. They result "from the arbitrariness [*Willkür*] of the parties" united by them. So far as the state is concerned, it "does not rest on contract, for contract presupposes arbitrariness [*Willkür*]. It is false to maintain that the foundation of the state is something at the option of all its members [in *der Willkür aller*]. It is nearer the truth to say that it is absolutely necessary for every individual to be citizen" (PR, ¶¶75, 75Z). Returning to Kant's view of marriage as a contract, Hegel notes that in such a marriage "the parties are bound by a contract of reciprocal caprice [*gegenseitige Willkür*], and marriage is thus degraded to the level of a contract for reciprocal use" (PR, ¶161Z).

The exercise of will exhibited by contract is described in the above passages as arbitrary, capricious, and optional. Of these three ways of rendering the German term *Willkür,* the last is most suited to Hegel's meaning. He does not mean to suggest that contractual relationships are arbitrary or capricious in the sense of being entirely random, unmotivated, or without reasons. In fact, as we shall see shortly, his third objection to contract is directed toward its underlying motivation. He rather means to say that contractual relationships are contingent or optional in the sense of being non-essential, extrinsic, or incidental both (a) in relation to the human condition as such and (b) in relation to the individual's own personal identity. It is not necessary to enter into such relationships to be fully human, and whether I do so or not does not significantly affect who I am.

Hegel views both family and state as necessary and essential rather than contingent and accidental in both of these senses. Regarding the first we have already noted him saying "that it is absolutely necessary for every individual to be a citizen." More boldly, he writes, "Our objectively appointed end and so our ethical duty is to enter the married state" (PR, ¶162). The point about personal identity is perhaps even more important. The family represents a unity unlike contractural unity as the absolute essence of oneself, with the result that one is not in it as an independent person but as a member" (PR, ¶158). Similarly, individual self-consciousness knows the state as its essence and "it is only as one of its members that the individual himself has objectivity, genuine individuality, and an ethical life" (PR, ¶¶257–58).

In this way the non-contractual bonds which Hegel earlier referred to as "substantial ties" are given further specification. Beyond being between whole or concrete persons, these relationships belong to the essence of the individuals related. The point is not that the I disappears before the We, for Hegel is answering the question how individuality occurs. His point is simply this. Who *We* are in the family and state to which I belong is an essential part of who *I* am, not some peripheral episode which takes place on the surface of my selfhood.

One practical consequence which Hegel is quick to draw from this view of "substantial ties" is that marriage is indissoluble. His point is eloquently expressed by C. S. Lewis in a theological context. Noting that Christian churches have not agreed with one another on the subject of divorce, he points to a deep underlying agreement.

> I mean, they all regard divorce as something like cutting up a living body, as a kind of surgical operation. Some of them think the operation so violent that it cannot be done at all; others admit it as a desperate remedy in extreme cases. They are all agreed that it is more like having both your legs cut off than it is like dissolving a business partnership or even deserting a regiment.[3]

What Hegel would appreciate most from this passage is not that Lewis happens to agree with him on the topic of divorce, but rather the phenomenological confirmation that certain kinds of relationship, of which marriage is a kind of paradigm, *are,* not merely ought to be, constitutive of our personal identity. That is the chief point of his polemic against *Willkür.* The irony is that while modern psychology and sociology illustrate and confirm this thesis again and again, we tend increasingly to view family and political relationships through contractual-contingent categories.

The third reason for repudiating contract thinking in our attempts to understand the "substantial ties" of family and state is the self-centered motivation of contractual relationships. This is perhaps the most obvious of the three features Hegel targets for criticism. People enter into contractual relationships, not in order to share themselves with someone else or to create some new reality larger than themselves, but for the sake of the personal advantages they will gain. The heart of the contractual posture is simply, I'll scratch your back if you'll scratch mine.

Since Hegel views the family relation as an essential part of a person's identity, it is not surprising that he would oppose any model which treats it as merely instrumental to the private ends of the individual as such. This is why, as we have seen above, he complains that with a contract model marriage is "degraded to the level of a contract for reciprocal use." He acknowledges that there is something quasi-contractual about the way a marriage comes into being, in the agreement between the parties or their parents. Nevertheless, "it is not a contractual relation. On the contrary, though marriage begins in contract, it is precisely a contract to transcend the standpoint of contract, the standpoint from which persons are regarded in their individuality as self-subsistent units" (PR, ¶163; cf. ¶75Z).

Just as Hegel extends his critique of the abstract and contingent nature of contract thinking both to family and state, in this case also he insists that the state, properly conceived, cannot be viewed as a means to my private ends. Hegel regularly insists that the state is to be viewed as an end, as the 'absolute' and 'final' end of individual self-consciousness (PR, ¶¶257, 258 and 260).[4] He is totally opposed to those who "conceive the state as a mere mechanical scaffolding for the attainment of external, non-spiritual ends . . . The state from this point of view is treated simply as an organization to satisfy men's necessities. . . . [It] is entirely deprived of any strictly ethical character." Such states have occurred, Hegel notes, "in times and under conditions of barbarism" (PR, ¶270). It was, in fact, the principle of such a society "which appeared in the ancient world as an invasion of ethical corruption and as the ultimate cause of that world's downfall" (PR, ¶185). In other words, the internal barbarism of egoism which destroyed Rome from within before the external barbarians administered the *coup de grâce,* is the very principle of modern civil society.

This alerts us to the fact that the passion of Hegel's critique at this point stems from his sense that the barbarism of which he speaks is anything but a thing of the past. Historically speaking nothing very noteworthy occurs when those in power view the state as a means to their personal ends.[5] The genius of social contract theory is that it teaches the ordinary citizen in the modern world to hold the same view.[6] Whether this becomes an ideological justification of the status quo, in which state power is accepted because it is said to serve the individual's interest, or becomes the revolutionary demand that the state actually serve those interests is not the primary concern from Hegel's perspective. In either case an assumption has been made to which he is totally opposed. It has been very succinctly expressed in our own time by an economist colleague who talks about the state as a kind of omni-insurance company. The crucial question, or, to be more precise, the only question to be asked is whether it is a good buy. Does a cost-benefit analysis reveal that the state scratches my back at least as hard and as long as I scratch its?

It is this sort of phenomenon which led to the earlier comment about the tendency, strong in Hegel's time and even stronger in our own, to view civil society as the model and goal of the state. For just as regularly as he denies that family and state can properly be understood in contract categories, he portrays civil society as the institutionalization of contractual relationships.[7] His opening description of civil society is the following:

> an association of members as self-subsistent individuals in a universality which, because of their self-subsistence, is only abstract. Their association is brought about by their needs, by the legal system—the means to security of person and property—and by an external organization for attaining their particular and common interests. This external state . . . (PR, ¶157)

It will be noted that civil society, by which Hegel understands the economic and legal organization of capitalist society, bears all three marks of contract thinking which Hegel has been denying to family and state. It is a means to the personal and economic security of individual property owners. For this reason its members are self-subsistent individuals related only by an abstract universality, a bond which relates them to each other only as owners of life, liberty, and property. This makes the resulting organization externally related to its members, not as something necessarily foreign or hostile, but as something essentially unrelated to who they are.[8] To belong to a different civil society would be like changing insurance companies or stockbrokers. If our immediate response to this is that we could not so easily exchange our citizenship for another, this only shows that Hegel is phenomenologically right, that the state is more than social contract theory allows it to be.

As a means toward the ends of its individual members, civil society's task can be defined both negatively and positively. It is necessary

> first, that accidental hindrances to one aim or another be removed, and undisturbed safety of person and property be attained; and secondly, that the securing of every single person's livelihood and welfare be treated and actualized as a right, i.e., that particular welfare as such be so treated. (PR, ¶230)

The negative task of removing human interference with the individual's livelihood and wealth Hegel calls 'the Administration of

Justice.' The positive task of affirmative action to assure the individual's livelihood and welfare he describes as 'the Police' or 'Public Authority' and 'the Corporation.' 'The Public Authority' is broader than what we today understand by police. For while it is concerned with crime control, and thus is directly related to the administration of justice, it also has responsibility for regulating prices, educating the citizens, and administering the antipoverty programs which will inevitably be needed.[9] By the Corporation Hegel means those voluntary associations which "come on the scene like a second family" for their members. The organized church is one example, but the primary model Hegel has in mind is economically oriented. It is something like a cross between a medieval guild and a modern labor union, assuring the livelihood of its members but also providing the recognition and respect that go with belonging. Thus, "as the family is the first, so the Corporation is the second ethical root of the state, the one planted in civil society" (PR, ¶¶250–56, 270).[10]

The point to be noticed here is simply this: civil society is organized in the pursuit of the goals to which it is a means and of the three structures Hegel discusses, 'the Administration of Justice' and 'the Public Authority' belong to what we call government while only 'the Corporation,' which includes features of genuine community within it, belongs to what we call the private sector. This makes it very easy to identify the state with the self-regulating organization of civil society. This is what is meant by speaking of civil society as the model and goal of the state. For when (1) the state is viewed simply as the further extension of civil society in pursuit of the latter's own goals and (2) civil society is composed of the network of contractual relationships which make up capitalist society, it is natural to think of political life as essentially a contractual affair with primarily economic goals.

Hegel resists this tendency. Having affirmed that the state is like the family in being non-contractual, Hegel consistently denies that it is like civil society in being contractual, without overlooking how deeply ingrained the latter assumption is upon modern thinking. "If the state is represented as a unity of different persons, as a unity which is only a partnership, then what is really meant is only civil society," he writes, immediately after noting that the creation of civil society is a distinctive achievement of the modern world.

> In the course of the actual attainment of selfish ends . . . there is formed a system of complete interdependence . . . This system may be prima facie regarded as the external state, the

> state based on need, the state as the Understanding envisages
> it. (PR, ¶¶182Z and 183)[11]

In other words, what may appear to be the state is not really the
state at all, not the state as it truly is, as Reason envisages it.

> Individuals in their capacity as burghers in this state are pri-
> vate persons whose end is their own interest. This end is me-
> diated through the universal which thus appears as a means
> to its realization.

But,

> this unity is not the identity which the ethical order re-
> quires . . . It follows that this unity is present here not as free-
> dom but as necessity. (PR ¶¶186–87)[12]

Neither the market nor the government regulation of the market
can be experienced as the freedom in terms of which the state is to
be understood. The second half of this essay, beginning on p. 45 with
the quotation from PR, ¶¶ 149, shows how Hegel's theory of community is also a theory of freedom. The double liberation embodied in
ethical life at the levels of family and state indicates that for Hegel
freedom is neither the absence of restraint on natural inclinations
nor the self-sufficiency of the independent individual but rather the
overcoming of both of these conditions.[13]

Perhaps Hegel's clearest attempt to distinguish the nature of
the state from that of civil society is the following:

> If the state is confused with civil society, and if its specific end
> is laid down as the security and protection of property and per-
> sonal freedom, then the interest of the individuals as such be-
> comes the ultimate end of their association, and it follows that
> membership of the state is something optional. But the state's
> relation to the individual is quite different from this. Since the
> state is spirit objectified, it is only as one of its members that
> the individual himself has objectivity, genuine individuality,
> and an ethical life. (PR ¶258)

We can summarize Hegel's negative thinking to this point with
two claims: like the family the state cannot properly be understood
in contractual terms, and therefore, the self-regulating organiza-

tion of a capitalist economy, even in its public or governmental structures, is only the appearance and not the true essence of the state. Negative results are always a bit frustrating, but these are likely to be more so than usual for many of us moderns. For if this is not what the state is, what could it possibly be? We have been so thoroughly conditioned to think of the state as that which protects us from enemy and criminal interference in our personal lives and which manages the economy so as to maximize our wealth that we can think of little or nothing else in terms of which to understand the state. After all, do the politicians ever talk about anything else during election time but national security, crime control, and who can best manage the economy? If Hegel is going to say anything to us that we can understand, he will have to become more positive.

What Hegel has been trying to evoke through all his negotiations is the central notion of his social theory, *Sittlichkeit*. It is the concept which underlies his talk about "ethical substance" and "substantial ties." Its etymological roots are in the terms *Sitten*, customs, and it is usually translated as ethical life, though for Hegel it connotes a whole theory of human community. There is perhaps no better brief summary of that theory than Charles Taylor's.

> '*Sittlichkeit*' refers to the moral obligations I have to an ongoing community of which I am a part. These obligations are based on established norms and uses, and that is why the etymological root in 'Sitten' is important for Hegel's use. The crucial characteristic of *Sittlichkeit* is that it enjoins us to bring about what already is. This is a paradoxical way of putting it, but in fact the common life which is the basis of my *sittlich* obligation is already there in existence. It is in virtue of its being an ongoing affair that I have these obligations; and my fulfillment of these obligations is what sustains it and keeps it in being. Hence in *sittlichkeit,* there is no gap between what ought to be and what is, between *Sollen* and *Sein.*[14]

It turns out that the parallel between the family and the state provides a positive articulation of what *Sittlichkeit* means as well as a negative evocation. Thus a closer look at what the family *is* will be our most helpful clue to understanding the kind of community Hegel understands the state to be.

As we have already seen, the institutions of ethical life provide "the duties of the station" to which the individual belongs.

> The bond of duty can appear as a restriction only on indeterminate subjectivity or abstract freedom, and on the impulses

either of the natural will or of the moral will which determines
its indeterminate good arbitrarily. The truth is, however, that
in duty the individual finds his liberation; first, liberation
from dependence on mere natural impulse . . . secondly, liber
ation from the indeterminate subjectivity which . . . remains
self-enclosed and devoid of actuality. In duty the individual ac-
quires substantive freedom. (PR, ¶149)[15]

The first instance of ethical life as this double liberation from
"mere natural impulse" and from "indeterminate" and "self-
enclosed," i.e., isolated subjectivity, is presented in the opening two
paragraphs of Hegel's account of marriage.
Paragraph 161 describes the first moment.

Marriage, as the immediate type of ethical relationship, . . .
contains first, the moment of physical life; and since marriage
is a substantial tie, the life involved in it is life in its totality,
i.e., as the actuality of the race and its life-process. But, secondly, in self-consciousness the natural sexual union, which is
only inward or undeveloped [*an sich*] and therefore exists only
as an external unity, is transformed into something spiritual,
into self-conscious love.

Alongside this notion that in marriage human sexuality is
raised from something merely natural and biological to something
spiritual and ethical, "that the consciousness of the parties is crys-
tallized out of its physical and subjective mode and lifted to the
thought of what is substantive" (PR, ¶164), Hegel places the idea of
marriage as reducing the importance of sex and putting it in its
place. In genuine marriage

physical passion sinks to the level of a physical moment, destined to vanish in its very satisfaction. On the other hand, the
spiritual bond of union secures its rights as the substance of
marriage and thus rises, inherently indissoluble, to a plane
above the contingency of passion and transience of particular
caprice. (PR, ¶163)

The view that marriage as an official, public act is alien to true love
"is a travesty of the ethical aspect of love, the higher aspect which
restrains purely sensual impulse and puts it in the background." In
the ethical bond of marriage

the sensuous moment, the one proper to physical life, is put
into its ethical place as something only consequential and accidental, belonging to the external embodiment of the ethical
bond, which indeed can subsist exclusively in reciprocal love
and support. (PR, ¶164)[16]

Hegel is not at war with himself here. True to the dialectical
spirit, he insists that marriage is at once the upgrading and the
downgrading of sexuality. He unites these two thoughts in a phrase
when he describes sex as "the external embodiment of the ethical
bond." The ethical bond of marriage is love, which is something spiritual. While Hegel defines spirit in inter-subjective terms as recognition rather than in metaphysical terms as incorporeality, it
remains the case for him as for the tradition that the physical can
never be fully adequate to the spiritual. Thus sexuality as a biological process can only be the *external* embodiment of the ethical bond.
But since Hegel is no dualist, the spiritual is that which reveals itself through incarnation. Hence the ethical bond, though spiritual,
is embodied. As the *embodiment of a spiritual relation* sex is caught
up into the realm of spirit and is no longer something merely natural or biological. In marriage sex takes on a sacramental role, for
it becomes the outward and visible expression of an inward and invisible love. This sacramentalism of the sex life is for Hegel the
mean between the naturalism of the sex life, which views it only in
terms of psychobiological needs and their fulfillment, and the romanticism of the sex life, which views it as the be-all and end-all of
human life and love.

If we ask about the spiritual or ethical bond of self-conscious
love whose expression or embodiment sexuality properly is, we
bring ourselves to the second moment of liberation. Ethical life in
general and marriage in particular bring liberation not only from
the merely natural but also from the isolation of autonomous selfhood. Paragraph 162 describes this second way in which social
structure and duty belong to the story of human freedom.

On the subjective side, marriage may have a more obvious
source in the particular inclination of the two persons . . . But
its objective source lies in the free consent of the persons, especially in their consent to make themselves one person, to re-
nounce their natural and individual personality to this unity of
one with the other. From this point of view, their union is a
self-restriction, but in fact it is their liberation, because in it
they attain their substantive self-consciousness.[17]

Just as in traditional metaphysics properties, qualities, or accidents cannot be themselves apart from the substance in which they inhere, so Hegel claims that human individuals cannot be themselves apart from the social wholes to which they belong. This is why he calls the union in which two persons become one their "substantive self-consciousness."[18] Neither in isolated self-sufficiency nor in contractual interdependency (which presupposes a genuine self prior to the relationship) does this kind of relationship exist and it is only in such ethical relationships, and thus in community, that true human selfhood and freedom are achieved. In Hegel's abstract language neither particularity nor abstract and external universality can satisfy the Idea, but only the genuine universality of substantial unity.[19]

The power and authority of this kind of ethical substance is not something alien to the individual who belongs to it.

> On the contrary, his spirit bears witness to them as to its own essence, the essence in which he has a feeling of self-hood, and in which he lives as in his own element which is not distinguished from himself. The subject is thus directly linked to the ethical order by a relation which is more like an identity than even the relation of faith or trust. (PR, ¶147)

Clearly the notion of contract would be even less appropriate for describing this relation of identity. I *am* who We are.

This is why Hegel says of the family in particular that

> one's frame of mind is to have self-consciousness of one's individuality within this unity as the absolute essence of oneself, with the result that one is in it not as an independent person but as a member. (PR, ¶158)[20]

Commenting on this passage, Hegel adds

> Love means in general terms the consciousness of my unity with another, so that I am not in selfish isolation but win my self-consciousness only as the renunciation of my independence and through knowing myself as the unity of myself with another and of the other with me . . . The first moment in love is that I do not wish to be a self-subsistent and independent person and that if I were, then I would feel defective and incomplete. The second moment is that I find myself in another person, that I count for something in the other, while the other

in turn comes to count for something in me. Love, therefore, is the most tremendous contradiction; the Understanding cannot resolve it since there is nothing more stubborn than this point of self-consciousness which is negated and which nevertheless I ought to possess as affirmative. Love is at once the propounding and the resolving of this contradiction. As the resolving of it, love is unity of an ethical type. (PR, ¶158A)

In love I am who We are. This is why We cannot view our relationship or the entity We comprise together simply as a means to our separate, individual ends.

The ethical aspect of marriage consists in the parties' consciousness of this unity as their substantive aim, and so in their love, trust, and common sharing of their entire existence as individuals. (PR, ¶163)

Several things need to be noted about this passage. First, this unity consists not only of attitudes (love and trust) but of activity as well (sharing of their entire existence). It is something to do. Second, though individuality renounces its ultimacy it does not disappear. The parties share their existence as individuals, though in sharing they create a reality which is more than the sum of their individualities. Third, it is "when the parties are in this frame of mind" that "their physical passion sinks to the level of a physical moment," becomes but one aspect, important as it is, of their total sharing together. Finally, by calling this unity the parties' aim Hegel indicates not only that it is a task and not a fact, something to be done, but also that it is valued for its own sake. It is not simply the means to something other than itself, but is itself the end, the goal, the aim of the attitudes and activities which constitute it. In Aristotelian terms marriage is *praxis,* not *poiēsis,* and the knowledge on which it depends is *phronēsis* rather than *technē.* Like all forms of virtue, the We formed by love is its own reward.

In sum, marriage as a noncontractual relationship is a double liberation. It frees our self-consciousness from self-centeredness so it can participate in a We which is larger than itself but with which it remains in a relation of identity. And it frees our sexuality from its state of nature so it can be an expression of the committed sharing which constitutes that We and not merely a means for reproduction or physical pleasure. If the family is to be the positive model for the state in its noncontractural rationality, we can expect the state to be a similar double liberation. And this is just what we find.

To begin with, the state is a We of the same sort as the family. There are differences, of course, most notably of scope. Hegel also suggests that while the family is based on love and thus feeling, the state is based on law and thus thought, though his discussion of patriotism as political sentiment (*Gesinnung*) complicates that distinction considerably.[21] Still the isomorphism is strong. The state is also a noncontractual unity in which the individual finds "substantive freedom" (PR, ¶257). Hegel makes this clear, I believe, in one of his first descriptions of the state.

> The state . . . is the actuality of the substantial will which it possesses in the particular self-consciousness once that consciousness has been raised to consciousness of its universality. This substantial unity is an absolute and unmoved end in itself, in which freedom comes into its supreme right. On the other hand this final end has supreme right against the individual, whose supreme duty is to be a member of the state. If the state is confused with civil society . . . then the interest of the individuals as such becomes the ultimate end of their association . . . But the state's relation to the individual is quite different from this. Since the state is spirit objectified, it is only as one of its members that the individual himself has objectivity, genuine individuality, and an ethical life. Unification pure and simple is the true content and aim of the individual, and the individual's destiny is the living of a universal life. His further particular satisfaction, activity, and mode of conduct have this substantive and universally valid life as their starting point and their result. (PR, ¶258)

Hegel returns to this theme of unity as an end in itself and not merely a means only a couple of paragraphs later. The state is the actuality of concrete freedom because individuals

> pass over of their own accord into the interest of the universal . . . they even recognize it as their own substantive mind; they take it as their end and aim and are active in its pursuit. The result is that the universal does not prevail or achieve completion except along with particular interests . . . and individuals likewise do not live as private persons for their own ends alone, but . . . their activity is consciously aimed at none but the universal end. (PR, ¶260)

In short, participation in the state is of value for its own sake and not instrumentally because the state, while transcending the individuals who make it up, remains in a relation of identity with them. It's a matter of ontology. I the citizen am who We the people are. Like the family, the state frees self-consciousness from self-centeredness.

The identity which Hegel affirms here does not exclude difference. In the family difference was reconciled with identity partly through the attitudes of love and trust and partly through the activity of sharing the whole of life together. All three, love, trust, and sharing, presuppose difference, identity, and the harmony of the two, such that the identity in question requires difference and vice versa.[22]

It is the sentiment of patriotism which corresponds to the love and trust in the family. By patriotism Hegel does not primarily mean "a readiness for exceptional sacrifices and actions," but rather an everyday attitude which "habitually recognizes that the community is one's substantive groundwork and end." He explicitly identifies this sentiment with trust, and though he has said that law is to the state what love is to the family, he continues to describe patriotism in terms similar to earlier descriptions of love. Obviously the sexual element is missing, but we have already seen that it is not the essence of the love which constitutes marriage. What is common to love and patriotism is that the other is perceived as not being other. We instinctively recognize this when we speak of patriotism as love of country.[23]

If the sentiment of patriotism is the individual's affective participation in the state, the active participation which would correspond to the sharing of life together in marriage remains to be determined. The We of marriage we have seen to be an aim or goal, not just because it is valued for its own sake, but also because it is something to do. How do we act in the state, so that, as Hegel insists, the individual self-consciousness finds the state to be not only its own essence and end, but also the "product of its activity" (PR, ¶257; cf. ¶258)?

Here it is necessary to distinguish "the strictly political state" from the state without qualification, the state as a people's system of government from the state as the whole of their life together, including in the broadest sense, their culture.[24] Hegel writes

> The spiritual individual, the nation—in so far as it is internally differentiated so as to form an organic whole—is what we call the state. This term is ambiguous, however, for the state and the laws of the state, as distinct from religion, science, and art, usually have purely political associations. But in

this context, the word 'state' is used in a more comprehensive sense, just as we use the word 'realm' to describe spiritual phenomena. A nation should therefore be regarded as a spiritual individual, and it is not primarily its external side that will be emphasised here, but rather what we have previously called the spirit of the nation, i.e. its self-consciousness in relation to its own truth and being, and what it recognises as truth in the absolute sense—in short, those spiritual powers which live within the nation and rule over it.[25]

It is clear from Hegel's account of patriotism that such a sentiment can exist only on the basis of an active participation in both the strictly political and the cultural life of one's people. In the former case the central notion is that freedom involves "self-determining action according to laws and principles ... " (PR, ¶258). Hegel echoes Rousseau's definition of liberty as "obedience to a law which we prescribe to ourselves."[26] It is debatable whether Hegel fully appreciates his own requirement for political participation and whether the constitutional monarchy he envisages provides sufficiently for it. (It is also debatable whether the parliamentary and presidential democracies of today really fulfill his criterion of rational government fully.)

What is clear is that Hegel's view of freedom requires active citizen involvement in determining the laws which regulate individual behavior. It is the quality of that involvement rather than effectiveness in promoting economic growth and consumption by which the political state is to be measured. Political participation (pursued for its own sake and not just as an instrumental necessity) is part of the sharing of one's life with one's people which constitutes the state.

The other part is obviously a sharing in the cultural life of the nation. Just as Hegelian philosophy cannot conclude with a philosophy of objective spirit but must go on to reflect on art, religion, and philosophy, so the active life of the individual must go beyond the narrowly political to the more broadly cultural aspects of national life.[27]

This is the first liberation which the state actualizes, participation in a We which frees the individual from the self-centeredness of natural selfhood. The other moment of liberation in the family is the transformation of sexuality from a natural to a spiritual activity by its incorporation into that community life (the family We) whose external embodiment it becomes. There is a human activity which undergoes a similar upgrading-downgrading by its incorporation into the life of the state. It is the economic activity which lies at the heart of civil society.

It should already be clear that the incorporation of economic life into the life of the state cannot mean government planning and regulation of the economy so far as these activities are determined by economic goals. For we have already seen that this dimension of government belongs conceptually to civil society and not to the state.[28] Just as sex for reproduction and pleasure does not belong to the essence of the family (though they get included in family life) so economics as production and consumption does not belong to the essence of the state (though they get included in political and cultural life). It is only as economic life is transformed by becoming an external embodiment of the We which is the state, rather than an end on its own terms which the political and cultural life of a society serve as means, thereby becoming its institutional and ideological superstructure, that the state completes the freedom which is its destiny. In this sacramentalism of economic life political and cultural values are the basis, production, and consumption of the superstructure of society.

Like social-contract theory, this one is capable of ideological or revolutionary readings. Hegel tells us that the state is rational because in the modern world it actually achieves these goals. Marx tells us it is irrational because the opposite is true. History has taken the side of Marx increasingly, as economic life has become more and more autonomous[29] and political participation and cultural expression have become more and more subordinate.

But let us linger with Hegelian theory long enough to notice the upgrading and downgrading of economic activity which it entails. Hegel is more explicit about the latter and is clearly as eager to put the pursuit of wealth in its place as he earlier was to put the pursuit of sexual pleasure in its. We have already seen him label barbaric any society which makes economic goals its ultimate goals.[30] The needs which economic life satisfies are in the first place merely animal needs. Beyond these there are artificial needs whose basis is culture and not biology. Still, the goal of satisfying economic needs, whether animal or human, is a goal so restricted, finite and particular that in the institutions of civil society which are given over to this goal we cannot hope to find the actuality of true human freedom.[31] One direct consequence of this is that it would be a travesty to conceive of education "as a mere means to those ends ... The final purpose of education therefore, is liberation and the struggle for a higher liberation still" (PR, ¶187), not the attainment of marketable skills.

There are perhaps two reasons why Hegel is less specific in discussing the elevation of economic life above the mere satisfaction of needs, natural and artificial, to the place where it is the external embodiment of the ethical bond of the state. First, the world he lived in, like our own, was not exactly brim full of instances where economic life had been subordinated to serve the political interests in shared decision-making, the aesthetic interests in beauty and equipoise, and the ethical and religious interest in justice. *Shalom,* the ancient Hebrew name for such a situation, has never been the most striking characteristic of capitalist society.[32] Second, Hegel regularly celebrates the freedom given the individual by the economic system of the modern world and focuses his praise of economic life on this feature. This is a constant theme in the *Philosophy of Right,* summed up in this claim:

> The principle of the modern state has prodigious strength and depth because it allows the principle of subjectivity to progress to its culmination in the extreme of self-subsistent personal particularity . . . (PR, ¶260)

But the freedom of free enterprise receives only penultimate praise from Hegel, who completes the claim just cited with these words: "and yet at the same time brings it back to the substantive unity and so maintains this unity in the principle of subjectivity itself." Since it is the substantive unity of the state and not the abstract unity of civil society which Hegel mentions here, it is clear that he understands the state to be rational only insofar as economic life is transformed to become the expression of noneconomic values.

If we compare Hegel's idealism of the community with the prevailing theory and practice of sexuality and economic activity in our own society we will be able to see how genuinely radical is the inner movement of Hegel's social thought.

4 Donagan's Critique of *Sittlichkeit*

No contemporary attempt to develop a theory of morality in the Kantian tradition would be responsible if it ignored the Hegelian critique of Kantian ethics. At the center of that critique is the claim that the principles and maxims of pure practical reason are insufficiently specific to give definite answers to basic moral questions arising in everyday life. Pure practical reason is here understood as the exercise of that rational capacity which I share with all rational creatures (at least all human ones) in all times and places. It thus abstracts from all aspects of my moral sensibility which derive from my own historical time and place in distinction from other cultures or societies.

It is just this act of abstraction which leads Hegel to call any morality which rests on pure practical reason abstract. "The moral point of view . . . is defective because it is purely abstract.[1] That is to say, it is "an empty formalism" into which specific moral guidance must be imported from without, since on its own terms "no transition is possible to the specification of particular duties nor, if some particular content for acting comes under consideration, is there any criterion in that principle for deciding whether it is or is not a duty. On the contrary, by this means any wrong or immoral line of conduct may be justified.[2]

Hegel's alternative is to insist upon placing the morality of pure practical reason, which he terms *Moralität,* in the concrete context of the laws and customs of an actual society, from which, in fact, he claims, the content attributed to pure practical reason actually comes. The morality of social mores he names *Sittlichkeit. Moralität* cheats, on Hegel's view, for it attributes to an unsituated, timeless reason the values actually derived from its own historical situation. It is, in the most precise sense, ideology.

Alan Donagan's *The Theory of Morality* is a challenging, contemporary attempt to develop an ethics in the Kantian tradition. Far from irresponsibly ignoring the Hegelian critique, he confronts it head on at the very onset. In doing so he first states Hegel's conclusions with considerable clarity,[3] setting aside in the process a couple of possible misunderstandings of what the issue is; secondly, he expresses his own rejection of those conclusions, identifying himself with those traditional moralists who "vehemently disapprove [Hegel's] . . . doctrine that morality has no content except that which the *Sittlichkeit* of ethical communities can supply . . . [and who] insisted that the restrictions ordained by practical reason on how one may pursue one's ends are specific";[4] thirdly, he complains that Hegel's "reasons for so degrading morality are obscure";[5] and, fourthly, he delivers an emotional *coup de grace* to Hegelian style reservations about Kantian style moral theory.

It is my purpose in this essay to suggest that Hegel's view, though far from being unproblematical, is worthy of more serious consideration than Donagan gives it. I shall try to show this by rendering his "reasons for so degrading morality" less obscure than they are to Donagan. But first it is both necessary and possible to consider the *coup de grace* just mentioned; for if its force is undiluted, the specifics of Hegel's reasoning really will not matter much. His theory of morality will be *morally* unacceptable.

Donagan dooms the morality of *Sittlichkeit* by telling the story of Franz Jägerstätter. He was a devout Catholic farmer in Austria during World War II who concluded from the church's teaching that it is morally wrong to serve in an unjust war and that he should refuse induction into the German army. Before his execution for refusing to serve he was told by his priest and bishop that nonparticipation was required by the moral law only if he was certain the war was unjust, and that neither they nor he could really be all that sure. After his death the bishop said that it was not Jägerstätter but the heroes of the *Wehrmacht* who were the moral example to be emulated.

Donagan's dismay begins with a theoretical question:

> Is it possible to find in this anything but the depravation of the *Sittlichkeit* of an ethical community whose members had lost the habit of moral self-criticism? . . . Hegel disparaged the point of view of morality on the ground that, being abstractly rational, it could find content for its judgments only in the mores of some actual community. The case of Jägerstätter reveals an opposite process . . . by recourse to the mores of their actual community, Jägerstätter's spiritual advisers were able to evaporate the precepts whose applicability to his case they could not dispute. . . . Here, what is exposed as empty, as lacking

specific content, as allowing any filling whatever, is not *Moralität,* but *Sittlichkeit.*[6]

I can only agree wholeheartedly with this verdict, as far as it goes. But it does not go far enough, and for that reason it is likely to suggest an unwarranted conclusion, one apparently accepted by Donagan. That conclusion may be stated fairly simply as follows: since the Hegelian strategy in moral philosophy, which gives priority to *Sittlichkeit* over *Moralität,* is insufficiently sensitive to the possibilities of distortions such as those in the Jägerstätter case, the Kantian moral strategy, which gives priority to *Moralität* over *Sittlichkeit* (to individual moral conscience or practical reason over social mores), is *morally* preferable.

Whether or not Donagan intends us to draw this conclusion, it is important to see why it does not follow. The human heart is indeed "deceitful above all things and desperately corrupt."[7] Just for that reason it knows more than one way to justify outrageous behavior. Jägerstätter represents a case where a rational *Moralität* is neutralized by a rationalizing *Sittlichkeit.*[8] But there can just as easily be cases where a rational *Sittlichkeit* is neutralized by a rationalizing *Moralität.*[9] One of Donagan's own objections to the "new" intuitionism of Broad and Ross is that its interpretation of pure practical reason invites just such abuse; for it "allows ordinarily respectable persons to do anything they are likely to choose, and to have a good conscience in doing it,"[10] and the presence of a contrary social consensus is at least theoretically no obstacle to this. Perhaps an even more pertinent example, given the Jägerstätter case, would be the behavior of Nazi groups and the Ku Klux Klan in the United States today. In direct defiance of laws and customs which repudiate their racism, they turn to their own private brand of practical reason, their *Moralität,* to justify some of the same kinds of behavior which, in the earlier instances, were justified by a thoroughly corrupt *Sittlichkeit.* To paraphrase Donagan: Is it possible to find in this anything but the depravation of *Moralität* in individuals who have lost the habit of moral self-criticism?

The Kantian moral philosopher will surely reply that he did not have the Klan's *Moralität* in mind, but a genuinely rational version. This only invites the Hegelian moral philosopher to reply, with equal ease, that it was not the anti-Semitic *Sittlichkeit* of central Europe which he had in mind either, but a truly rational community of values. Hegel himself, indeed, is fond of summarizing his theory of *Sittlichkeit* in the following manner: "When a father inquired about the best method of educating his son in ethical conduct, a Pythagorean replied: 'Make him a citizen of a state with *good laws.*' "[11]

Kierkegaard was as offended as Donagan at the primacy given by Hegel's critique of conscience in the *Philosophy of Right* to the social universal over the reflective individual.[12] He knew about the idolatrous tendency of every social order to absolutize itself, automatically justifying all its behavior.[13] But he was just as keenly aware of the individual's tendency to do the same. His warning against the self-serving bad faith of human moral autonomy therefore goes farther than would be suggested by reflection on the Jägerstätter case alone.

> Every individual ought to live in fear and trembling, and so too there is no established order which can do without fear and trembling. Fear and trembling signifies that one is in process of becoming, and every individual man, and the race as well, is or should be conscious of being in process of becoming. And fear and trembling signifies that a God exists—a fact which no man and no established order dare for an instant forget.[14]

This reminder of the historicity of human existence in both its individual and social dimensions, cautions us against assuming that pure practical reason thinking *sub specie aeternitatis* is ever anything but a regulative ideal. Neither Aquinas nor Kant was sufficiently sensitive to this point. If we would learn from their extraordinarily rich contributions to moral philosophy, we need to be especially careful not to duplicate one of their great weaknesses.[15] *Caveat philosophus.*

This warning, however, leaves the central issues before us. What were Hegel's reasons for "so degrading morality"? And are "the restrictions ordained by practical reason on how one may pursue one's ends" sufficiently specific to justify the claim that our common morality (which we learn in large measure, to be sure, from participation in the ethical life of our people rather than from philosophical deliberation) can always, or, for the most part, be validated by the exercise of pure practical reason?

It will be helpful in addressing these questions to understand the logical structure of the system of morality Donagan has in mind.[16] (We are talking here about what he calls the "first-order system," the one which concerns the permissibility or impermissibility of actions objectively considered, as distinct from the culpability or inculpability of moral agents.) This system, as he understands it, has a single first principle. From this first principle various "specificatory premises" are "derived" which, in conjunction with the first principle, permit rigorous deductions of the following form:

    a) All actions with a certain characteristic are impermissible.
    b) Actions of kind K have this characteristic.
    c) Therefore, actions of kind K are impermissible.[17]

This argument has the same form as the familiar

    d) All men are mortal.
    e) Socrates is a man.
    f) Therefore, Socrates is mortal.

Since it consists of arguments of this form, the system of morality Donagan has in mind could be called a "simple deductive" system. But this could be misleading by suggesting a status for the specificatory premises (b and e) which they do not have. They are *not themselves axioms* of the system, independent and on a par with a and d. They are rather derived from a and d, but *not strictly derived* by means of definition and substitution. The derivation, in other words, is not itself deductive. It involves the attribution of a general concept to a particular (in the first case, to a particular action kind). Not wishing to call this derivation process "arbitrary and unreasoned," Donagan describes it both as "informal analytical" and as "unformalized analytical" reasoning.[18] Since it involves the subsumption of a particular, e.g., Socrates, under a universal, e.g., man, it could also be called judgment.

    Thus it is clear that while the presentation of the system of morality will have a strictly deductive form, its justification will not; for as Donagan is careful to point out, everything depends on the nondeductive establishment of the specificatory premises. That is where "virtually all the philosophical difficulties" lie.[19] The question is whether specificatory premises (which are sufficiently specific "for the solution of serious moral problems")[20] can be convincingly derived from the first principle. To the degree that such premises cannot be convincingly derived, and serious moral problems remain unresolved by the system, the first principle will show itself to be empty and abstract. Score points for Hegel. To the degree that such premises can be convincingly derived, and serious moral problems resolved, the first principle will show itself fecund and fruitful. Score points for Kant.

Donagan suggests that there have been two primary candi-
dates for the role of first principle in terms of which our common
morality can be rationally justified.[21] One of these is the Golden
Rule: Do (do not do) unto others as you would (would not) have them
do unto you. Donagan takes Kant's first formulation of the categorical imperative—"Act only according to that maxim by which you
can at the same time will that it should become a universal law"—to
be the philosophical equivalent of the Golden Rule,[22] and he rejects
it as an inadequate first principle. As a principle of impartiality it
is not wholly vacuous, for it precludes acts in which I make an exception of myself from rules I expect others to follow. Still,

> what a man would or would not have another do to him is in
> part a function of the mores he has made his own. Hence in
> cultures whose mores differ radically, what the Golden Rule is
> taken to require or forbid will differ radically too. And so any
> system of conduct that can be put forward as rational can in-
> clude it. . . . But obviously, no principle of impartiality that is
> common to different systems of mores can serve as the sub-
> stantive first principle that distinguishes any one of them
> from the others.[23]

Perhaps Hegel's critique of Kant has never been put so succinctly
before.

It is possible now to answer Donagan's question about Hegel's
reason for "so degrading morality." His discussions of Kantian morality are in terms of the first formulation of the categorical imperative, and he simply agrees with Donagan that it is compatible with
too much, that it is too empty to be the first principle of duty and
virtue. At this point it needs to be noted that the phrase "too empty"
is not logically and grammatically inappropriate in the way the
phrases "too unique" or "not unique enough" are. Whereas the logic
of "unique" is an either/or matter, the logic of "empty" is not; it
rather permits of degrees. Depending on the context, something can
be too empty to be satisfactory without being completely empty,
and that is just the judgment which Donagan has made about
Kant's first formula. It is not entirely empty, since it does preclude
some behavior, but it is too empty to be the first principle of
morality because it is compatible with too many morally significant
alternatives.

Though the rhetoric of Hegel's critique of Kant sometimes suggests that he takes Kant's principle to be completely empty, a more
charitable and philosophically fruitful reading would be something

like this: by seeking to ground morality on a reason which abstracts from historical-social conditioning, Kant can only produce a principle which is manifestly too empty. It leaves too many serious moral problems unresolved. Human ethical life requires more specific guidance.

Donagan and Hegel are in agreement against Kant on this point, so far as the first formula is concerned. This settles the matter of Kantian ethics for Hegel, since he accepts at face value Kant's claim that all subsequent formulations of the categorical imperative are equivalent to the first. It is precisely by rejecting this view, which Kant and Hegel share, that Donagan is able to sustain his defense of Kant against the Hegelian critique. His case depends on showing that the second candidate for the role of moral first principle is clearly not equivalent to the first, since from it can be derived "restrictions ordained by practical reason on how one may pursue one's ends" which are sufficiently specific "for the solution of serious moral problems." Just as it was both uncharitable and philosophically unfruitful to expect Hegel to show that Kant's first formula was completely empty, it would be uncharitable and philosophically unfruitful to expect Donagan to show that the second principle is completely full, that it can solve all serious moral problems. Between the two extremes no a priori definition can be given as to how empty is too empty, and how full is full enough. All that can be said a priori, as noted earlier, is that to the degree that it can solve serious moral problems, the Kantian strategy is supported, and to the degree that it cannot, the Hegelian critique is sustained.

Like the first candidate, the second has both its popular and its philosophical versions. The popular formulation is familiar from both the Old and New Testament: Love your neighbor as yourself. Donagan gives both Thomistic and Kantian formulations of this rule. The former he expresses this way: "act so that the fundamental human goods, whether in your own person or in that of another, are promoted as may be possible, and under no circumstances violated." The latter is Kant's second formula: "act so that you treat humanity, whether in your own person or in that of another, always as an end, and never as a means only." After giving reasons for preferring the Kantian version, Donagan reformulates it in terms of respect: "act always so that you respect every human being, yourself or another, as being a rational creature." And, since for purposes of logical elegance he wants to express the forbidden, obligatory, and permitted in terms of permissibility, he offers the final reformulation: "it is impermissible not to respect every human being, oneself or any other, as a rational creature."[24] The question then becomes whether the love-respect principle is sufficiently more fecund as a source of specificatory premises than the impartiality principle to rescue Kant's strategy from the Hegelian critique.

In view of the broad cross-cultural consensus that murder, theft, and adultery are serious moral issues, Hegel's doubts can be put in this way. A *Moralität* which takes the love-respect principle as its basis may be able to derive such moral imperatives as Thou shalt not kill, Thou shalt not steal, and Thou shalt not commit adultery. But this is not enough. *Thou shalt not kill* remains fatally indeterminate until I know whether it precludes all taking of human life or whether it permits abortion, euthanasia, just war, capital punishment, human sacrifice, private vengeance (the feud), the treatment of wives, children, or slaves, as property rather than persons, or suicide. Similarly, *Thou shalt not steal* becomes sufficiently determinate only when I know whether what rightfully belongs to another is to be defined in terms of pre-Lockean natural law conceptions, Lockean capitalist conceptions, socialist property-is-theft conceptions, or ancient Hebrew Jubilee conceptions. And *Thou shalt not commit adultery* becomes a genuine moral precept only when I know whether it permits or forbids polygyny, polyandry, divorce, or even Plato's scheme in the *Republic* about how the best and brightest are to breed.

Donagan accepts responsibility for answering questions of the sort raised in the previous paragraph. While he does not address every issue just mentioned, he does deal with a goodly percentage of them, and, just as important, he seeks to answer them by applying the concept of respect for a rational creature to each specific action kind. In accepting this responsibility and working carefully to fulfill it, Donagan acknowledges that the Hegelian critique of the Kantian project is not really disposed of by Jägerstätter type examples, but only by successfully cashing in the Kantian promissory notes.

The Hegelian view, of course, arises from the suspicion that it is just this sort of question which typically cannot be answered convincingly simply by asking what it means to respect persons as rational creatures, and that we inevitably depend on the laws and customs of our own people (*Sittlichkeit*) for answers. Or, to put it a bit differently, we find answers to these questions in terms of respect for rational creatures convincing only by mistakenly identifying the funded value of our own particular *Sittlichkeit* for the transhistorical rationality required by the approach of Aquinas, Kant, and Donagan.

Hegel's critique of Kantian formalism predates the formulas of the *Philosophy of Right* to which Donagan directs our attention.[25]

In the *Phenomenology* he develops essentially the same critique we find later in the *Philosophy of Right,* except that it focuses specifically on the question of property, seeking to show that Kantian ethics is compatible with too much, that it does not sufficiently specify the precept, Thou shalt not steal.[26] Since Hegel's complaint is directed against the categorical imperative formulated as the impartiality principle, and since Donagan has a fairly extended discussion of the property in terms of the respect-love principle which he takes to be more specific, this issue may well be a good one for evaluating Donagan's success in cashing in the promissory notes of the Kantian project which he and Hegel agree in finding irredeemable in terms of the former principle. From the principle of respect for persons as rational beings can he derive, convincingly, though not deductively, specifications of the rule against stealing sufficiently stringent for "the solution of serious moral problems"?[27]

The following recollection of Tony Campolo, an American sociologist, may help to give focus to the issue.

> I was talking to a young Marxist on the main state university campus in the Dominican Republic. We were talking about Christianity and he said that the people of the Dominican Republic do not need Jesus. What they needed, he said, is Gulf & Western off their back. He put it in those terms. He said, "When Trujillo was in power, every time he needed money he would send his troops out and they would drive peasants off the land. Then that land was put up for sale and one of the biggest buyers was the American sugar companies. Now large amounts of our land that ought to be used to grow food for our children are being used to grow sugar to provide candy bars for people in the United States." He continued, "In your country, if one man steals from another and a third party sees that the thief has stolen goods and buys those stolen goods knowing they are stolen, isn't he an accessory to the crime?"
> I said, "Yes."
> Then he said, "What does that make Gulf & Western? What does that make any of the sugar companies that bought up the land that was put up for sale by the dictator that took it from the people. Doesn't it make them accessories to the crime?"
> I said, "Yes."
> He said, "Someday we're going to all get together and have a revolution and get our land back from those who have taken it from us. You know what will happen then? Your country will send in the marines." I couldn't argue with that because we did

it in '65 and we've done it other times this century. And it's that kind of thing that really raises an ethical question for Christians. Namely, do we support a political system which so far as foreign policy is concerned is not interested in fostering self-determination or freedom, but is interested in one primary thing: protecting the investments of multi-national corporations based here in the United States. And I really feel that as you go into the Old Testament, you can get some very, very negative judgments pronounced by God on that kind of seizure and that kind of exploitation. I think that the Old Testament prophets would have a heyday analyzing the American economic-political structure.[28]

According to the Dominican student, three acts of stealing underlie the poverty of the majority of the population in this country. The land grab by Trujillo and his troops is the first theft; the purchase of that land by American sugar companies is the second; and the purchase of cheap candy bars by ordinary North American citizens is the third, extending the purchase of stolen goods one step farther. Whether or not we would view the first "theft" as justified in terms of some principle of eminent domain, most of us would view the second and third acts, subject to neither legal nor extralegal sanctions in our culture, as perfectly acceptable, and would be more than surprised to hear them labeled stealing.[29] But the socialist, who is inclined to see the world from the perspective of the dispossessed peasant rather than the comfortable candy bar buyer, is more likely to generalize his experience into a slogan like "Property is Theft." He will seek to keep before our eyes the violent processes by which property accumulation all too frequently occurs and which are often left out of view in capitalist discussions of property rights.[30] He will view private property *per se* to be a violation of people's right to respect as ends and not merely as means because of its habitual links to violence, domination, and exploitation.

It is not because he shares this socialist perspective that Campolo is sympathetic to the Dominican student. It is rather because he takes the Old Testament prophets so seriously. They do not argue that property is theft; they appeal rather to a law which takes private property more seriously than capitalism, which insists that it is so important everyone should have some. According to the Jubilee legislation of Leviticus 25, the land, which had been divided more or less equally among the families of Israel when they came to Canaan, was to return to its original owner every fifty years. Being the primary productive wealth in a agrarian society, land could not be sold. It could only be leased for the remainder of the fifty-year period. According to this view, it would be stealing not to return land to the family which originally owned it at the year of Jubilee, no matter what price had been paid or what agreement had been made. It would equally be stealing for the state to claim ownership of the means of production, for, to repeat, this model is even more committed to private ownership than capitalism and therefore excludes the primary feature of capitalist property, the right to alienate.[31]

It should be clear that the Jubilee model is as different from the socialist model as it is from the capitalist model. We have here three distinct frameworks for the definition of stealing. Whether any or all of them can be institutions compatible with the respect we owe one another as human persons is surely a "serious moral problem." Let us see how Donagan's treatment of property is able to deal with these issues.

His view is that property arises from agreements within a given society, and that while there is no natural right to property and that property is not in itself a moral institution, the principle of morality nevertheless places constraints on the sort of agreements which are permissible. This is in keeping with the more general notion that morality in part concerns "the restrictions ordained by practical reason on how one may pursue one's ends."[32] Even when socially accepted, forms of proprietorship may be morally impermissible for failing to respect persons as rational beings in various ways. The rights of future generations to what they need for their own preservation might be compromised by forms of property which (a) permit open ownership of human beings (chattel slavery); (b) permit concealed ownership of human beings (forced labor); (c) prevent individuals from using their productive powers in a non-destructive manner (systemic unemployment?); or (d) permit confiscation of what workers produce (unfair wages?).[33]

These are important and timely issues. By raising them Donagan makes it clear that he does not mean his theory of property to be all permissive. Yet there are at least two ways in which Hegelian doubts remain. First, while the prohibition against slavery is quite explicit, it is far from clear that any of the other restrictions against impermissible forms of property holding are specific enough to be meaningful. Donagan has not even attempted to answer the extremely difficult questions that arise. What constitutes forced labor? What levels and types of unemployment make a particular form of ownership of productive wealth into systematic, legalized theft? What are fair wages, and below what levels does employment

become theft? Perhaps answers to these questions can be derived
convincingly from the concept of respect for rational beings as such,
but in the absence of even a sketch of how this could be done, skepticism does not seem unwarranted. In Donagan's hands the prohibition against stealing is left to be given its specific definition by the
laws and customs of each society. He raises the right questions, but
leaves them unanswered.

A second layer of Hegelian doubt arises from more general
comments which Donagan makes. For example, "In general, the
ownership of property of all kinds may be transferred from one pro-
prietor to another on whatever terms they may agree upon."[34] The
meaning of the qualifying phrase, "In general," is not entirely clear
here. In spite of Donagan's critique of the intuitionist notion of
prima facie duties, he may mean that there is a *prima facie* right to
alienate property, subject to the general restrictions on social institutions of property previously mentioned. He notes that this principle places some constraint on transfers of public property, since
future generations are not in a position to give consent to agreements dealing with what is in an important sense theirs. Apart
from the fact that the rights of future generations, as Donagan himself has stated them, cannot be restricted to publicly owned property, this principle seems to avoid or beg questions of moral
significance posed by socialist and Jubilee alternatives to the capitalist system of private property.

In relation to socialist thought it leaves undiscussed the question what sorts of property, if any, should be publicly owned, leaving
it to historical accident what properties are public and then addressing the question of exchange. From the socialist perspective
this represents the bias of a capitalist *Sittlichkeit,* one effect of
which is to omit moral discussion of the historical process by which
any given set of property relations has come into being. For example, while Donagan's principle has a bearing on the government's
right to dispose of national park and wilderness reserve lands in its
holding, it does not encourage any reflection on the moral implications of the way land was first acquired from the native Americans.
From the Jubliee perspective, the assumption that property brings
with it the right of alienation or sale to anyone with whom I can
agree to terms begs the crucial question about the nature of those
property rights which pertain to productive wealth.

Another example of this second sort concerns Donagan's discussion of the pre-Lockean natural right theory of property. Among
the natural law restrictions which Locke first mentions and then

discards[35] is the one which requires that the private appropriator of property (land in particular) leave as much and as good for others. Donagan also sets this aside, noting that "the happy situation in which, in appropriating something, the appropriator leaves as much and as good to be appropriated by those who come after, almost never exists. Even in societies with a moving frontier, in which it is believed to exist, it is usually an illusion."[36]

But what is the moral relevance of this observation that there does not now exist, and rarely if ever has existed, a frontier situation in which this principle could be applied without pain? The principle originated not in the context of a frontier situation, but in a Europe where it obviously had real bite. It arose as an effort to think through the implications of something like Donagan's own respect principle, and it would appear to be one of the more easily derivable specifications of that principle. That Donagan dismisses it as quickly as Locke did, suggests that his thinking may be less that of a timeless practical reason and more than he realizes the product of the capitalist *Sittlichkeit* in which he is immersed. For it is just some such principle of radical equality that underlies both the socialist and the Jubliee differences with capitalist systems of property.

Donagan's theory is no moral laissez-faire, to be sure. As far as it permits capitalist forms of property we would have to talk about capitalism with a conscience. But his restrictions do not begin to approach the radical egalitarianism implicit in alternative conceptions. They merely serve (as far as they can be given any specific definition) to preclude certain extreme abuses all too much a reality in the world in which we live. Yet it should not be the task of moral theory to chart even an ambitious reform program, but to tell us (in this instance) what is forbidden by the injunction not to steal. Given the *prima facie* strength of the egalitarian principle in relation to the respect principle and the absence of an argument to show why it is not required by that principle, the impression is once again left that Donagan's attempt to specify the principle of respect is governed more by his own historical milieu than by a practical reason he shares with Kant and Aquinas (and all humans everywhere and at all times).

No doubt more "Hegelian doubts" could be generated by further discussion of Donagan's attempt to derive specificatory premises from his first principle. But in an important sense Donagan seems to concede the Hegelian case before he even gets down to dealing with specifics. He does so in disputing Hare's analysis of the kind of reasoning involved in the application of a concept to instances not unambiguously included or excluded from its scope. Hare's example concerns legal reasoning.

> If we make a law forbidding the use of wheeled vehicles in the park, and somebody thinks he can go in the park on roller skates, no amount of cerebration, and no amount of inspection of roller skates, are going to settle for us the question of whether roller skates are vehicles 'within the meaning of the Act' if the Act has not specified whether they are; the judge has to decide whether they are *to be* counted as such. And this is a further determination of the law. The judge may have very good reasons of public interest or morals for his decision; but he cannot make it by any physical or metaphysical examination of roller skates to see whether they are *really* wheeled vehicles.

In making this application the judge has to "decide," and "we are not going to be able to use the principle to decide cases on the borderline without doing some more normation or evaluation."[37]

Donagan notes that there are indeed positivist legal systems in which such questions of application are

> to be settled by additional acts of 'normation or evaluation' by judges. But only a tiny minority of students of the law consider that a logically coherent legal system must be of that kind, much less that British and American common or statute law is. Any British or American bench, called upon to determine whether the words of an Act forbidding the use of wheeled vehicles in a public park apply to roller skating, the Act itself specifying neither that it does nor that it does not, would normally be able to do so by the ordinary process of statutory interpretation. It is almost unthinkable that it would have to legislate under the guise of giving judgment.[38]

I do not find it at all unthinkable that a British or American court would do much the same as a legislative committee holding hearings about the wheeled vehicle law in the first instance. It would not study roller skates nor the dictionary definition of wheels, but rather would hear testimony about the degree to which roller skating in the park is a threat to the safety and comfort of persons walking in the park. Upon hearing that there was a broken elderly hip at least once a month attributable to roller skating, the court would have no trouble deciding to include roller skates within the meaning of "wheeled vehicles." Upon hearing that no injuries were traceable to roller skating during the ten-year history of the park and that the present plaintiff had not even been inconvenienced by roller skaters, but was a well-known local grinch who always seemed most unhappy when children were having fun, the court would with equal ease decide to exclude roller skates from the meaning of the law. Obviously somewhere in between these two extremes there would be a set of facts which would make the decision much more difficult, but the judicial decision would remain essentially the same as the legislative one which forbade wheeled vehicles in the first place.

It is not, however, my account of the court's behavior which really matters here, but Donagan's own. For I have said that Donagan gives away his own case even before getting down to specifics. He seems to me to do so when he says "Any British or American bench" could determine whether the concept of wheeled vehicles applies to roller skates by a nonlegislative act of interpretation, one which involves no further "normation or evaluation." Why does it have to be a British or American bench? Donagan answers this question himself.

> While the predicate 'wheeled vehicles within the meaning of the Act' has fuzzy edges in the superficial sense that disputes can arise about what it applies to, it does not follow that it has fuzzy edges in the deeper sense that those disputes can be resolved only extrinsically: that is, by considerations, whether of public interest or of morals, which according to received canons of statutory interpretations are not implicit in the words of the Act.[39]

What is crucial here is the reference to "received canons of statutory interpretation." The derivation of the more specific judgment, "roller skates are forbidden in the park," from the less specific judgment, "wheeled vehicles are forbidden in the park," is legitimated by an inference ticket which is culturally particular. It is by participation in the Anglo-Saxon tradition of law, the legal world's *Sittlichkeit*, that the judges are able, on Donagan's account, to derive the specificatory premise they need to render judgment in the case before them. Thus it is only the combination of principle (the statute) and the tradition (the "received canons of statutory interpretation") which permits the specific legal question to be answered.

There are, of course, important differences between legal and moral reasoning. But in this case it is the similarity that is relevant. Donagan himself makes this clear when immediately after his discussion of Hare and the roller skate problem he says,

> The fundamental concept of respecting every human being as a rational creature is fuzzy at the edges in the superficial sense that its application to this or that species of case can be disputed. *But among those who share in the life of a culture in which the Hebrew-Christian moral tradition is accepted,* the concept is in large measure understood in itself; and it is connected with numerous applications, as to the different weights of which there is some measure of agreement. This is enough for it to be possible to determine many specificatory premises with virtual certainty and others with a high degree of confidence.[40]

Once again Donagan has stated Hegel's own position as clearly and succinctly as Hegel was himself ever able to express it. The application of the concept of respect for persons as rational creatures to specific moral problems is acknowledged to be dependent upon participation in a *particular* cultural tradition; or, to put it in Hegelian language, *Moralität* is dependent upon *Sittlichkeit*. Would it be unfair to ask whether Donagan is really more willing to be an Hegelian than he seems, as long as he is able to specify which *Sittlichkeit* (the Hebrew-Christian) is called upon to give content to the principle of neighbor love and respect for rational creatures?

In any case, it remains puzzling that Donagan offers to save us from ethics in the dangerous Hegelian traditions (remember Jägerstätter) by offering us a theory of morality which is so overtly Hegelian, not only in its critique of the impartiality principle, but more importantly in the account it gives of its own self-understanding. In the light of Kierkegaard's argument in *Philosophical Fragments* and *Training in Christianity,* this is more than puzzling; it is sadly ironic. For those two works, taken together, show that nothing contributes so directly to the deification of one's own established order (the absolutizing of a particular *Sittlichkeit* which renders any accepted behavior acceptable—remember Jägerstätter) as the identification of a particular society's assumptions with universal Reason. It is just this identification which silently occurs when Donagan equates the rational principle of respect for rational creatures with the interpretation it would be given in a particular culture, one which has traditionally accepted Hebrew-Christian morality.

These last comments have a bearing on the purpose of the present essay. It is neither to detract from the value and importance of Donagan's work, to which I feel personally much indebted, nor to suggest that Hegel has satisfactorily solved the problems I have been discussing. Hegel's legacy has largely been, contrary to his intention, an historicism and relativism which are genuinely troubling. And this is no doubt due to the fact that he did not himself find a satisfactory way to identify which societies have good laws and customs, to distinguish a good *Sittlichkeit* from an evil one. But if Kierkegaard's analysis is correct, and I am persuaded that it is, then Donagan's strategy only compounds the problem.

THE FAILURE OF NERVE

5 Dialectic and Intersubjectivity

Hegel's dialectic can be expressed as a transcendental holism. It is a transcendental enterprise because it seeks to make manifest the conditions of the possibility of whatever is to be understood. Thus a phenomenological dialectic brings to light the conditions of the possibility of experience, the various modes in which the world appears to us; a logical dialectic shows forth the conditions of the possibility of the thoughts with which we think the world; and an ontological dialectic expresses the conditions of the possibility of the things themselves which make up the world we think and experience.

Like Kant's, Hegel's transcendental search is Augustinian. It is driven on by a restlessness which leaves it no repose until the search for conditions has led to the Unconditioned. Introducing his phenomenological dialectic, Hegel describes it this way:

> But the goal is as necessarily fixed for knowledge as the serial progression; it is the point where knowledge no longer needs to go beyond itself . . . Hence the progress towards this goal is also unhalting, and short of it no satisfaction is to be found at any of the stations on the way.

There is something like violent death in being uprooted from every achievement, but:

> . . . consciousness suffers this violence at its own hands: it spoils its own limited satisfaction. When consciousness feels this violence, its anxiety may well make it retreat from the truth, and strive to hold on to what it is in danger of losing. But it can find no peace. If it wishes to remain in a state of unthinking inertia, then thought troubles its thoughtlessness, and its own unrest disturbs its inertia. Or, if it entrenches itself in sentimentality, which assures us that it finds everything to be good in its kind, then this assurance likewise

75

suffers violence at the hands of Reason, for, precisely in so far
as something is merely a kind, Reason finds it not to be good.
(PhG, 69/51–52)[1]

Though Kant and Hegel agree in understanding reason to be
this very restlessness, there are important differences in their interpretation of it. Perhaps the most fundamental is that for Kant
the ideas of reason designate a special subset of entities, soul,
world, and God, rendered distinctive by their nonempirical character, while for Hegel the search for the conditions of the possibility of
experience, thought, and reality leads to ever larger wholes to
which the original subject matter belongs and without which it
could not be itself. Instead of a transcendental foundationalism
which seeks the Unconditioned in the aseity of causally (or logically) prior particulars, Hegel offers a transcendental holism which
seeks the Unconditioned in the aseity of the totality of the
conditioned.[2] This makes it possible for Hegel's most profound summary of the meaning of his dialectic also to be the most succinct:
"The true is the whole" (PhG, 21/11).
   It is for just this reason that no distinction between phenomenological, logical, and ontological dialectics can be anything but
preliminary. Distinctions between them can indeed be drawn, and it
is the glory of the understanding to do this with precision. But if one
inquires about the conditions of the possibility of any one of these,
the context in which alone it ultimately makes sense will turn out
to involve the others. Just as within any one of these modes of dialectic the movement will be from the foreground to the background
or context which it presupposes, which in turn becomes a new foreground whose background must be sought, so in thinking the relation of these modes to each other, the task will be to seek each as a
part of the whole made up by their mutual implication of each other.
Or, to put the point a bit differently, just as the three syllogisms
with which the *Encyclopedia* concludes show how Idea, Nature, and
Spirit imply one another, no matter which is taken as the point of
departure, a similar threefold pattern could show the same relation
among the phenomenological, logical, and ontological aspects of
dialectical rationality. Kant's transcendental logic has already
pointed to the inseparability of the phenomenological (experiential)
and the logical (conceptual) moments of rational intelligibility, but
"overawed by the object" *(aus Angst vor dem Objeckt,* WL 1:32/51), it
left the gap between conceptualized experience and the thing-
in-itself unbridgeable. For this reason Hegel is especially eager to
affirm the ultimate unity of logic with metaphysics or ontology.

"Logic therefore coincides with metaphysics, the science of things set and held in thought,—thoughts accredited able to express the essential reality of things" (EL, ¶24; cf. WL, I, 46–47/63–64). Perhaps the reason Hegel is so tormentingly vague about the relation of his phenomenological dialectic to his logical dialectic,[3] never giving us a very clear account of their identity and difference, is that he is so preoccupied with the refutation of Kant which consists in showing the unity of logic with ontology.

It is just because it is holistic that dialectical thinking is negative thinking.

> The true is the whole. But the whole is nothing other than the essence consummating itself through its development. Of the Absolute it must be said that it is essentially a *result,* that only in the *end* is it what it truly is; and that precisely in this consists its nature, *viz.,* to be actual, subject, the spontaneous becoming of itself. Though it may seem contradictory that the Absolute should be conceived essentially as a *result,* it needs little pondering to set this show of contradiction in its true light. (PhG, 21/11)[4]

But such a result will never be reached if reason takes its repose anywhere short of totality. It will have to turn against all claims to finality on behalf of what is partial, revealing its partiality in the search for the whole which is its home. For:

> . . . everything actual, in so far as it is true, is the Idea, and has its truth by and in virtue of the Idea alone. Every individual being is one aspect of the Idea: for which, therefore, yet other actualities are needed, which in their turn appear to have a self-subsistence of their own. It is only in them altogether and in their relation that the Concept is realized. The individual by itself does not correspond to its concept. It is this limitation of its existence which constitutes the finitude and the ruin *[Untergang]* of the individual. (EL, ¶213)[5]

This passage forms an important commentary on an earlier account of the finite, which simply states that "all finite things involve an untruth: they have a concept and an existence, but their existence does not meet the requirements of their concept. Therefore they must perish *[zugrunde gehen]*" (EL, ¶24Z).[6] It is easy to take this to mean that rutabagas rot because none is the perfect exemplar of the species and that the ideal iguana would be immortal.

But our commentary passage indicates a different reading. Finite things do not require others because they are imperfect. They are imperfect (limited or finite) because they require others. Their concept is the concept of a whole to which they belong, and by themselves, in isolation, they do not correspond to their concept. The task of philosophy is neither to find nor define the perfect porpoise, but rather, when it has occasion to deal with porpoises, to see how they fit into the larger scheme of things.

The unrelenting drive toward totality is the positive or speculative moment of dialectical reason, but it essentially involves the negative moment of exposing the finite and conditioned as lacking the character of the rational, "to be self-contained, self-determining" (EL, ¶82Z). In its totality dialectical thinking is affirmative, but when the negative moment is isolated from the movement toward the Idea of which it is properly a part, dialectic is like anything else—in its abstract, that is, partial mode, it is untrue to itself. Just as in theology heresy so often consists of a truth cut off from other truths and made absolute in isolation, so in philosophy the most deeply anti-philosophical movements result from making penultimate insights ultimate. "Thus *summum jus summa inuria:* which means, that to drive an abstract right to its extremity is to do a wrong" (EL, ¶81Z). In this case that means that dialectical negation falls into the service of skepticism or sophistry.

It is not the "grand skepticism of antiquity" (EL, ¶24Z) which Hegel has in mind here. It is a part of genuinely dialectical thinking. Especially in its Socratic-Platonic from it serves as an indispensable introduction to metaphysics by refusing to treat as final either the obviousness of ordinary consciousness or the cleverness of the sophists,[7] for its possesses a "complete hopelessness about all which understanding counts stable" (EL, ¶81Z).

It is the modern skepticism, associated in Hegel's mind especially with Hume and Kant, which represents the heresy of half-truth.[8] It recognizes the inadequacy of the finite categories of understanding for apprehending the infinite and unconditioned, but draws positivistic conclusions from this insight. It affirms "the sensible, that is, what is present in immediate sensation, as what we have to keep to." Thus "the skeptic mistakes the true value of his result when he supposes it to be no more than a negation pure and simple" (EL, ¶81Z). At the same time the positive character of this positivism goes unnoticed, its absolutizing of the immediate. "We must take what is given as it is . . . " (EL, ¶38Z).

When motivated by self-interest, this skepticism passes over into sophistry. For "the essence of sophistry lies in giving authority to a partial and abstract principle, in its isolation, as may suit the interest and particular situation of the individual at the time. For example, a regard to my existence, and my having the means of existence, is a vital motive of conduct, but if I exclusively emphasize this consideration or motive of welfare, and draw the conclusion that I may steal or betray my country, we have a case of sophistry" (EL, ¶81Z). We are reminded of Kierkegaard's later definition of sophistry as "the perpetual life-and-death struggle of knowledge with the phenomenon in the service of egotism."[9]

What we are dealing with here is an "adventitious art *[äussere Kunst]*, which for very wantonness *[Willkür]* introduces confusion and a mere semblance of contradiction into definite concepts." This is why dialectic often connotes only "a subjective swinging back and forth of arguments, where mere emptiness is disguised by the cleverness of such thinking as the content which is actually lacking" (EL, ¶81). This is indeed the charge brought against Socrates by those who confused him with the sophists.

If Hegel's account of sophistry as skepticism in the service of self-interest reminds us of Kierkegaard's similar account, this further account of sophistry as cleverness masquerading as real thought has its echo in Rorty's account of much contemporary analytic philosophy as cleverness trying to pass itself off as wisdom, claiming a kind of scientific status solely by virtue of a formal ability to argue skillfully.[10] In fact, the whole account of Hegel's dialectical holism to this point provides a helpful frame of reference for thinking about the contemporary philosophical scene.

In both the analytic and continental camps, much of contemporary philosophy can be summarized in terms of holistic reactions to Cartesian foundationalism and its atomistic assumptions. In the continental context, the Husserlian project of phenomenology as a rigorous science has given way, first to the hermeneutic phenomenology of Heidegger and Gadamer, then to the historicist structuralism of Foucault, and then to the textualism of Derrida.[11] On the analytic front, a Cartesian empiricism resting on the "myth of the given" and the "dogma" of reductionism has largely succumbed to holistic attacks.[12] First the logical atomism and logical constructionism of early analytic philosophy gave way to the practical holism of Wittgenstein's language games and the theoretical holism of Quine's pragmatic logic. Then the foundationalism of positivistic, hypothetico-deductive philosophy of science gave way before the holistic critiques of Hanson, Kuhn, and Feyerabend.[13]

We have seen that Hegel's holism is similarly directed against Cartesian foundationalism. It implies that we look for the truth in results rather than in starting points, and its sustained critique of appeals to immediacy entails that no intuition, rational or empirical, produces a givenness which is fixed and final, thereby capable of serving as the starting point of Cartesian method. Should we say then that the emergence of holism in contemporary philosophy represents the triumph of Hegel over Descartes? So far as holism has tended to replace foundationalism, along with its presupposed atomism and implied reductionism, we can say yes.

But this is conspicuously less than the whole truth and as such it is seriously misleading. For the holisms of contemporary philosophy tend to be relativist and skeptical. They tend to assume that philosophy should not "try to find natural starting points which are distinct from cultural traditions," but instead, that "all philosophy should do is compare and contrast cultural traditions," since they see "all criteria as no more than temporary resting places." They have "the sense that there is nothing deep down inside us except what we have put there ourselves, no criterion that we have not created in the course of creating a practice, no standard of rationality that is not an appeal to such a criterion." Since there are no "self-evident principles" or "basic values" to be the "foundations of moral obligation," it can be concluded that a free society needs no moral or metaphysical foundation, that "our culture, or purpose, or intuitions cannot be supported except conversationally," and that "there are no constraints on inquiry save conversational ones—no wholesale constraints derived from the nature of objects, or of the mind, or of language, but only those retail constraints provided by the remarks of our fellow-inquirers."[14]

Perhaps no single version of contemporary holism would choose to express itself in this way without amendment, but these formulas, taken from Rorty, surely express a powerful tendency at work in both the analytic and continental traditions. When we learn to say, for example, "This language game is played—we can say no more," or, "To be in the hermeneutic circle is the human condition," or, "What texts are about is other texts; writers are interpreters of interpretations," it is clear that only the first of the two following Hegelian theses is being affirmed: (1) Human thought and experience are inextricably caught up in their historical, cultural situation,[15] and (2) Though philosophical thought cannot be based on any immediacy which frees us from this conditionedness at the outset, our thought can end with a systematic mediation which enables us to transcend our conditionedness without either denying or abandoning it. From Hegel's perspective, contemporary holism is only dialectical negatively. It knows how to reveal the finitude of anything that would claim foundational status, but that is all.

Whether, in Hegelian eyes, contemporary holisms are better viewed as a renewal of modern skepticism or of ancient sophistry depends on the interpretation, not of their philosophical conclusions but of the motivations which have led to them. If relativist holism represents a failure of nerve *aus Angst vor dem Objekt,* it would count as a form of skepticism. If, on the other hand, it represents an excess of nerve, a kind of intellectual chutzpah or adolescent rebellion against all constraint, it would count as a form of sophistry. (The possibility that it represents the virtue of humility is, of course, precluded within the Hegelian horizon.) But in neither case would it count as a genuinely dialectical mode of thinking. Its ability to recognize all criteria as "temporary resting places" is not matched by the restlessness which drives it onward toward totality, to "the point where knowledge no longer needs to go beyond itself." From Hegel's perspective the contemporary debate between foundationalism and holism reenacts the struggle between a Cartesianism and a Kantianism, both of which need to be transcended.

* * *

From this brief glance at developments during our own century we turn back to Hegel himself. Having seen his dialectic at work as a frame of reference for interpreting and evaluating aspects of contemporary philosophy, we are in a good position to watch his own holism at work and to inquire whether it lives up to its own demands. It will be my thesis that in at least one important respect it does not, that Hegel himself suffers from a failure of nerve and allows his own dialectical thinking to stop short of the totality it demands.

The point of departure for this suggestion is Hegel's holistic critique of the transcendental ego of traditional transcendental philosophy from Descartes through Kant and Fichte (and Husserl). This ego can be a foundation for knowledge only because it has been radically de-situated. In the move from consciousness to self-consciousness in the *Phenomenology* subjectivity and theory get taken up into the larger context of intersubjectivity and practice. Spirit is the I that is We and the We that is I, since the I apart from the We is only an abstraction, which philosophy must treat as such. Because of the individualism and intellectualism with which it is understood, the "I think" of the transcendentalism Hegel wishes to surpass is doubly abstract. It is individual thought isolated from its social context, and, as such, it is thought isolated from the practice in which it is embedded. Knowing can only be understood in the context of social praxis, which is why the analysis of Newtonian science in chapter three leads, not arbitrarily and abruptly, but altogether appropriately, to social praxis guided by desire and thus, in chapter four, to the struggle for recognition. Hegel's reminder that scientific thinking must be seen in the larger context of human social interaction indicates the dramatic epistemological implications his holism has from the very beginning.

The most important of these implications is the historicity of all human knowing. The attempt "to demonstrate the finite, historically situated character of reflection," has been described as "an explicit countermove to Hegel."[16] But in fact it is to Hegel that we must turn for the first clear statement of situational epistemology. For not only is the I that thinks caught up into the We of social praxis as its context, the condition of its possibility, but the We of social praxis is caught up in the history of traditions as its context. It is always located somewhere, but not everywhere, within that history.

That is why, although consistently stressing that the *Phenomenology* is a treatise on knowledge, whose goal "is Spirit's insight into what knowing is," Hegel can say that "now is the time for philosophy to be raised to the status of a science." And why? Because the historical conditions for this possibility are now actual. "If we apprehend a demand of this kind in its broader context, and view it as it appears at the stage which self-conscious Spirit has presently reached, it is clear that Spirit has now got beyond the substantial life it formerly led . . . " This means that "it is not difficult to see that ours is a birth-time and a period of transition to a new era. Spirit has broken with the world it has hitherto inhabited and imagined, and is of a mind to submerge it in the past, and in the labor of its own transformation" (PhG, 27/17, 12–13/3–4, 15/6). Precisely because the transcendental subject who makes knowledge possible is not the abstract "I think" but Spirit in the concreteness of its historical social praxis, historical change is the condition of the possibility of cognitive transformation.

Though it may come as a surprise to most readers, Hegel begins the *Science of Logic* by making the same point. He bemoans the fact that "the complete transformation which philosophical thought in Germany has undergone in the last twenty-five years and the higher standpoint reached by Spirit in its awareness of itself, have had but little influence as yet in the structure of logic." Though unlike the older metaphysics, logic is still taught, it "shows no traces so far of the new Spirit which has arisen in the sciences no less than in the world of actuality. However, once the substantial form of Spirit has inwardly reconstituted itself, all attempts to preserve the forms of an earlier culture are utterly in vain; like withered leaves they are pushed off by the new buds already growing at their roots" (WL 1:3–5/25–26). Hegel clearly views his task as bringing this branch of philosophical reflection up to date, bringing to actuality the possibility inherent in changed historical conditions.

We have already seen that the goal is "the point where knowledge no longer needs to go beyond itself." But now we see that knowledge is always beyond itself, that it can never be complete in itself inasmuch as social praxis is the condition of its possibility. What then can it mean for knowledge no longer to need to go beyond itself? Perhaps it means that knowledge is able fully to thematize the social praxis which is its ground, to render fully transparent to thought the social identity of the transcendental ego. By bringing the extratheoretical conditions of the possibility of knowing back into the realm of theory, knowing would somehow become rational in the sense specified earlier, unconditioned, self-contained, self-determining.[17]

Whatever plausibility this suggestion has depends on the ahistorical character of social praxis. For if it is genuinely historical, as we have already seen it to be, then to thematize it would simply be to make conspicuous the finitude of knowing by showing the finitude of its condition. For seen in historical context, each particular social praxis will be seen as the particular, i.e., limited, reality which it is. No matter how large is the whole into which a given social praxis must be fitted as a part, that is, no matter how close this thematizing comes to being a genuine universal of world history, nothing is changed. For what is revealed as partial in a small totality is even more obviously partial in a larger totality. What has been offered as a possible cure for the vertigo of relativity is really nothing more than the emergence of a fully self-conscious historicism.

Let us try again. If knowledge is always already beyond itself in the social praxis which makes it possible, what can it mean to speak of "the point where knowledge no longer needs to go beyond itself"? Strictly speaking we should not say that knowledge is beyond itself in social praxis, for once we see the latter as the ground of the former we realize that the latter is part of the former's concept when it is properly understood. To think knowledge is to think social praxis. Knowledge corresponds to its concept by being embedded in social praxis. But surely this lends no support to "the rapturous enthusiasm which, like a shot from a pistol, begins straight away with absolute knowledge" (PhG, 26/16). It is not the relativity to social praxis as such that renders knowing finite. Might it be that the finitude of knowing is the finitude of its ground, and that only a social praxis which no longer needs to go beyond itself could ground a knowing which could legitimately rest at its goal? If so, under what conditions does social praxis correspond to its concept and no longer need to move on to its fulfillment?

The first of these two questions receives an affirmative answer in the transcendental deduction of Spirit as the transcendental subject in the first half of Hegel's *Phenomenology*. It is the task of the second half to work out an answer to the second question, for these two questions do indeed indicate what strategy Hegel adopts. If the first and negative task of his dialectical holism is to unmask the historical finitude of human knowledge against the ahistorical and thereby abstract assumptions of Cartesian foundationalism, rationalist and empiricist, the second and positive task is to press on beyond the resulting relativism, which is at best skeptical and at worst sophistical. We have already seen enough of the first task to be ready for at least a sketch of the second.

Hegel would not deny that "every human society is, in the last resort, men banded together in the face of death."[18] But he is keenly aware that mere biological existence is not the deepest motive of human behavior. At the crucial turning point of the *Phenomenology* he interprets that deepest drive as the uniquely human desire for recognition. In Kantian language this can be expressed as dignity or respect, in biblical language as love. For to be recognized by another is to be treated as an end and not merely a means and it is to be united with another at the center of the circle of value and interest rather than pushed to the periphery by the self-assertion of the other.[19]

At the culmination of the *Phenomenology* it is in and as the community of reciprocal recognition that Spirit emerges as absolute and absolute knowing becomes a possibility. Knowledge no longer needs to go beyond itself when and only when it is embedded in a social praxis which no longer needs to go beyond itself, and when the social praxis occurs in the community whose distinctive mark is reciprocal recognition.[20] To understand the nature of such a community we need to take a closer look at Hegel's understanding of recognition.

As Hegel unfolds the concept of recognition it turns out that to be itself it must be not only reciprocal but also uncoerced and universal. In these respects continuity with the Kantian and Judeo-

Christian traditions is clear. But Hegel adds a distinctive consideration to the argument for reciprocity and non-coercion: I want to be recognized. But recognition is the sort of thing that can only be given freely by someone with the moral status of a person. To take a crude but pointed example, I can condition a parrot to say, "I love you," whenever I enter the room, but this will not be love nor will I feel loved. Whenever I fail to recognize the one from whom I seek recognition I deny the moral status of spiritual selfhood to that individual, and if I seek to extract recognition through coercion I deprive any "recognition" I succeed in extorting of the freedom which it needs to be, in fact, recognition. In neither case is genuine recognition possible.

I can receive the recognition I seek only from one whom I already recognize, and, correspondingly, from whom I seek recognition without resort to coercion. In his famous account of lordship and bondage Hegel is explicit about the impossibility of gaining recognition by resort to physical violence or its threat. But it is easy to see that the same considerations which lead to this conclusion preclude any kind of resort to manipulation. For to the degree that you are manipulated into "recognizing" me, your "recognition" becomes like that of the parrot, an appearance without reality, a spiritual check that bounces.

The import of these results is greatly increased when they are combined with the third essential mark of recognition, its intrinsic universality. So far as the history of traditions is concerned, Hegel's universalism is a chapter in the *Wirkungsgeschichte* of Judeo-Christian ethics via Kant. But in terms of method, it is the product of Hegel's holism at work. The concept of recognition starts with the individual's desire and shows that the individual as such does not correspond to his or her concept. To be a human individual is to be part of a community (at first only a twosome) in which reciprocal recognition occurs. But once this process begins there is no stopping it short of universality. For not only does each member of the twosome seek recognition from each other individual to be encountered, but the twosome and every other community constituted by the resultant recognition also want to be recognized by the individuals and communities external to them. So the dialectic of reciprocal recognition occurs at the level of families, tribes, clans, cities, and nations. I correspond to my concept as a human individual insofar as I belong to a community constituted by reciprocal recognition, but to the degree that that community is not in turn recognized by other, similar communities, I do not correspond to my concept.

This, at any rate, is the form taken by Hegel's holism in the *Phenomenology*. The universalism implicit in his holism leads to the definition of the ultimate community in moral and religious rather than political terms. But that very same holism requires that our moral and religious life not be isolated from our political life, and the concept of recognition has very direct political implications. Human beings correspond to their concept only when they belong to a universal human community whose life has been freed of physical violence and manipulation. Hegel is envisaging a world from which not only war but also the media as we know them have been eliminated. For even in societies which proudly call themselves free, the media represent the most powerful forces of political, economic, social, and cultural manipulation.[21]

Hegel's treatise on knowledge began with the relatively innocuous insight that knowing is grounded in social praxis. It has now reached the conclusion that the historicism or relativism implicit in that relationship can be overcome, not by resort to some refurbished foundationalism, but by pressing onward to a radically new form of social life. The knowing which would emerge out of the social praxis of the universal, nonviolent, and nonmanipulative community would indeed be relative to the social praxis. But the relativity would not produce vertigo, for it would be a relation to and thus the expression of a social praxis which itself no longer needed to go beyond itself, having reached the goal of corresponding to its concept.

A global community without war or propaganda! How utopian it sounds! How subjunctive our language has become, talking about what *would* be the case if. How much more down to earth Hegel sounds later in the *Philosophy of Right* and the *Philosophy of History*. To be sure, the particular state is not absolute there, and Hegel retains a kind of universalism. But it is primarily the diachronic universalism of world history rather than the synchronic universalism of a global community; and while the states do belong (synchronically) to a community in which they recognize each other, the rationality of the world order does not seem, in Hegel's eyes, to be compromised by the fact that their relations are mediated by war and contractual relations, though the former is a fundamental violation of the concept of recognition and the latter Hegel has shown at smaller levels of totality to be entirely too abstract to constitute genuine recognition.[22]

It is not just that Hegel abandons the clear implications of his dialectic as developed in the *Phenomenology*. The very same holism is powerfully at work in the *Philosophy of Right* itself, and represents Hegel's greatness as a political theorist. But the kind of thinking that generates a theory of the state, not simply as power keeping order, but as the genuine community of all the individuals and subcommunities which make it up, is abandoned without justification at paragraph 321 when Hegel turns from treating the state as the whole in relation to its parts and begins to treat it as a part of the larger international whole. This is the failure of nerve of which I spoke earlier.

If we ask why it occurs, we must say first of all that it is not that Hegel is either a chauvinistic nationalist or a warmonger.[23] We might put the point by saying that if Hegel is more wedded to the international political situation of his times (and ours) than his own dialectical holism permits, it is not for political reasons. The problem lies elsewhere.

To follow the implications of his own dialectical holism for an understanding of both knowledge and the intersubjectivity which underlies it, Hegel would have to say that no human society yet corresponds to its concept, that the present world order is in specifiable respects irrational, and that a specifiably different state of affairs ought to exist. But Hegel is adamant against all suggestions that the task of philosophy is to tell the world how it ought to be. And here we encounter what might be called Hegel's *Angst vor dem Sollen.*[24]

There seem to be three reasons underlying this anxiety of Hegel's, ethical, epistemological, and metaphysical. First, there is the warning that "philosophy must beware of the wish to be edifying," on the grounds that such a desire opens the door to replacing serious, disciplined thought with a shallow, empty, emotional enthusiasm which lives in a fantasy world of dreams (PhG, 14–15/5–6). In Hegel's view this is morally irresponsible.

Second, there is the question of timing:

> One word more about giving instructions as to what the world ought to be. Philosophy in any case always come on the scene too late to give it. As the thought of the world, it appears only when actuality is already there cut and dried after its process of formation has been completed. . . . When philosophy paints its grey in grey, then has a shape of life grown old. . . . The Owl of Minerva spreads its wings only with the falling of the dusk. (PR, preface)

The claim that philosophy is always too late to give advice is not a dogmatic assertion. It is an epistemological consequence of Hegel's understanding of the historical situatedness of human thought:

As a work of philosophy, [Hegel's political theory, as expressed
in the *Philosophy of Right*] must be poles apart from an attempt to construct a state as it ought to be. The instruction
which it may contain cannot consist in teaching the state what
it ought to be. . . . Whatever happens, every individual is a
child of his time; so philosophy too is its own time apprehended
in thoughts. It is just as absurd to fancy that a philosophy can
transcend its contemporary world as it is to fancy that an individual can overleap his own age, jump over Rhodes. (PR,
preface)

In the midst of this last statement Hegel alludes to a third reason
why philosophy gives no advice. He writes, "To comprehend what is,
this is the task of philosophy, because what is, is reason." This is an
echo of the earlier, much discussed claim that "what is rational is
actual and what is actual is rational." Hegel expands on this as
follows:

If on the other hand, the Idea passes for "only an Idea," for
something represented in an opinion, philosophy rejects such a
view and shows that nothing is actual except the Idea. Once
that is granted, the great thing is to apprehend in the show of
the temporal and transient the substance which in immanent
and the eternal which is present. . . . To recognize reason as
the rose in the cross of the present and thereby to enjoy the
present, this is the rational insight which reconciles us to the
actual, the reconciliation which philosophy affords. . . . (PR,
preface)

These commentary passages on Hegel's identification of the
rational and the actual imply the differentiation carefully expressed in EL, ¶6 between actuality [*Wirklichkeit*] and mere empirical existence [*Dasein, Existenz*]. The point of his slogan is not to
claim rationality for everything that happens to happen, but rather
to protest against the "precocious wisdom" that would tell the world
what ought to be "as if the world had waited on it to learn how it
ought to be, and was not!" Rather, to say that the actual is rational
is to say that the rational has the power to actualize itself. To doubt
this is to suppose "that Ideas and Ideals are something far too excellent to have actuality, or something too impotent to procure it for
themselves. . . . The object of philosophy is the Idea: and the Idea is
not so impotent as merely to have a right or an obligation to exist
without actually existing." Not to recognize this is equivalent to de-

nying the divine governance of the world. It is the metaphysical heresy Hegel calls "the atheism of the ethical world" (PR, preface).

These considerations are serious, but not sufficient, I believe, to establish Hegel's conclusion. First, there is indeed a superficial and sentimental pacifist internationalism from which philosophy would do well to keep its distance. But the requirement for a new international order free from war and propaganda which we are considering did not arise out of a "conceptophobic" emotionalism, but rather out of the severe conceptual discipline of Hegel's own dialectical holism. If shallowness should happen to hit on the same truth, we should not let that drive us to embrace error so as to be guiltless by nonassociation.

Second, in the present case philosophy is manifestly not too late. The philosophically grounded requirement for perpetual peace comes on the scene and is carefully articulated quite noticeably before rather than after the fact of its realization. There is, however, the question of its epistemological credentials. Since this putative insight is grounded in a social praxis which is not the ultimate social praxis to which it purports to point, it can lay no claim to being the expression of absolute knowing. There is an element of faith (epistemic risk) involved in claiming the ability to recognize what would be the fulfillment of history prior to its occurrence. But for the reasons given in the previous paragraph we can think of it as a rational faith as distinct from a faith grounded merely in wishful thinking.

Finally, if philosophy sees the rose in the cross of the present, this can only be because it sees the cross, the pain which cries out for some kind of reconciliation. This means that philosophy not only apprehends "the substance which is immanent and the eternal which is present" in "the show [*Schein*] of the temporal and transient," but also the degree to which the substance remains transcendent and the eternal absent. And what does philosophy do then? In the first place, it transcends itself in action. The time has come for understanding the world to become the guide for changing it. If dialectical holism points to a mode of human intersubjectivity not yet actual, belief in the ability of the rational to actualize itself may well take the form of hearing the call to do whatever one can to assist in the actualization. Philosophy becomes political action.

In the second place, philosophy may be called upon to transcend itself in faith. This is different from the faith just mentioned. In the process of working for an international community free from war and propaganda, it may well become evident that the best of human efforts are insufficient to the task. We may be forced to join with Heidegger in acknowledging that only a god can save us now. Here faith is not merely the willingness to take epistemic risks. It is the willingness to take existential risks, to hope for what cannot be guaranteed and to trust another for what I (and We) cannot do.

Insofar as philosophy transcends itself in this kind of faith and works, it knows that it is not absolute knowing. If faith and works are virtues, they are inseparable from another virtue, humility, the humility involved in admitting the philosophy has not yet reached "the goal where it can lay aside the title 'love of knowing' and be actual knowing" (PhG, 12/3). It would seem to be the conclusion of the present, allegedly Hegelian, argument, that a philosophy which wants to become absolute knowing must give up all pretensions of having arrived at that goal and, so long as the world has the shape it presently has, overcome itself in humble faith and works. At first glance this self-overcoming seems as remote from Hegelian thinking as anything possibly could be. But perhaps it is not so. For if it was Jesus who taught that only those who lose their life can really find it,[25] who was it who wrote the following?

> But the life of Spirit is not the life that shrinks from death and keeps itself untouched by devastation, but rather the life that endures it and maintains itself in it. It wins its truth only when, in utter dismemberment, it finds itself. (PhG, 29–30/19)

Like the Christendom of which he considered himself to be a part, Hegel succumbed to triumphalism, was ready to celebrate victory before the battle was over. But that does not mean that there is not some powerful food for thought and action in his work for any of us who, in his aftermath, are willing to acknowledge that, so far as the kingdom of God is concerned, we are at best the church militant and not the church triumphant.[26]

6 HEGEL AND GADAMER

At the heart of Hans-Georg Gadamer's philosophical hermeneutics is the claim that the "fundamental prejudice of the Enlightenment is the prejudice against prejudice itself, which deprives tradition of its authority."[1] He counters with the claim that "the prejudices of the individual, far more than his judgments, constitute the historical reality of his being," and he seeks to bring about a "rehabilitation of authority and tradition."[2]

No one has understood this as a call for resurgent bigotry. The etymological sense of prejudice as prejudgment (*Vor-urteil*) and thus as the fore-sight that guides all sight, has been noticed.[3] But the charge has been made that philosophical hermeneutics represents an uncritical conservatism *vis-à-vis* the past. To this Gadamer responds that being open to tradition, allowing it to address us and make its claim upon us *before* we make it into an object over which we preside as subjects, is not the same as blindly accepting everything it says. Perhaps there is no better example of what Gadamer means than his own relation to Hegel.

Gadamer describes the relation as a "tension-filled proximity."[4] We are not likely to improve on that formula. Gadamer is powerfully drawn to Hegel's thought as a source of insight he cannot do without. At the same time he sees it as a seductive force that he must use every energy at his disposal to resist, lest it lead him to forsake his own deepest insights. Still it would not be helpful to call him ambivalent, as if he isn't able to make up his mind and vascillates, finding Hegelian dialectic attractive on Monday, Wednesday, and Friday, but dangerous on Tuesday, Thursday, and Saturday. It is just because he knows who he is and where he stands that he finds it necessary to say both yes and no to Hegel.

One way to express this is to see contemporary debates as re-enactments of debates in which Hegel took part. In the debate over whether the full self-transparency of self-consciousness can provide a foundation for philosophy as a rigorous science, Gadamer (with Heidegger) plays Kant to Husserl's Hegel and comes down

consistently on the side of the unsurpassable finitude of human cognition. But in the debate over whether an energetics of nature creates a boundary beyond which hermeneutical understanding
cannot pass, needing to give way to a more nearly natural scientific
way of thinking, Gadamer plays Hegel to Habermas's Marx.[5] His
proximity to Hegel is indeed tension filled.

The Post-Transcendental
Understanding of Knowledge

An important part of this proximity arises from an agreement that
the nature of the finitude of human knowledge is to be understood
in existentialist rather than empiricist terms. The question is
whether it is ultimately the sense-bound character or the situation-
bound character of knowledge that renders it finite.

Empiricism sees cognitive limitations in quantitative and spatial terms. There are some areas (metaphysics) into which our capacities will not reach, and some portions of those areas that they
will reach will remain at any given time unexplored. But this latter
limitation is in principle remediable, and the sense-based knowledge we gain through exploration of the sensible world is territory
genuinely brought under our control. We have objective knowledge.
This remains the case even if no definitive answers can be given to
problems about induction and confirmation.

By contrast, existentialism sees the limitations of human
knowledge in qualitative and nonspatial terms. While asserting
that no territory can be ruled out of bounds to human investigation
a priori, it even more vigorously insists that there is no territory
where the situatedness of human cognition does not place a qualification on the knowledge achieved.

This second view is common ground shared by representatives
of philosophical traditions that often disagree among themselves
sharply on other issues. Among these can be mentioned Marxism;
the sociology of knowledge; the Frankfurt school; pragmatism; phenomenology; hermeneutics (including Gadamer); and, I shall argue,
Hegel. To label this view 'existentialist' is not to suggest a monopoly
on the part of those who claim or merit that title. It is rather to note
the combination in the existentialist tradition of the theme of human finitude on the one hand, and its explication in terms of being
in a situation on the other. This applies to Heidegger's analysis of
being-in-the-world as much as the analyses of Jaspers, Marcel,
Merleau-Ponty, and Sartre, who explicitly use the term 'situation'.[6]

Most often reference is to the so-called *Geisteswissenschaften,* where the claims of situation epistemology are most easily supported. But epistemological existentialism is not limited to what we call the humanities and social sciences; it extends to the natural sciences as well. When Marcuse and Habermas can debate not whether but how the natural sciences function as ideology, when Heidegger can suggest that the exact sciences give us correct answers but in so doing direct us away from the truth, when Whitehead similarly suggests that Cartesian-Galilean science leads us metaphysically astray because of the fallacy of misplaced concreteness, when Husserl suggests that all of the sciences have their foundation in the life-world, when Gadamer claims that the methodical character of the natural sciences requires both a historical derivation and an epistemological restriction, and when even within the philosophy of science it is increasingly doubted that there are any theory-free data, it is clear that the philosophical issue is broader than the conflict of political ideologies in the human sciences.[7]

It is clear that for any philosophy that gives what I've been calling an existentialist interpretation to the finitude of human knowledge, transcendental philosophy can be only preliminary and in no sense final. This is not because there is no a priori element in our knowledge, but because the situatedness of knowing implies that beneath the necessity and universality of the a priori elements there lies a contingency that renders them particular.

Thus, for example, Habermas speaks of a "transitory a priori structure" underlying our knowledge, because "apparently the empirical conditions under which transcendental rules take shape and determine the constitutive order of a life-world are themselves the result of a socialization process." He concludes that "a radial critique of knowledge is possible only as social theory."[8]

Gadamer agrees, for this is the point of his "defense" of prejudice. With reference to the hermeneutical circle as described by Heidegger, he writes, "It is not so much our judgments as it is our prejudices that constitute our being . . . the historicity of our existence entails that prejudices in the literal sense of the word, constitute the initial directedness of our whole ability to experience. Prejudices are biases of our openness to the world. They are simply conditions whereby we experience something—whereby what we encounter says something to us."[9] For Gadamer the concept of prejudice and that of tradition are closely linked, as is clear in this summary of his views by Ricoeur.

A human being discovers his finitude in the fact that, first of all, he finds himself within a tradition or traditions. Because history precedes me and my reflection, because I belong to history before I belong to myself, prejudgment also precedes judgment, and submission to traditions precedes their examination. The regime of historical consciousness is that of a consciousness exposed to the effect of history [*wirkungsgeschichtliches Bewusstsein*]. If therefore we cannot extract ourselves from historical becoming, or place ourselves at a distance from it in such a way that the past becomes an object for us, then we must confess that we are always situated within history in such a fashion that our consciousness never has the freedom to bring itself face to face with the past by an act of sovereign independence.[10]

This kind of conclusion, along with the implication it has for the possibility of our being free to bring ourselves directly face to face with any object of knowledge at all, is what has pulled contemporary hermeneutics away from Husserlian phenomenology. David Linge has written, "The life-world was overlooked by constitutional analysis as Husserl had practiced it [though it] functioned precisely as the horizon of intentional objects without ever becoming thematic itself. How could the phenomenologist's own enterprise avoid presupposing the self-evident validity of a life-world in which his praxis had its meaning? Indeed, this life-world, present as a non-objectified horizon of meaning, seems to encompass transcendental subjectivity itself and in this sense threatens to displace it as the absolute foundation of experience. The ego at this point appears to be 'in' the life-world."[11]

This is exactly the conclusion that Gadamer wishes us to draw. One way he puts it is to give to philosophical hermeneutics the task of moving "back along the path of Hegel's phenomenology of mind until we discover in all that is subjective the substantiality that determines it."[12] The main point Gadamer wants to make about the life-world that grounds the transcendental ego, thereby giving substantiality to the subjective, is its linguistic nature, "for language is not only an object in our hands, it is the reservoir of tradition and the medium in and through which we exist and perceive our world." This means we can speak of the "linguistic constitution of the world."[13] It also means we must speak of the historically conditioned constitution of the world; for as the "reservoir of tradition," each particular language is both a specific and a changing "medium in and through which we exist and perceive our world."

This central theme of post-transcendental philosophy, that all human knowledge is inextricably situated in some historically specific life-world or other, makes the question of history and truth the central philosophical problem. It is not merely an issue for the methodology of the *Geisteswissenschaften* or even for a general epistemology. It concerns our very being. For historicity seems to be as essential to our nature as truth is to our destiny or calling (*Bestimmung*). But if being historically situated means that our knowing is always perspectivally partial (disclosure entailing concealment) and not merely quantitatively partial, is there not a discrepancy between our nature and our destiny? Are not epistemological existentialism and the "vertigo of relativity" it brings with it just the Sartrean conclusion that we are a useless passion coming at us from another direction?[14]

Rather than try to answer these questions at this point, we need to note that Hegel stands with Gadamer in this post-transcendental tradition. In fact, it is to him that we owe its first clear formulation. As early as his essay on natural law he expects "to see the empirical condition of the world reflected in the ideal mirror of science," because "the condition of all sciences will express also the condition of the world."[15]

Though it is especially the political-ethical sciences he has in mind here, he means it when he says *all* the sciences are historically conditioned, and he applies this idea to systematic philosophy as a whole. Throughout his career as a philosopher Hegel remarks with wonder at the new era that has dawned for European civilization in his own lifetime.[16] And he regularly states that this birth of a new historical epoch has epistemological significance. Thus, for example, in the preface to the first edition of the *Science of Logic* he complains that "logic shows no traces so far of the new spirit which has arisen in the sciences no less than in the world of actuality." This cannot last, however, for "once the substantial form of the spirit has inwardly reconstituted itself, all attempts to preserve the forms of an earlier culture are utterly in vain." What is now called for is "the labour required for a scientific elaboration of the new principle."[17] Much too little attention has been given to this clear indication that when Hegel calls philosophy "its own time comprehended in thoughts,"[18] he means not only his political philosophy but also his Logic itself!

We get an equally clear statement (and more) in the *Phenomenology*. It's goal is "to show that now is the time for philosophy to be raised to the status of a Science." The reason this hasn't already happened is not that Hegel's predecessors were not as clever as he, but because they lived too soon. It will therefore be necessary for this treatise on knowledge to take account of "the stage which self-conscious Spirit has presently reached." Once the question is put, "it is not difficult to see that ours is a birth-time and a period of transition to a new era." Again the task is to articulate the significance of the new era by bringing the whole, rich content of Spirit's life into a systematic knowledge structured by the principles of Spirit's latest advance.[19]

But the *Phenomenology* contains more than this programmatic commitment to incorporating history into epistemology. It inaugurates the post-transcendental era by teaching us to ask a new question: Who is the transcendental subject? Both the answer implied in chapter 1 "Sense-Certainty," and the explicit answer of chapter 4 "The Truth of Self-Certainty," make the same point: the transcendental subject, or the totality of conditions of possible experience, is a particular perspective on the world by virtue of being historically situated.

The phenomenological critique of sense-certainty's claim to immediacy in knowing brings to light not only the mediated character of sense perception, which thereby has the status of interpretation, but also the central role of language in this mediation. Especially when read against the background of the Jena lectures on the philosophy of Spirit, this analysis both teaches us to ask Who is the transcendental subject? and to answer by saying that, the transcendental subject is the speaker of a language, or perhaps, the transcendental subject is language itself. And because language is always some specific language and never language in general, we find reflection on consciousness turning into reflection on language, which in turn becomes reflection on tradition. The I is not fundamental here. Individual consciousness is rather the vehicle of the tradition embedded in language. As Hegel puts it, "Through consciousness Spirit intervenes in the way the world is ruled," and language is "the true being of Spirit as Spirit in general."[20]

This is but one of two Hegelian routes to the Gadamerian conclusions that "understanding is not to be thought of so much as an action of one's subjectivity, but as the placing of oneself within a process of tradition. . . . The anticipation of meaning that governs our understanding of a text is not an act of subjectivity, but proceeds from the communality that binds us to the tradition."[21] When Hegel turns from the interpretations of sense perception to the more sophisticated interpretations of the understanding, which we would call natural science, a second "transcendental deduction" of the post-transcendental perspective occurs.

Here the often neglected continuity of chapters 3 and 4 of the *Phenomenology* is crucial. The latter contains the famous section on lordship and bondage as these emerge from the fundamental human desire for recognition. The ineradicable need for reciprocal recognition is what leads to the revolutionary definition of Spirit as " 'I' that is 'We' and 'We' that is 'I'."[22] But the *Phenomenology* has not abandoned the task, clearly announced in preface and introduction alike, of solving the problem of knowledge. We have already noted that in the Jena lectures Spirit replaces the transcendental ego of Kantian-Fictean idealism. Here, too, the emergence of Spirit has epistemic meaning. For in chapter 3 Hegel gives an essentially Kantian interpretation of understanding, leading to the conclusion that every consciousness is a self-consciousness, that the world is *given* only to the self which *takes* it in a certain way. But that self is no individual, theoretical self, as the Cartesian assumptions of the transcendental tradition take for granted. The concrete human self is a desiring as well as a judging self, and because the desire for recognition is what distinguishes human from animal desire, the social, interactive self that is We as much as I and thus Spirit is the subject of any concrete and thus fully adequate knowing. But Spirit is not static structure and the struggle for recognition has many historical moments. The theory of knowledge inescapably becomes the history of Spirit. The transcendental framework is *aufgehoben* through asking the question Who is the transcendental subject?[23]

The Critique of Method

The proximity of Hegel and Gadamer finds expression in a second important agreement. If the situational interpretation of cognitional human finitude gives rise to a post-transcendental self-understanding threatened by "the vertigo of relativity," some will seek to desituate themselves by recourse to method.[24] This can be called the Cartesian strategy, for Descartes makes it clear in the *Discourse* that the goal of his method is not just the power of predictability but the transcendence of tradition, with its interminable disputes. Hegel and Gadamer are united in uncompromising opposition to the Cartesian strategy and to the paradigmatic privilege of mathematics and the matematico-experimental sciences that belongs with it.

In Hegel's case, it is immediately after noting the historically situated character of the Logic that he repudiates any borrowing of method from "a subordinate science like mathematics."[25] His

reference is to the critique of mathematical (geometrical) knowledge in the preface to the *Phenomenology*. The key word is 'external'.
In geometry I set out to prove a theorem. Because this goal guides
the construction of the proof, "an external purpose governs this activity." Correspondingly, in this mathematical cognition "insight is
an activity external to the thing; it follows that the true thing is altered by it." The result may be "true propositions," but "the content
is false." For, to put it one way, the subject matter that can be
treated in this way is lifeless in itself, incapable of being adequate to
the philosophical concept. Or, to put in the other way, this external
knowing "proceeds on the surface, does not touch the thing itself. . . . and therefore fails to comprehend it."[26]

By explicitly repudiating the idea that philosophy can borrow
its method from mathematics, Hegel makes it clear that his critique
is not merely directed toward mathematics but toward any method
modeled after it and sharing its character. That character has two
closely related features, a purpose that comes from the knowing
subject rather than the subject matter, and, consequently concepts
and procedures that are external to the subject matter and imposed
upon it rather than arising from within it. This subjectivity of
thinking and this independence of the object thought can be called
the creation of subject and object, for the relation between knower
and known it entails is by no means universal or necessary. Calculative thinking, rooted in the desire to control, is a specific, historical project. Like Heidegger's analysis, Hegel's shows it to be a road
taken, but not necessarily.[27]

In the *Science of Logic* Hegel reemphasizes the connection between externality and subjectivity in seeking to look beyond them.
What is needed is "the point of view which no longer takes the determinations of thought to be only an instrument and a means" of
the knower's purposes; "more important is the further point connected with it, namely that it is usual to regard them as an external
form."[28] This also must go. It must be replaced by the method that
is no method, which no longer allows an external relation between
method and content because the method of knowing is at once "the
manner peculiar to cognition" and "the *objective* manner, or rather
the *substantiality,* of *things*" being known.[29] By contrast to external
reflection "it can only be the nature of the content itself which spon-
taneously develops itself in a scientific method of knowing. . . . This
spiritual movement . . . is the absolute method of knowing and at
the same time is the immanent soul of the content itself."[30] Perhaps
it is a bit misleading to speak of the method arising by spontaneous

generation. But the point Hegel wants to make is the same as when he says that true philosophical knowledge "demands surrender to the life of the object, or, what amounts to the same thing, confronting and expressing *its* inner necessity."[31] And it is the same point once again when he says of true philosophic knowledge, "It is not *we* who frame the concepts."[32]

Hegel's analysis of the Concept as the union of Universality, Particularity, and Individuality is in terms of the freedom whose most immediate forms are friendship and love. Because this includes a theory of the theoretical as well as the practical self, we can say that Hegel attempts to spell out a relation of loving intersubjectivity between knower and known.[33] We can even speak here of epistemological nonviolence. For "the universal is therefore *free* power; it is itself and takes its other within its embrace, but without *doing violence* to it . . . for it bears itself towards its other as towards *its own self.*"[34] This Golden Rule of the theoretical self is in striking contrast to the triumph of Cartesian method, whose inner secret Kant betrays when he admits that the scientific revolution assumed "that reason has insight only into that which it produces after a plan of its own, and that it must not allow itself to be kept, as it were, in nature's leading strings, but must itself show the way . . . *constraining nature to give answer to questions of reason's own determining.*"[35]

This methodical violence Hegel abjures, so that knowledge will let the known be itself and show itself as itself. But such an encounter of loving and nonviolent intersubjectivity, in which the knower's openness means "surrender to the life of the object," can only occur in the world. Both knower and known belong to the closeness of a situation. The former has not become a subject outside the world for whom the world in its totality has become object, over which it presides like a judge and from whom it demands answers like a prosecuting attorney. The methodical attempt to desituate the knowing self turns out to be not so much a form of escape as of aggression. It arises from the will to dominate.

The same themes recur in Gadamer's critique of the Cartesian strategy. He tells us that "the title of *Truth and Method* never intended that the antithesis it implies should be mutually exclusive."[36] But the title does imply an antithesis, so that even if the 'and' in it isn't the 'and' of 'black and white', it is surely closer to that 'and' than to the one in 'love and marriage'. He repeatedly insists that the hermeneutical problem is not one of method but rather of truth (and of being);[37] but his regular introduction of hermeneutics, with reference to the way a work of art seizes us and makes a truth-claim upon us, makes it clear that he is concerned with kinds of truth not available to method.[38]

No more than Hegel does Gadamer propose that the sciences whose glory is their method forsake their Cartesian heritage. He wants them rather to acknowledge its meaning. Only by becoming aware of their estrangement from natural consciousness, of the price they have paid for the achievements made possible thereby, of the presuppositions guiding the entire enterprise, and of the necessary return to the larger language context in which they are but one of the language games played, can they regain their integrity.[39]

When all this is fully brought to light the cognitive primacy of methodically secured science will be undermined.[40] The concept of experience will be freed from the concept of science. With the concepts of life and the life-world, respectively, Dilthey and Husserl were in a position to achieve this freedom. But their Cartesian roots were too deep, and the ideal of science governs both the concept of history grounded in romantic hermeneutics and the concept of philosophy grounded in intentional analysis.[41] What Gadamer says about experimental and historico-critical methods applies with at least equal force to the methods Dilthey and Husserl derive from Schleiermacher and Brentano, namely that they "are concerned to guarantee, through the objectivity of their approach, that these basic experiences can be repeated by anyone."[42]

But this denial of the historical nature of experience, which Hegel had already spelled out so emphatically in the *Phenomenology,* this attempt to desituate the knower, remains plausible only as long as self-deception about the logic of question and answer is allowed to prevail. As an example Gadamer points to the objective answers statistical research can give to precisely formulated questions. Everything is under the strict governance of method except the choice of questions to be asked. This shows that "science always stands under definite conditions of methodological abstraction and that the successes of modern sciences rest on the fact that other possibilities for questioning are concealed by abstraction. This fact comes out clearly in the case of statistics, for the anticipatory character of the questions statistics answer make it particularly suitable for propaganda purposes. . . .Thus what is established by statistics seems to be a language of facts, but which questions these facts answer and which facts would begin to speak if other questions were asked are hermeneutical questions."[43] The Kantian claim that the questions asked are of "reason's own determining" only serves the self-deception that remains oblivious to the historically specific purposes that guide such questioning. By calling itself reason this particular project seeks to hide from itself its own finitude.

Because "there is no such thing as a method of learning to ask questions,"[44] science is delivered over to history and tradition at its very foundation, the selection of questions to be asked. Moreover, the particular historical project at work in the sciences, which have come to be paradigmatic, is not hard to identify. Bacon already formulated it at the birth of modern science with the slogan Knowledge Is Power. For this reason the concepts of method and of control are intimately connected as Gadamer restates Hegel's objection to the "external purpose" that governs any methodical inquiry that is not a "surrender to the life of the object."[45]

This "surrender" Gadamer expresses in terms of the distinction between openness to the truth claims placed upon us by text or tradition and knowledge as domination (Scheler), in which appropriation means taking possession of the subject matter and placing it at our disposal. For every true question, he holds, involves the openness that puts ourselves in question.[46] Such true questioning is unknown by the knowledge that rests upon objectifying procedures in the investigation of its subject matter

> Abstracted out of the fundamental relation to the world that is given in the linguistic nature of our experience of it, it seeks to become certain about entities by methodically organizing its knowledge of the world. Consequently it condemns as heresy all knowledge that does not allow of this kind of certainty and hence is not able to serve the growing domination of being. As against this, we have endeavored to liberate the mode of being of art and history, and the experience which corresponds to them, from the ontological prejudice that is contained in the ideal of scientific objectivity.[47]

Because hermeneutics "does not intend an absolute mastery over being by the one who understands,"[48] it finds in the Greek understanding of theoria a further account of the openness that surrenders to the object. As the Greeks understood it, theory meant being so present to the object as to be "outside oneself." "This kind of being present is a self-forgetfulness." It "arises from the attention to the object," which, in turn makes it "possible to forget one's own purpose." Instead of being a "self-determination of the subjective consciousness," theory is rather "a true sharing, not something active, but something passive (pathos), namely being totally involved in and carried away by what one sees."[49] But it would be a mistake to interpret this passivity as inertia or listlessness. For this passivity is the activity of "uninterrupted listening."[50]

The Dispute over Absolute Knowledge

It can be said that the concept of life is central to Hegel's attempt "to distance himself critically from the subjectivity of modern philosophy."[51] But the crucial form of life in and through which this occurs is human social life. For this reason much of what Gadamer appreciates in Hegel is implicit in his regular praise of the concept of objective spirit, the I that is We and vice versa.[52] This concept enables Hegel to break with the individualized self-consciousness fundamental to idealist transcendentalism, including Kantian moral philosophy, which rests on the moral certitudes of the Cartesian ego.[53] It is the same concept with its critique of subject and object that assists Gadamer in the attempt to free himself from post-Kantian Cartesianism, whether in Schleiermacher, neo-Kantianism, or Husserlian phenomenology.[54] By recognizing that there is a reason in history greater than that of the individual, this concept not only opens up our understanding of understanding to history, but also permits the reappropriation of the Greek *logos* tradition of a rationality above that of individual self-consciousness. Ancient substantiality and modern subjectivity are united in a relationship that deepens and enriches both.[55]

But proximity gives way to tension when Hegel seeks to go beyond objective spirit to absolute spirit, to that knowledge of spirit by itself, which can be called absolute knowledge. Here, in Gadamer's view, Hegel's struggle with the Cartesian spirit proves itself to be halfhearted, and he succumbs to it in a threefold manner. First, he remains within the transcendental framework in that knowledge of the world and knowledge of knowing the world are inseparable. Or, to put it another way, knowledge remains self-knowledge, even if the self is not the static, individualized self of the earlier tradition, but the expanded self expressed in the notions of *nous* and spirit.[56] Next, there is the idea of "the transparency of the idea to itself or spirit's self-consciousness," which represents the "self-apotheosis of thought implied in Hegel's idea of truth."[57] Finally, there is the notion that when knowledge is this kind of self-knowledge, the certainty of the self's full transparency to itself, philosophy can be science as the "perfection of experience." The philosophy that in its anti-Cartesian moments is a "self-defense against the sciences" turns out to claim the status of science for itself, a claim "which ultimately is founded upon Descartes' idea of method and which, within the framework of transcendental philosophy, is developed from the principle of self-consciousness."[58]

There are, to be sure, important differences between Hegel's philosophical science and the sciences against which it is meant to stand as a self-defense. Its method seeks to be immanent rather than external. It seeks to deal with the whole rather than some part of the real.[59] Most important, it does not seek to ground itself in a timeless, desituated ego, but holds fast to the notion that the true subject of human knowledge is the historically situated social self. It is at this point that Hegel is perhaps most ingenious. Biblical eschatology becomes the key as he regularly relates the notion of science to that of the kingdom, meaning the Kingdom of God. Then, instead of seeking to make thought absolute by freeing it from all conditioning by life, he puts the question of the cognitive implications of the fulfillment of historical life in the Kingdom of God. As we have already seen, he makes thought in both his *Phenomenology* and his *Science of Logic* relative to the new age that has dawned in his own lifetime, but instead of producing vertigo, this relativity is affirmed simultaneously with the claim of scientific status for both works. This is possible because the route to absolute knowledge is not that of fleeing every historical situation, but that of being born in the absolute historical situation, the Kingdom in which history achieves its goal. And it is precisely the birth of that Kingdom that Hegel believes the tumult of his own times to represent.[60]

But whatever awe we may experience before the grandeur of Hegel's project, Gadamer finds it irrelevant to our situation. It shatters, and we need to understand why. "The ancient Greek, 'Know thyself!' still holds good for us as well, for it means, 'know that you are no god, but a human being.' What self-knowledge really is is not the perfect self-transparency of knowledge but the insight that we have to accept the limits posed for finite natures."[61] In other words, scientific philosophy as absolute knowledge is *hubris*.

As it stands this charge is mere assertion. To support it Gadamer finds it necessary to turn his phenomenology of the hermeneutical situation against Hegel. Whereas for much of the journey Hegel has been, in Gadamer's view, a major partner in the development of this understanding of understanding, he now becomes its target. Not surprisingly it is the historical and linguistic character of understanding to which Gadamer appeals.

With reference to history Gadamer emphasizes both the openness and the opaqueness of the historical situation. There are two aspects, in turn, to the openness of historical experience, general and specific. Against Hegel's insistence that knowledge be self-knowledge and experience become science in order that absolute knowledge be possible, the openness of historical experience in general is affirmed. "We can now understand why Hegel's application to history, insofar as he saw it as part of the absolute self-consciousness of philosophy, does not do justice to the hermeneutical consciousness. The nature of experience is conceived in terms of that which goes beyond it; for experience itself can never be science. . . . The truth of experience always contains an orientation towards new experience."[62] This means that historical experience has the marks of what Hegel calls the "bad infinite," and that historical understanding is given over to the "tireless self-correction" of the Socratic dialogues, which join "the metaphysical question concerning the infinite and absolute with the ineradicable finitude of the questioner."[63]

More specifically, the openness of history is evidenced in the at best partial realization of the fulfillment Hegel claimed for his historical moment. Gadamer willingly grants that the final principle of history has emerged. Since Hegel's time "history is not to be based upon a new principle. The principle of freedom is unimpugnable and irrevocable. It is no longer possible for anyone still to affirm the unfreedom of humanity. The principle that all are free never again can be shaken. But does this mean that on account of this, history has come to an end? Are all human beings actually free? Has not history since then been a matter of just this, that the historical conduct of man has to translate the principle of freedom into reality? Obviously this points to the unending march of world history into the openness of its future tasks and gives no becalming assurance that everything is already in order."[64]

Hegel might reply that the last sentence is dogmatic and without foundation. Biblical eschatology in both its Jewish and Christian forms envisages a decisive fulfillment of history's goal, which, while not violating the general character of historical experience, would put us in a situation so different from all previous situations that their finitude would be overcome. Does not Paul promise that in that day we shall know as we are known by God?[65] Gadamer might well grant the theoretical possibility of such a historical transcendence of the normal limits of historical understanding. (How else avoid the charge of blatant dogmatism?) But his response to Hegel's actual claim would not be changed. It would take an eschatological transition far more dramatic than anything that took place in Hegel's life or since to merit being called the Kingdom of

God. The promise of "liberty and justice" for all would have to become a reality and not merely a promise and a dream.

In addition to this openness of the historical situation, there is also its opaqueness. "It is precisely our experience of history that we are located so completely within it that we can in a certain sense always say, We don't know what is happening to us."[66] The point can be put in Hegelian terms. "That the consciousness of the individual. . . is no match for reason in history Hegel had illuminatingly demonstrated in his famous doctrine about the cunning of reason (*List der Vernunft*). But must not this knowledge of the finitude and limitedness of the individual who stands as an agent in history affect any individual who thinks? What must this mean for the claim of philosophic thought to truth?"[67] This is not to say that reflection is utterly impotent, only that it is finite. "Reflection on a given pre-understanding brings before me something that otherwise happens *behind my back*. Something—but not everything, for what I have called *wirkungsgeschichtliches Bewusstsein* is inescapably more *being* than consciousness, and being is never fully manifest."[68]

Beyond its historical character, Gadamer sees the linguistic character of experience as a barrier to the possibility of its being perfected as science. The same linguisticality of all understanding, including philosophical reflection, which drives beyond the Cartesian-transcendental perspective in the first place keeps us from returning to it at the level of spirit, as Hegel wishes to do. This is the meaning of Gadamer's claim that "dialectic must retrieve itself in hermeneutics."[69] The claim of the dialectic of Hegel's *Logic* to be scientific may well be consistent. "It is another question, however, whether that purpose, which he proposes for his *Logic* as transcendental logic, is justified convincingly when even he himself relies on the natural logic which he finds in the 'logical instinct' of language."[70]

It seems that Gadamer never tires of finding new ways to make this point, including the following:

1) The multiplicity of languages implies the multiplicity of logics and places the scientific status of any particular logic in question.[71]

2) The categories of thought presuppose language as the home of thought, and we can never reflect ourselves out of that home. Since language is not an instrument in the service of our purposes but the medium in which we live, it can never be objectified so that it ceases to surround us and define a limited horizon for our thinking.[72]

3) This becomes even clearer if we notice that even the speculative proposition, which Hegel so carefully distinguishes from ordinary prediction, needs to be interpreted. Philosophical reflection is language that points to what it cannot fully say.[73]

4) This point in turn is deepened by the realization that philosophical discourse not only implies ongoing philosophical discourse (interpretation), and thus its own finitude, but it also implies an ongoing dialogue with nonphilosophical discourse. The language of philosophy is always in dialogue with the language of the world.[74]

5) Finally there is the fact that language places us within tradition and thereby within history. The linguistic character of experience implies its historical character and all the implications of finitude already noted with reference to the latter.[75]

6) All five of these points are implied by and summed up in the conversational nature of language, which Gadamer indicates by speaking of the logic of question and answer. This logic limits the dogmatic claims of Hegelian Logic by calling attention to the historical situatedness of language and the unending conversation it represents, both within and among ourselves. Because objective spirit is this conversation it can never become absolute spirit. The truth of absolute spirit is precisely the finitude of the questioner. We are "exposed" to the questions that "befall" us in art, religion, and philosophy. In fact, "these questions hold us in suspense." As long as we allow ourselves to be addressed by these questions the conversation continues, and as long as this happens, dialectic will need to retrieve itself in hermeneutics, because speculation will remain open to new interpretation.[76]

Though mostly spelled out in essays subsequent to *Truth and Method,* this critique of the Hegelian doctrines of absolute spirit and absolute knowledge from the perspective of the historical and linguistic character of objective spirit relies entirely on themes developed carefully in Gadamer's magnum opus. The more recent of these essays, however, include a third line of argument against Hegel, one derived from what Ricoeur calls the hermeneutics of suspicion. This was not a part of Gadamer's project originally, and much of the Gadamer-Habermas debate, with the larger discussion of hermeneutics in relation to ideology critique, is best understood as the challenging of a "hermeneutics of recovery" with a "hermeneutics of suspicion." Like Ricoeur, Gadamer does not see in the arguments of Marx, Nietzsche, and Freud (along with Schopenhauer and Bergson) a limit to the hermeneutical claim to universality. Suspicion is to be incorporated into hermeneutics.

The possibility of including suspicion in the hermeneutical task is grounded in a refusal to make the Cartesian assumption that the mind is more easily known than the body. In the transcendental tradition up through Husserl this becomes the assumption that consciousness is fully transparent to itself, once it makes the decision to become reflective. By accepting the critique of this position, which stems from Habermas and the "school of suspicion," Gadamer broadens the hermeneutical perspective by indicating yet another way (beyond history and language) in which revealing and concealing are the convex and concave sides of the same curve even for reflective self-consciousness. If there is always more going on "behind the back" of consciousness than it can get out in front of itself, so to speak, this refers not only to the impossibility of thematizing the horizon of one's thinking without remainder, or making the background of perception the foreground without creating a new background. In addition to the implicit, the unconscious also makes its home "behind my back." The attempt to understand must include the search for meanings unnoticed (because unwelcome) by those in whom they function.

So far as Hegel is concerned, this means that in addition to the ordinary opacity of historical life and the "tacit dimension" involved in every conversation, there is also the unconscious as a barrier to the full transparency of self-consciousness. Whether one speaks of repression or bad faith, the shared rationalizations of ideology are as intractable as the personal ones of neurosis, leaving the self-consciousness of spirit always in need of therapy.[77]

This third argument against Hegel plays a relatively minor role, and perhaps this is fitting. For to the degree that he can base his quarrel with Hegel on perspectives developed in the first place with help from Hegel, the quarrel becomes an example of the immanent critique that Hegel's own theory of dialectical "method" requires. This, in turn, is perhaps the best way of indicating how openness to tradition and respect for its authority need not involve an uncritical conservatism that worships the past. As long as distance and involvement, tension and proximity are kept in polar tension, the conversation continues.

7 HEGEL AND HUSSERL:
TRANSCENDENTAL PHENOMENOLOGY AND THE REVOLUTION YET AWAITED

It turns out that 1984 is not only the year for reflection on contemporary nightmares about Big Brother but also the year for recollecting the somewhat older dreams of these two giants on whose shoulders we seek to stand—dreams of rigorous science and of rational human life. It was in 1964 that George Schrader gave us an illuminating comparison of Hegel and Husserl.[1] Then in 1974 Quentin Lauer did the same,[2] suggesting to us that at least once a decade we need to reconsider what can be learned by generating a dialogue between these two thinkers, of whom it is not easy to tell whether it is the similarities or differences that run deeper. Now in 1984 we turn once again to that task.

The temptation is all but irresistible to focus on the *Phenomenology of Spirit* for Hegel's part of the conversation. Without even trying to resist, I do suggest that a comparison based on the theme of logic might also be very fruitful. But I shall stick to phenomenology rather than logic as the point of contact, and since I take Hegel's *Phenomenology* to belong to the tradition of transcendental philosophy (however un-Cartesian and un-Kantian it may be), the Husserl I shall seek to engage is the overtly transcendental phenomenologist we meet from 1907 on.[3]

To begin, let us note four major points of agreement between Hegel and Husserl. They are not, to be sure, total agreements in every detail. In fact, there are substantive disagreements related to each of these points. But the agreements are not for that reason merely verbal or superficial. On the contrary, they are deep and basic.

Philosophy as Rigorous Science

Two of these agreements are indicated by this familiar passage from Hegel's famous preface:

to help bring philosophy closer to the form of Science, to the
goal where it can lay aside the title *"love* of knowing" and be
actual knowing—that is what I have set myself to do. The
inner necessity that knowing should be Science lies in its nature. . . . To show that now is the time for philosophy to be
raised to the status of a Science would therefore be the only
true justification of any effort that has this aim, for to do so
would demonstrate the necessity of the aim, would indeed at
the same time be the accomplishing of it.[4]

In the first place, then, Hegel agrees with Husserl that philosophy must be a rigorous science. It goes without saying that by
this they do not mean that it should somehow try to imitate the procedures of the experimental sciences or that it should seek to
ground itself on the results of the *Natur-* or *Geisteswissenschaften.*
Both take the sciences in the most familiar sense of the term to
be unfulfilled promises, themselves in need of clarification and
grounding in spite of their dramatic successes.

Hegel's most general account of what would make philosophy a
rigorous science has two key elements, each of which has strikingly
Husserlian overtones. On the one hand, philosophy can be scientific
only if it is without presuppositions. Hegel develops this point in detail in the introduction to the *Phenomenology,* an utterly crucial
text for understanding his relation to Husserl.[5] But this freeing of
thought from prejudice, this negative preparation has a positive
goal. And so, on the other hand, philosophy can be scientific only if
it gets beyond the superficiality of first-order conceptualizations of
experience and descends into the conceptual depths to encounter
die Sache selbst. "Culture and its laborious emergence from the immediacy of substantial life must always begin by getting acquainted
with *general* principles and points of view, so as at first to work up
to conceptual thought of the subject matter [*der Sache über-
haupt*] . . . " Even when this includes the ability to develop precise
classifications and to give reasons for and against various claims, it
is not enough. "From this beginning culture must leave room for the
seriousness of life in its concrete fullness, which leads to the experience of the heart of the matter [*die Erfahrung der Sache selbst*]."
But even this is not enough, for Hegel is no romantic. Just as the
immediacy of substantial life requires conceptualization, so this
deeper level of experience which gets beyond what Hegel views as
mere Understanding must be brought to conceptual form. This final
stage of *Bildung* occurs "when the heart of the matter has been pen-

etrated to its depths by serious speculative effort [*der Ernst des Begriffs*]."[6]

This experiential and conceptual turn from superficial reasoning (*Verstand* in Hegel's sense) *zu den Sachen selbst* is not an automatic feature of everything that calls itself philosophy. It occurs only when philosophy gets beyond being "no more than a device for evading the heart of the matter [*die Sache selbst*]." Hegel's account of this latter kind of philosophy gives the negative image of a truly scientific philosophy. "For instead of getting involved in the real issue [*der Sache*], this kind of activity is always away beyond it; instead of tarrying with it, and losing itself in it, this kind of knowing is forever grasping at something new; it remains essentially preoccupied with itself instead of being preoccupied with the real issue [*der Sache*] and surrendering to it."[7] It is for the sake of this tarrying and this surrendering that philosophy seeks to free itself from presuppositions.[8]

Philosophy and Cultural Crisis

A second major agreement between Hegel and Husserl comes to light when Hegel says that "now is the time" for philosophy to become truly scientific. This seemingly incidental reference to Hegel's historical present is in fact anything but innocent. For he takes his time to be the *kairos* (in Tillich's sense) for scientific philosophy. On the one hand, it is a time of desperate need. If we consider "the stage which self-conscious Spirit has presently reached," we will see

> that Spirit has now got beyond the substantial life it formerly led in the element of thought, that it is beyond the immediacy of faith, beyond the satisfaction and security of the certainty that consciousness then had, of its reconciliation with the essential being, and of that being's universal presence both within and without . . . Spirit has not only lost its essential life; it is also conscious of this loss, and of the finitude that is its own content. Turning away from the empty husks, and confessing that it lies in wickedness, it reviles itself for so doing, and now demands from philosophy, not so much *knowledge* of what *is*, as the recovery through its agency of that lost sense of solid and substantial being.[9]

Only the imagery of the prodigal son is adequate to convey the current cultural crisis.

On the other hand, however, Hegel sees the hopeful beginning of new things. For him

> it is not difficult to see that ours is a birth-time and a period of transition to a new era. Spirit has broken with the world it has hitherto inhabited and imagined, and is of a mind to submerge it in the past . . . But just as the first breath drawn by a child after its long, quiet nourishment breaks the gradualness of merely quantitative growth—there is a qualitative leap, and the child is born—so likewise the Spirit in its formation matures slowly and quietly . . . The frivolity and boredom which unsettle the established order, the vague foreboding of something unknown, these are the heralds of approaching change. The gradual crumbling that left unaltered the face of the whole is cut short by a sunburst which, in one flash, illuminates the features of the new world.[10]

We could summarize this second agreement between Hegel and Husserl by saying that both place the demand for a truly scientific philosophy in the context of an historico-cultural crisis whose resolution they hope it will be.

There are two fairly obvious objections to this way of putting their second point of agreement. From Hegel's side it has been said, "The very idea of a true crisis of man, with the fate of the human spirit undecided and hanging in the balance, is unthinkable in the context of the Hegelian 'theodicy.'"[11] Put this way the statement is unobjectionable, for Hegel surely has a deep, theologically rooted confidence about history which is lacking to Husserl. But the dictionary uses the term "crisis" to speak of the turning point or climax of a process and of an unstable situation which requires transformation or resolution; and I think it is clear that in these senses Hegel might well have entitled his book "The Crisis of European Culture and the Phenomenology of Spirit." The genuine difference must not be allowed to obscure the equally genuine similarity.

The other objection comes from the Husserlian side and goes like this. While the crisis motif is obviously central to Husserl's last great introduction to transcendental phenomenology, it is missing from *Ideas I* and from *Cartesian Meditations*. It does not belong to his idea of transcendental phenomenology as such. But this would be to overlook the way in which "Philosophy as Rigorous Science" serves as a kind of introduction to all the introductions. For the crisis motif is conspicuously present there. The task of a scientific philosophy concerns not only the demands of theory but also the requirement "from an ethico-religious point of view [of] a life regulated by pure rational norms." Yet not only has there never been a rigorously scientific philosophy, but also in the modern world the separation of science from wisdom and its ability to "unravel for us the riddles of the world and of life" has become so total that "the spiritual need of our time has, in fact, become unbearable. Would that it were only theoretical lack of clarity regarding the sense of the 'reality' investigated in the natural and humanistic sciences that disturbed our peace... Far more than this, it is the most radical vital need that afflicts us, a need that leaves no point of our lives untouched."[12] This is the passion which drives the sometimes tortured, hypertheoretical analyses of *Ideas I* and *Cartesian Meditations*.

Philosophy and Natural Consciousness

The third and fourth fundamental agreements between Hegel and Husserl concern, not the historical setting in which the need for scientific philosophy is keenly felt, but the further specification of its nature. They identify a twofold turning which philosophy must undertake, the turn against natural consciousness and the transcendental turn, the turn from the primacy of the world and the turn toward the primacy of the subject. If in Husserl the epoche and the phenomenological reduction are to be distinguished rather than identified, it is because the former prepares for the latter, clearing the way for the turn to transcendental subjectivity by suspending or putting out of play all beliefs in the world's existence and explanatory value, the whole of the natural attitude, which pervades both everyday common sense and the sciences.[13]

Husserl puts it dramatically by saying that from the perspective of the self-evidence which philosophy must achieve, "every ordinary appeal to self-evidence, insofar as it was supposed to cut off further regressive inquiry, [is] theoretically no better than an appeal to an oracle through which a god reveals himself. All natural self-evidences, those of all objective sciences (not excluding those of formal logic and mathematics), belong to the realm of what is 'obvious,' what in truth has a background of incomprehensibility. Every [kind of] self-evidence is the title of a problem, with the sole exception of phenomenological self-evidence, after it has reflectively clarified itself and shown itself to be ultimate self-evidence."[14]

Hegel speaks of natural consciousness rather than the natural attitude or standpoint, but he means the same thing. It includes common sense, the sciences, even philosophy insofar as it is not yet truly scientific. Already in his Jena essay on scepticism he had praised the scepticism of antiquity for being directed, not against philosophy but against the "dogmatism of common sense."[15] Now in the central third of the introduction to the *Phenomenology* he presents his phenomenological journey as a radical scepticism directed against all forms of natural consciousness, from which philosophical science can liberate itself "only by turning against it."[16] In describing the systematic dispossession of natural consciousness, his imagery is more violent than Husserl's. True philosophy seems to natural consciousness like the attempt to walk on one's head and is experienced as a kind of death and despair.[17] It would not be surprising to find an implacable hostility in natural consciousness toward philosophical science.[18]

But while different metaphors bespeak a different rhetorical tendency, the issue is the same for Hegel as for Husserl.[19] Philosophy must free itself from natural consciousness because the latter is prejudiced; it proceeds on unexamined presuppositions. It appeals to principles whose truth has not been established and to concepts whose meaning has not been clarified.[20] This is why Hegel finds it necessary to say that "the familiar, just because it is familiar, is not really understood."[21] The willingness to let go of the familiar and undertake a self-transformation that at first looks like death, but is really the path to life, is the courage without which philosophy is impossible.[22]

Philosophy as Transcendental Reflection

The journey from the familiar into new and unknown territory leads into the domain of the cogito, discovered but unexplored by Descartes. The fourth and, for the present, final agreement between Hegel and Husserl is that we enter the path toward scientific philosophy by taking the transcendental turn.[23] Hegel's preface indicates this in the most general way by saying that "the goal is spirit's insight into what knowing is."[24] By itself, of course, this is not the phenomenological reduction, for there is no guarantee that the subjectivity which comes to view will not be naturalized, leaving us in the snares of psychologism.[25] This, on Husserl's view, is exactly what happened to the founders of the transcendental tradition he seeks to perfect, Descartes, Locke, and Kant. But we cannot overlook the fact that they, along with Fichte, are the founding fathers of that tradition precisely by virtue of this first step of redirecting attention from the object known to the subject knowing. Reflection as such may not be the sufficient, but it is the necessary condition of transcendental philosophy.

In the introduction Hegel becomes a bit more specific about the meaning of the reflective move. The task at hand is "an exposition of how knowledge makes its appearance [*Darstellung des erscheinenden Wissens*]."[26] This involves distinguishing the observed from the observing consciousness, what appears to the former and what appears, namely the former's activity, *für uns*. We, that is the phenomenological we, which is so crucial to Hegel's methodology, do not participate in the acts of the consciousness we observe. We are rather the *reine Zuseher* of reflection. "All that is left for us to do is simply to look on." For this reason phenomenology can be called the "Science of the experience of consciousness."[27]

It is only, however, in the chapters on Consciousness that the intentional nature of consciousness and its constitutive role come to full light.[28] These chapters are the phenomenological retelling of the Aesthetic and Analytic of Kant's first *Critique*. The analysis of the Here, the Now, and the I in the chapter on Sense-Certainty is Hegel's deduction of space, time, and the transcendental unity of apperception as conditions of possible experience; and the chapters on Perception and Understanding develop the a priori nature of the concept of nature, substances (things with properties) in the totality of causal reciprocity. Moreover, it is in the analysis of Sense-Certainty that we first encounter a phenomenological refutation of the view that sense experience is something that the object does to us. "The truth of Sense-Certainty is in the object as *my [meinem]* object, or in *my intending* it [*im Meinen*]; it is, because *I* know it."[29] This expelling of Sense-Certainty from the object is not the final truth of Sense-Certainty, for merely as just stated it is capable of misinterpretation. Like Husserl, Hegel insists that the constituting I is not the momentary immediacy of the Cartesian "each time I think." It is a moment in the total life and thus is always the mediated part of a whole. But this discovery of its essential activity in knowledge is never abandoned.

On the contrary, it is reinforced in the transition from Sense-Certainty to Perception, made with the help of a pretty bad pun. Hegel tells us that "experience teaches me what the truth of Sense-Certainty in fact is: I point it out as a Here, which is one Here among other Heres, or as in itself a simple togetherness of many Heres; i.e., it is a universal. I take it up then as it is in truth, and instead of knowing something immediate, I take it truly or perceive it [*ich nehme so es auf wie es in Wahrheit ist, und statt ein Unmittelbares zu wissen, nehme ich wahr*]."[30]

Hegel is here summarizing his phenomenological demythologizing of the myth of the given. He is translating the logical notion
that every determination is a negation into the phenomenological
insight that every perception (or any other knowing, for that matter) is the taking of something as something. I can perceive my copy
of Kant's first *Critique* only by taking it to be there and not elsewhere, now and not then, book and not typewriter, red and not blue,
hardbound and not paperback, etc. Without this taking, nothing is
given. In Husserlian language intentionality constitutes its object
in the act of meaning bestowal.

It is important to notice that while Hegel here focuses on the
referential features of the object, the Here and the Now, this analysis looks ahead to the descriptive features as well, its properties,
as the example of the book illustrates. And, in terms of properties,
this same analysis applies just as fully to the material, empirical
properties as to the formal, categorial properties. So I cannot but
repeat my claim that "in this respect the theory of transcendental
subjectivity which emerges from the discussion of the Now and the
Here is, in spite of its obvious Kantian overtones, closer to the Husserlian principle of strict correlation between intentional act and
intentional object, noesis and noema."[31] It would seem that Hegel
and Husserl agree with Merleau-Ponty that philosophy is "the vig-
ilance which does not let us forget the source of all knowledge."[32]

Turning now to the differences between Hegel and Husserl, I
want to mention three. They are so closely interrelated that it is not
easy to find the ideal order for presentation. I shall proceed from
the theme of freedom to that of method and thence to that of transcendental subjectivity, the theme of the most basic disagreement.

Two Views of Freedom

My sketch of the different concepts of freedom in Hegel and Husserl
will be sketchy indeed, leaving the fuller development of what I take
to be a very important issue for another occasion. Borrowing a clue
from Ricoeur, we might say that Husserl has a Cartesian concept of
freedom while Hegel has a Spinozist concept.[33] According to the
former, freedom is a permanent possession which can be exercised,
so to speak, "at will," at any time and in any circumstances. According to the latter, freedom is not a permanent possession to be exercised "at will" but a characteristic of my doings only under special
circumstances, which we might call liberation. On both views it is

possible to say that it belongs to our essence as human to be free, but in the one case it means we are always free while in the other it means we are not fully free until we achieve liberation.

In the case of Hegel and Husserl this difference is closely related to another. For Husserl the primary meaning of freedom seems to be that freedom from prejudice and sedimented tradition which makes it possible for me to be fully self-responsible (primarily for my cognitive acts). Performing the epoché and the phenomenological reduction are the primary acts of freedom. For Hegel, the primary meaning of freedom, in the *Phenomenology* at least, is reciprocal recognition (a primarily non-theoretical relationship). I do not become free by becoming a phenomenologist. In the one case freedom is independence, in the other interdependence.

I mention this difference between freedom as autonomy and freedom as community, if ever so incompletely, to alert us all to the political ramifications of the issues before us. It may well be true that Husserl has no politics, but his image of the self and its freedom is that of classical liberalism. The free self is the thin self, unemcumbered by any worldly identity, and therefore fully free, no matter what its choices, so long as it makes those choices in sovereign independence. The theory of right and of freedom is independent of all theories of the good. By contrast, Hegel's image of the self and its freedom belongs to the critique of classical liberalism.[34] Because the self which requires freedom is the concrete self, a thick self with worldly identity, freedom cannot be defined independently of its proper goals, nor can it be realized in circumstances where those goals are unrealized. In so far as the classically liberal concept of freedom prevails in our society, we can say that Husserl's phenomenology performs an ideological function, Hegel's a utopian function.[35]

Two Views of Method

I want to approach the second disagreement a bit obliquely. There is a conspicuous tendency in Husserl to identify certainty and truth. His passion not merely for apodicticity but for absolute apodicticity, even when he does not identify apodictic evidence with adequate evidence, is the permanent core of his project.[36] By contrast Hegel regularly distinguishes certainty from truth. It could be said, of course, that (as previously noted) neither takes the certainties of natural consciousness for truth and both see it to be the task of philosophy to find a knowing where truth and certainty coalesce.[37] But Husserl's path to this goal has a noticeably different direction from Hegel's, a difference we might indicate by calling Husserl's the path of piecemeal certainty.

Hegel places enormous emphasis on the requirement that philosophy be systematic, while this seems of little consequence to Husserl. I think it can be said that Husserl's recurring sketches of a comprehensive classification of regional ontologies is about as close as his phenomenology comes to being a philosophic system. Hegel's concept of system, inextricably tied up with such substantive theses as (a) Substance is Subject, (b) the Absolute is Spirit, and (c) the True is the Whole, is dramatically more demanding.[38]

Quentin Lauer sees a link between these two differences. "Unlike Husserl, however, [Hegel] refuses to believe that the apodictic certainty of knowledge will guarantee its rational adequacy. It is not the certainty of knowledge which constitutes its rationality; rather it is the grasp of reality in its total interrelatedness. Husserl can institute a phenomenology which piles up—and even relates—bits of certain knowledge . . . In this view phenomenology is phenomenology antecedent to any concrete investigation it undertakes; it is a sort of blueprint for future investigations. For Hegel phenomenology . . . is not complete as phenomenology until it somehow embraces the totality of consciousness. . . . "[39]

If, indeed, these two differences are linked, it may be that they will show themselves to be expressions of a deeper and more basic disagreement. And so they do. Far from being random or accidental, the differences on the issues of certainty and system show themselves to be corollaries of antithetical models of what genuine knowledge must be. Husserl is a foundationalist, Hegel a holist. Even if there were no other interesting point of contact between them, the crucial contemporary debate over foundationalism and the meaning of holistic alternatives to this long reigning epistemic paradigm in the larger philosophical community would make our *Auseinandersetzung* of Hegel and Husserl all but unavoidable.

The heart of classical foundationalism, whose paradigm of normal philosophy Husserl seeks to reformulate and perfect, is not simply the distinction between basic and derived or inferred beliefs by itself, but this distinction combined with a certain kind of restriction on what kinds of beliefs can be properly basic.[40] The three traditional criteria, self-evidence, evidence to the senses, and incorrigibility are clearly expressions of the same passionate quest for certainty which we find at work in Husserl's intuitionist theory of evidence. He moves immediately from the distinction between immediate and mediate or grounded judgments to the theory of evidence in terms of the fulfillment of intention. Fulfillment occurs when what is merely supposed or meant "from afar" or "at a distance" is fully present itself, a presence expressed in terms of viewing or mental seeing, on the one hand, in terms of having or possession, on the other.[41]

The mixture of metaphors is essential to Husserl's intuitionism. Not just any seeing will do, for, as just mentioned, to see "from afar" or "at a distance" is to see through a glass darkly, and this seeing cannot lay the sure foundation which the edifice of knowledge requires. Only the seeing which derives from the presence of possession will do. Husserl also expresses this in terms of the crucial concept of immediacy. So he can write, "*Immediate 'seeing', not merely sensuous, experiential seeing, but seeing in the universal sense as an originally presentive consciousness of any kind whatever, is the ultimate legitimizing source of all rational assertions.*"[42]

By making clear that the appeal to intuition is an appeal to immediacy, Husserl indicates the radicality of his foundationalist requirements. For on this theory of evidence, to be properly basic a belief must not only be *uninferred* from other beliefs, but also *free of all interpretation*. We are talking not only about *underived* propositions, but especially about *theory-free data*.[43]

It is perhaps in terms of immediacy that Hegel's holism is best distinguished from Husserl's foundationalism. For Hegel sets his phenomenological procedure against any appeal to immediacy, not just against the immediacies of everyday obviousness. For him science is mediated knowing, and the central text of Hegel's holism, the claim that "the True is the whole," is the introduction to an exposition of the essentially mediated character of true knowing. There can be no results unmediated by the process of their development, no part unmediated by the whole to which it belongs, and vice versa.[44] Hegel seeks to provide phenomenological grounding for this claim not only in his critique of any use of the mathematical model to support a rationalistic kind of intuitionism,[45] but above all in his critique of Sense-Certainty, which functions in the *Phenomenology* as a critique not only of empiricist foundationalism but by extrapolation of all appeals to immediacy. It seeks to show that the object of knowledge is always doubly mediated, on the one hand by the context (world, horizon) in which it appears, and on the other hand by the subject to and for whom it appears, a subject which turns out itself to be mediated by its own temporality.[46] It is not language which introduces mediation into experience. Rather, language refutes every appeal to immediacy just because the experience it seeks to express is already filled with mediation.[47]

This difference over immediacy has two important ramifications. First, it brings the difference over system into clearer focus. For Hegel it follows directly from the mediated character of knowing that true knowledge must have the form of system.[48] For if no bit, piece, part, or building block of knowledge is intelligible or justified by itself but only in relation to something else, each relational constellation short of the whole will itself be a bit, piece, part, or building block. Only in the totality of relatedness or mediation can meaning or truth be adequately established. Short of that totality knowing cannot rest.[49]

Hegel's philosophy has to be a system, because it is a dialectical holism.[50] It is dialectical because everything immediate or finite shows itself to be relationally dependent rather than self-sufficient, and it is holistic because given the absence of anything immediate upon which to build, everything remains in flux until totality is reached. Perhaps the metaphor of the arch is helpful here, in which none of the stones will stay put until all of them are in place.

By contrast, Husserl's phenomenology cannot be a system, for there are only three methods for building a philosophic system, and he is cut off from all three. In addition to the dialectical system there are the constructive and deductive systems. Constructionist philosophical systems are not easy to characterize. What is clearest about the way Leibniz or Whitehead, for example, proceed, is that it is neither deductive nor dialectical. Beyond that I am tempted to characterize this strategy as nondialectical holism, but that is more a promissory note than adequate exposition.[51] We need not be too concerned with this alternative, however it is to be defined and whoever its best exemplars are, for it is not at issue between Hegel and Husserl. Each repudiates it as failing to live up to his own standards of genuine science.

If both dialectical and nondialectical holism are unavailable to Husserl because of his intuitionism, there remains the deductive route, which Descartes, at least, found compatible with his own intuitionist foundationalism. But on Husserl's view, this was one of Descartes's most serious errors. For, to give but one reason, this involves presupposing the validity of logic, which rather requires its own grounding, one which obviously cannot be deductive.[52] This leaves Husserl with a foundationalism like that of the empiricists, which I earlier called "the path of piecemeal certainty," and which Quentin Lauer, more vividly, called "a phenomenology which piles up—and even relates—bits of certain knowledge." Given their shared repudiation of deductive and constructionist approaches, Hegel and Husserl find the question of immediacy deciding the question of system. Hegel denies immediacy and finds himself a dialectical holist. Husserl seeks to retain immediacy and finds the way to system blocked.

There is a second significant ramification of the disagreement over immediacy. The foundationalist model obviously lends itself to thinking of knowledge as built from the ground (a loaded word for both Hegel and Husserl) up. It is not difficult to find Husserl tying this imagery of *"Philosophie von unten"* as tightly as possible to the concept of scientific rigor.[53] But there are times when this spatial metaphor turns into or is joined by a temporal metaphor, as when Husserl writes that there

> emerges, as the *question of the beginning,* the inquiry for those cognitions that are *first in themselves* and can support the whole storied edifice of universal knowledge. Consequently . . . we mediators . . . must have access to evidences that already bear the stamp of fitness for such a function, in that they are recognizable as *preceding* all other imaginable evidences.[54]

Sometimes that which is "first in itself" is "prior" in a literal temporal sense. But usually, as the interchangeability with the spatial metaphor would indicate, the point is epistemic independence. The foundation can be what it is without the superstructure, and that which comes first can be what it is apart from what comes later. The primary priority is the "logical" priority of conceptual autonomy. In either case, the movement of thought is from what is subsequent to what is antecedent or primordial.

Hegel's thought moves in just the opposite direction. For him, as Ricoeur puts it,

> consciousness is a movement which continually annihilates its starting point and can guarantee itself only at the end. In other words, it is something that has meaning only in later figures, since the meaning of a given figure is deferred until the appearance of a new figure. Thus the fundamental meaning of the moment of consciousness called Stoicism in the *Phenomenology of spirit* is not revealed until the arrival of skepticism, since it itself reveals the absolute unimportance of the relative positions held by Master and Slave before the abstract thought of freedom. The same is true for all the spiritual figures . . . We

can say, therefore, in very general terms that consciousness is the order of the terminal, the unconscious that of the primordial.[55]

Ricoeur is obviously developing his contrast between Hegel and Freud, but on this point, ironically, Husserl's philosophy of consciousness plays the same role as Freud's theory of the unconscious. Like Freud, in spite of obvious differences, Husserl plays archeologist of the spirit to Hegel's teleologist of the spirit. When this difference is applied to the philosophy of history we get the difference between mythological and eschatological thought. On the one hand, the historical process has its meaning only in relation to what happened *in illo tempore*. On the other hand, historical events have a meaning which is only fully available in the culmination of the historical process.

But even when historical temporality is not an issue, there is all the difference in the world between seeking to explain a phenomenon (or justify it, or interpret it, or whatever) by reference to what is prior to it in the sense of being fully independent of it and seeking to explain (or whatever) the same phenomenon with reference to what presupposes, includes, and fulfills it. Husserl's foundationalism involves the one habit of thought, Hegel's holism the other. Perhaps both are necessary, and the real challenge is to find a way of uniting them. Perhaps we must choose between them. Perhaps we'll find that one is appropriate for some tasks, the other for other tasks. (Which for scientific philosophy?) In any case we need to see how sharply different they are from each other and how the debate between "causal" and "teleological" thinking in the philosophy of science is but one expression of a larger issue that cannot be left to the philosophers of science, though we might learn a good deal from their debates.

Two Views of Transcendental Subjectivity

The third disagreement between Hegel and Husserl that I want to discuss concerns the nature of transcendental subjectivity. Our point of departure can be Husserl's lament: "Philosophy as science, as serious, rigorous, indeed apodictically rigorous, science—*the dream is over*."[56] There is general agreement that neither this lament nor Husserl's later work in its totality is, in David Carr's words, a "deathbed renunciation" of the dream on the part of Husserl himself.[57] There is a second agreement, less general, but more interesting, that Husserl's lament is the verdict which *he* did his best to ward off, but which *we* are compelled to draw, not because of Dilthey or Heidegger, but on the basis of insights growing out of Husserl's own tenacious radicality.[58]

Thus, for example, Landgrebe speaks of Husserl's "reluctant" departure from Cartesianism. At issue, clearly, is not just the adequacy of the "Cartesian way" to the Cartesian goal, but the viability of the very goal itself. Husserl's breaking up of the traditions he sought to fulfill begins as early as 1923–1924 in *Erste Philosophie,* II, where, "*before the eyes of the reader,* occurs the shipwreck of transcendental subjectivism, as both a nonhistorial a-priorism and as the consummation of modern rationalism [read: foundationalism]. Today, primarily as a result of Heidegger's work, the 'end of metaphysics' is spoken of as though it were quite obvious. We shall first properly understand the sense of such language if we follow closely how, in this work, metaphysics takes its departure *behind Husserl's back.* . . . To be sure, neither Husserl nor those who were his students at that time were explicitly aware of this." For this reason the full impact of his later work in the *Crisis* is "partially obscured by the self-interpretation he gave it."[59]

No doubt the most familiar formulation of this thesis is Merleau-Ponty's:

> The most important lesson which the reduction teaches us is the impossibility of a complete reduction. . . . If we were absolute mind, the reduction would present no problem. But since, on the contrary, we *are in the world,* since indeed our reflections are carried out in the temporal flux on to which we are trying to seize . . . there is no thought which embraces all our thought. The philosopher . . . is a perpetual beginner, which means . . . that *radical reflection amounts to a consciousness of its own dependence on an unreflective life which is its initial situation,* unchanging, given once and for all. Far from being, as has been thought, a procedure of idealistic philosophy, phenomenological reduction belongs to existential philosophy: Heidegger's *"being-in-the-world"* appears only against the background of the phenomenological reduction.[60]

Whether one is sympathetic to this movement of phenomenology toward existentialism and hermeneutics, or, like Husserl himself, would prefer to resist it, Merleau-Ponty's formulation has the advantage of defining the issue with real precision. By juxtaposing two ways of putting the issue he helps us to see their equivalence.

On the one hand, there is the question whether reflection can ever become total by freeing itself from its origins in life. Can I ever "grasp myself in pure reflexion," or is it rather the case that "human consciousness never possesses itself in complete detachment"?[61] In the *Ideas I* Husserl presents the phenomenological reduction as precisely the sought-after triumph of reflection over life without which rigorous science would not be possible. In response to the question whether we can really do this, he replies that it is not all that hard. Just as the geometer does it when doing geometry, so the philosopher does it when doing phenomenology.[62] In the *Crisis* the reduction is still understood in the same way.[63] But the discovery in the meantime that geometry itself has origins and that it was already tradition and not rigorous science for Galileo makes it clear that the quick assurance of 1913 will need to be more carefully supported.[64]

The other way of putting the question asks whether we who philosophize are inextricably in the world. For reflection to win full independence of its "initial situation" in "unreflective life" is for the transcendental ego to be established as "outside" the world in a sense Husserl seeks to make precise.[65] There are two ways of being-in-the-world, the Cartesian and the Heideggerian. Husserl seeks to overcome them both.

Husserl complains regularly and bitterly that Descartes is a kind of Moses who leads us to the promised land but fails to enter in himself. A central reason why his discovery of transcendental subjectivity falls short of fruition is that he identifies the ego with the soul, which remains substantially and causally part of the world as nature. Descartes is a dualist, of course, and not a materialist, but his psychophysical dualism leaves us with a psychic world which, "because of the way in which it is related to nature, does not achieve the status of an independent world."[66] Husserl names the resultant point of view transcendental realism or transcendental psychologism, and regularly blesses it with the epithet Absurd.[67] This absurdity can also be expressed as what Husserl calls "the paradox of human subjectivity: being a subject for the world and at the same time being an object in the world."[68] The problem is obvious. A subjectivity which is part of the world cannot be the ground of the world. The acts of an ego conditioned by the world to which it belongs cannot be the unconditioned acts which have the foundational status required for rigorous science.

But on Husserl's view the paradox is only apparent. It disappears the moment we distinguish the empirical ego, which is clearly in the world as, for example, situated in the lived body, from the transcendental ego, for whom the world as a whole is transcendent.[69] In short, it is the work of the phenomenological reduction to dissolve the paradox. As Ricoeur puts it, "The subject which [in the natural attitude] is hidden from itself as part of the world discovers itself [in the reduction] as the foundation of the world."[70]

But there is another way of being-in-the-world. If we call it the Heideggerian way, this is not meant to imply that Husserl's attention is drawn to it only through his reading of *Being and Time*. David Carr has shown us convincingly that there are powerful internal motives which lead Husserl to reconsider the adequacy of the reduction as first formulated for its liberating task.[71] To be in the world in the Heideggerian sense is to be given over to and thus conditioned by a universal network, not of causal interactions but of meaning constellations.[72] This world of meanings, which Husserl calls the life-world, is "the always already pregiven world."[73] Like the world of nature this is an actual world which "always precedes cognitive activity as its universal ground," and for this reason "we will not so easily find [in it] that ultimately original self-evidence of experience which we seek."[74]

But unlike the world of nature, this world stands as a challenge to the reduction and the goal of rigorous science as an explicitly historical world. For this world is "always a world in which cognition in the most diverse ways has already done its work." It is "always already pregiven to us as impregnated by the precipitate of logical operations. The world is never given to us as other than the world in which we or others, whose store of experience we take over by communication, education, and tradition, have already been logically active, in judgment and cognition." Thus "the world of our experience is from the beginning interpreted . . . "[75] In short, to be in the world in this Heideggerian sense is to be caught up in the hermeneutical circle.

In the *Ideas* and the *Cartesian Meditations* Husserl had already recognized that the world in which we always already find ourselves is a world of both nature and culture,[76] that this "already" represents a bondage or restriction from which we must be freed,[77] that it is the task of the phenomenological reduction to reflect us out of the world, both as nature and as culture,[78] and that phenomenology must flesh itself out as a theory of the constitution of both nature and culture.[79] But he came to think that in those works he had only developed the first step of the epoché.[80] The bracketing of nature and culture as defined by the sciences had left untouched the pre-theoretical life-world within which and on the basis of which

the sciences arise, and this world, whose opacity must be transformed into transparency, is itself largely the product of cultural
history. It is a world of linguistically mediated tradition.

In this context the reduction is redefined in order to be completed. One must still speak of the movement from *doxa* to *epistēmē*.
But whereas *doxa* originally had the sense of belief as that which
lacks the apodictic certainty of knowledge, it now comes to have the
more determinate sense of tradition as that which lacks the self-
grounding character of knowledge. In the Vienna Lecture, the
Greek ideal of theory, of truth-in-itself as knowledge without presuppositions, is interpreted as freedom from every form of bondage
to tradition.[81] Hence the identification of tradition with prejudice.[82]
The reduction, which can now be called the historical reduction, becomes the "discovery-overthrow" of historical prejudices, the "dismantling" of sedimented tradition.[83]

This task amounts to moving the life-world from the subject
side of the equation to the object side. When Husserl speaks of the
life-world, with all its sedimentations of historical tradition, as the
ground of all our cognitive activity, he gives it a constitutive role in
everyday experience, in scientific research, and even in philosophical reflection.[84] As such he identifies it with the subject of knowing
and speaks of "mankind as the subjectivity which, in community, in-
tentionally brings about the accomplishment of world validity."[85] It
is, to be sure, an "anonymous" subjectivity, marred by the opacity of
unconscious mediation.[86] It is an intersubjectivity whose We is
much closer to Heidegger's They (*das Man*) than to any I myself. But
it nevertheless participates in subjectivity.

But the subjectivity which is enveloped in this anonymous subjectivity is not capable of *epistēmē*, for it is swimming in the *doxa* of
traditional prejudice. Just as in the first instance rigorous science
was to be possible only for a knower which had reflected itself out of
the world of theoretical objectivity, so now it will be possible only by
the switching off of one's interested involvement in the world of pre-
theoretical subjectivity. This involves doing what has never been
done before, making the life-world itself into a theme of scientific
(phenomenological) investigation. The historical reduction and the
science of the life-world are the same thing. In both cases the life-
world itself becomes phenomenon, constituted not constituting, object not subject.[87]

Like the original version of the reduction, this one involves the
eidetic reduction. The life-world has an essence, general structures
which are not themselves historically relative, and these can be
brought to intuitive clarity.[88] But the eidetic reduction is never suf-

ficient. Here as in the *Ideas* it must be completed by a reduction which arises out of the epoché by which I disengage myself from interested involvement *within* the world in question so as to rise *above* it. It is this rising above which constitutes the phenomenological, and now, its completion, the historical reduction.[89]

As the Sartrean self seeks to neutralize the threatening look of the other by returning the gaze so as to objectify the other, I now seek, as Husserlian philosopher, to neutralize the anonymous subjectivity of the life-world, looking not at but through me, by making it the object of my own philosopical gaze. At this point

> the gaze of the philosopher in truth first becomes fully free: above all, free of the strongest and most universal, and at the same time most hidden, internal bond, namely, of the pregiveness of the world. Given in and through this liberation is the discovery of the universal, absolutely self-enclosed and absolutely self-sufficient correlation between the world itself and world-consciousness. By the latter is meant the conscious life of the subjectivity which effects the validity of the world. . . . [90]

But this subjectivity is no longer the anonymous subjectivity of the life-world. The self has raised itself above that in the very act of "the reduction of mankind to the phenomenon 'mankind', [which] makes it possible to recognize mankind as a self-objectification of transcendental subjectivity which is always functioning ultimately and is this 'absolute'."[91]

True philosophy for Husserl, like true religion for St. James, is to "keep oneself untarnished by the world."[92] It now looks as if this task is a good deal harder than it had looked earlier. The simple reflection of the "Cartesian way" will have to be supplemented by an historical reflection which is much more complicated.[93] But the passages cited in the previous paragraph suggest that Husserl has little doubt that the freedom and purity he sought could indeed be found. This impression is confirmed in *Experience and Judgment.* Once the need is seen to distinguish between the pregiven world, the life-world as spoken of up to now, and the *original* life-world, Husserl is confident that the regression from the former to the latter can be accomplished. In doing so we move from a realm of experience which is already the result of interpretation to "experience in its immediacy," to "pure experience," to "immediate intuition," and to "original experience," which is "experience in the ultimately original sense . . . an experience still unacquainted with [unaffected by] any of these idealizations [historical traditions] but whose necessary foundation it is."[94] This is the realm of pure experience which has been Husserl's goal since 1907. It is the home of that utterly antimundane subjectivity which Husserl calls transcendental.

It can easily be argued against this background that Heidegger, for example, is not a transcendental philosopher. Far from seeking a subjectivity "untarnished by the world," he emphasizes the inescapably worldly character of *Dasein,* not in the Cartesian sense of worldly but in the, well, Heideggerian sense. And he draws the obvious consequences about the hermeneutical circle and the possibility of philosophy as rigorous science. If Husserl is taken to be the paradigm of transcendental philosophy, we simply have to acknowledge that Heidegger stands outside its pale. In doing so we gain an important insight, but also close ourselves off from other insights. For in important senses Heidegger is a transcendental philosopher. *Dasein* is the totality of the conditions of possible experience, a "subjectivity" which gives meaning to the nature and culture in which it lives. It does so, of course, not absolutely, but as a mediated and conditioned source of meaning. Instead of simply denying that Heidegger is a transcendental philosopher, it might be more accurate to speak of his first taking the transcendental turn and then a post-transcendental turn, in which the worldly and relative nature of transcendental subjectivity is acknowledged without denying the import of the second Copernican Revolution.

I make this point in order to suggest the same for Hegel. Like Husserl, as I have already argued, he takes the transcendental turn.[95] But like Heidegger, he also takes the post-transcendental turn, and he does so by asking essentially the same question posed by the existential analytic of *Dasein:* Who is the transcendental subject? This Who? implies a thick self with a worldly identity which guarantees the historical relativity of all its acts. And yet Hegel is not, as Heidegger is, among those for whom the dream of rigorous science is over.[96] Precisely this is the genius of the *Phenomenology of Spirit,* that (to speak anachronistically) with Heidegger it takes the post-transcendental turn but with Husserl retains the dream of rigorous science. How does Hegel think it possible to do this?

The transcendental turn is essentially completed as the transition from Consciousness to Self-Consciousness takes place with "the necessary advance from the previous shapes of consciousness for which their truth was a Thing, an 'other' than themselves," to the discovery "that not only is consciousness of a thing possible only for a self-consciousness, but that self-consciousness alone is the truth of those shapes."[97] The post-transcendental turn begins immediately with the introduction of desire. As animal desire, self-consciousness is embodied, and thus embedded in nature. As human desire for recognition, self-consciousness is embedded in spirit, the I that is We and the We that is I. And this We to which I belong is not the We of Husserl's Fifth Meditation, but the historically concrete We whose struggles for reciprocal recognition include the brutalities of alienated labor. Who is the transcendental subject? The transcendental subject is Spirit embodied, working, dominating, fighting, and dying.[98] The subject which gives meaning to my life is the partially individuated self I am, immersed in a life-world, a *Sittlichkeit* which is as much a part of my identity as I myself am. And just as my practical freedom does not consist in the autonomy of dominating the other self, so my theoretical freedom does not consist in the autonomy of freeing myself from immersion in the world. In Hegel's eyes Husserl has been seduced by the most tragic of modernity's heresies, the equation of freedom with independence. He does not recognize that, beyond the inherent impossibility of ever becoming truly independent, to the degree that I do become independent, I become, not more free, but more abstract, less real.[99]

Philosophical thought is not immune to this worldliness. Already in his Jena essay on *Naturrecht* Hegel had spoken of "the historical aspect of Science," and invited us to see "the empirical condition of the world reflected in the conceptual [*ideellen*] mirror of Science." Philosophy pays its dues to necessity not by disdaining particularity as something merely positive and contingent, tempting it to flee the world. It rather rescues [*entreisst*] the ethical life of its people from contingency when "it permeates and animates it [*sie durchdringt, und belebt*]."[100] Here Hegel anticipates the famous formula from the preface to the *Philosophy of Right,* "Whatever happens, every individual is a child of his time: so philosophy too is its own time apprehended in thoughts."[101]

In the *Phenomenology* Hegel expresses this theme not only by presenting philosophy as essentialy mediated by its own history,[102] but also as the fulfillment and expression of its own spiritual world. Thus, Science is the "crown of a world of spirit, the product of a widespread unheaval in various forms of culture, the prize at the end of a complicated tortuous path of historical development."[103] One can feel Husserl's shudder when he hears Hegel saying, "That the True is actual only as system, or that Substance is essentially Subject, is expressed in the representation of the Absolute as Spirit—the most sublime concept and *the one which belongs to the modern age and its religion.*"[104] Prior to Marx we have here the makings of a theory of ideology, of philosophical thought as essentially conditioned by its world. But Hegel is not traumatized, for he sees no conflict between this relativity and the absoluteness philosophy requires to be scientific. Again we are forced to ask, How can this be?

It turns out that when Hegel says that "now is the time for philosophy to be raised to the status of a Science," he implies a double disagreement with Husserl as well as the double agreement pointed out at the beginning of this essay. On the one hand is the acceptance of science as having historical-cultural conditions, as being possible only in a life-world of a particular kind. On the other hand is the claim that these conditions are, at least in principle, currently actualized. When Hegel finds it not difficult "to see that ours is a birth-time and a period of transition to a new era," he is not speaking of just any historical transition but of the decisive one which finally makes philosophy possible as science. We are face to face with Hegel's so-called end of history thesis.[105]

It is easy to make either absolute or relative nonsense of Hegel's claim that his philosophy somehow brings the historical process to its conclusion, or, as he puts it at the end of the *Phenomenology*, that the triumph of the concept which he presents "annuls time" (*die Zeit tilgt*) or "sets aside its time-form" (*hebt er seine Zeitform auf*).[106] We get absolute nonsense if we make Hegel into a kind of evolutionary McTaggert, for whom at a particular time events cease occuring. We get relative nonsense if we hear Hegel saying, as I fear we must, that the historical world of his own time is the fulfillment of human history. But I want to try to see if we can find some sense rather than nonsense here.

We can begin to do so, I believe, by answering the question we have twice left hanging: How does Hegel harmonize the relativity of philosophical thought, on which he insists in terms of the thick, historical identity of the transcendental subject, with the absoluteness of philosophical thought, on which he insists with equal vigor, in terms of its scientific, systematic rigor? Hegel's "solution" is as simple as it is bold. Relativity is not bad in itself. Relatedness belongs to the very nature of the real (this being the ontological foundation of the holistic methodology). Thought is finite in a sense to be surpassed, not simply by virtue of its ties to its world, but by virtue of the finitude of that world. But what if the world had overcome its finitude by fulfilling the inner telos of human history? The thought which was the crown of that world would be the ideology of freedom actualized. It would be relative and absolute at the same time, relative to its world instead of being self-grounding, but absolute because that world would be unsurpassable. Knowledge would no longer need to go beyond itself because its world would no longer need to be transcended.

If we inquire how Hegel describes such a world, which others have called the Messianic age, the Kingdom of God, the classless society, and so forth, we find that in the *Phenomenology* Hegel defines the fulfillment of history in terms of reciprocal recognition. On the analysis he develops there reciprocal recognition must be both uncoerced and universal to be completely realized. Since mental manipulation is as much a violation of freedom as physical force, this means that the world whose ideology would be science would have to be a global community free from both war and propaganda.[107]

Hegel's time may well have been a birth-time of revolutionary change, but neither his time nor ours has been the advent of a global community free or war or propaganda. That fact counts against the element of realized eschatology in Hegel's thought but not in the least against his concepts of transcendental subjectivity, science, and freedom. Because of his deep affinities with Husserl he would find it important to be as clear as possible about the differences between them, and he might well summarize them this way, with apologies to Marx: the phenomenologists have only sought to perfect the reduction, the task is to hold forth a vision that will help to change the world. The task of philosophy as such is not directly to change the world. But precisely because its own fulfillment as science depends upon the world's fulfillment as the global reign of peace, justice, and love, its task is to be a partner in the revolution still awaited. This revolution will not be the triumph of either capitalism or communism in anything like the forms in which we know them. For while both aspire to be the global community, both have sold their souls to war and propaganda as the means to universality. The philosophy which wishes to be scientific in the spirit of Hegel's *Phenomenology* will be a subversive agent in relation to both contemporary theory and praxis—for its own sake and for the sake of the world from which it seeks no divorce.

THE SEARCH FOR A NONSECTARIAN SPIRITUALITY OF COMMUNITY

8 HEGEL, HINDUISM, AND FREEDOM

In a recent review of the new German edition of Hegel's lectures on "Determinate Religion," Dale Schlitt says that Hegel "gave a surprisingly appreciative reading of the various religions . . . "[1] If 'appreciative' is meant here to signify affirmative, it is hard to agree with this claim. Schlitt himself indicates why, when he writes, "Hegel was so appreciative of the various religions that, even with his often negative judgments on them, he consistently presented them as necessary instances without which the consummate, absolute, or true religion could not have come into being" (p. 194). With regard to the Indian traditions we know as Hinduism, it is true that Hegel finds within them "the instinct of the concept" (DR, 586).[2] But that is hardly high praise, especially when Hegel more frequently emphasizes that in Hinduism the moments of the concept regularly fall apart. As a result, and to me this seems the central theme of Hegel's accounts, Hinduism is irremediably a religion of unfreedom.

The reference to freedom in the midst of logical talk about the concept and its moments may seem sudden. But it is quintessentially Hegelian. Nowhere is this clearer than in an illustrative and all but passing reference to Hinduism in the *Philosophy of Right*.[3] It comes in the introductory discussion of the concept of freedom in paragraphs five through seven.[4] There Hegel identifies the triadic structure of the Concept in terms of Universality, Particularity, and Individuality, which he also identifies as Indeterminacy, Determination, and Self-Determination. Each of the first two moments is essential to freedom, but when the moments fall apart and either tries to be the basis of freedom independent of the other, the result is disastrous. Only when the opposition between the two is overcome and they are reconciled and united in the third moment is true freedom found.

What concerns us here is the attempt to understand freedom wholly in terms of Universality = Indeterminacy. This is "negative freedom, or freedom as the Understanding understands it." It is the identification of freedom with independence. Freedom does indeed involve this moment of "pure reflection into itself which involves the

135

dissipation of every restriction and every content either immediately presented by nature, by needs, desires, and impulses, or given
and determined by any means whatever. This is the unrestricted infinity of absolute abstraction or universality, the pure thought of
oneself." But when this is taken to be the whole story, the result is
"my flight from every content as from a restriction." This is empty
escapism or "the freedom of the void which rises to a passion and
takes shape in the world; while still remaining theoretical, it takes
shape in religion as the Hindu fanaticism of pure contemplation,
but when it turns to actual practice, it takes shape in religion and
politics alike as the fanaticism of destruction . . . " (PR, ¶5).

In the *Zusatz* to this paragraph, Hegel makes it clear that the
latter reference is to the Terror of the French Revolution, which he
had discussed at length in the *Phenomenology;* and the former reference is to the techniques of meditation and concentration known
as Yoga.[5] Of these he writes, "Amongst the Hindus, for instance, the
highest life is held to be persistence in the bare knowledge of one's
simple identity with oneself, fixation in this empty space of one's inner life, as light remains colorless in pure vision, and the sacrifice of
every activity in life, every aim, and every project. In this way one
becomes Brahman; there is no longer any distinction between the
finite self and Brahman. In fact in this universality every difference
has disappeared" (PR, ¶5Z).

Three facts emerge with great clarity. For Hegel (a) the question of freedom is unthinkable (quite literally) apart from categoreal, logical analysis, (b) Hinduism is wedded to a false, abstract,
escapist freedom, and (c) the proper method for the interpretation
and critique of Hinduism involves the categoreal analysis both of its
theory and practice and of freedom. It is in these terms, I believe,
that our own interpretation and critique of Hegel's reception of Hinduism will prove most fruitful.

In his review of Wilhelm von Humboldt's essay on the
Bhagavad-Gita, Hegel follows Humboldt in treating the *Gita* as a
key to the heart of Hinduism and in discussing it in terms of theory/
knowledge and practice/action (BG, 133–36). This is in keeping with
the structure of his philosophy of religion in general, which first
treats of the basic *Begriff* and the various *Vorstellungen* which
make up a religion's knowledge and then turns to its cultus, the actions which constitute the relation of the believing soul to the sacred. However, in keeping with Hegel's claim that religion is the
foundation of the state,[6] his analysis of Hindu practice moves at two
levels, one narrowly directed to the cultus as such and the other directed to the ethics and polity (*Sittlichkeit*) which Hindu "theology"

and "worship" together sustain. His critique of Hinduism (and his treatment is overwhelmingly negative) is therefore threefold: the metaphysical critique, the cultic critique, and the political critique. Because the same logical analysis is at work in all three, they have the character of variations on a theme.

In emphasizing the role of Hegel's Logic in his treatment of Hinduism I want to be as clear as I can about the sense in which his hermeneutics is a priori. Peter Hodgson has written that "far from imposing an abstract, preconceived, a priori structure on the history of religion, [Hegel] approached this subject matter as an experimental field in which virtually nothing should not be tried, at least once" (DR, 87). That may be a little bit strong—after all, Hegel never presented the history of religion as culminating in Hinduism—but it surely points in the right direction. The separation of the four lecture series in the philosophy of religion reveals a great deal of variety in both the form and the content of the exposition. But there is also a great deal of continuity. In the lectures of 1824, 1827, and 1831, for example, we find the following orders for the presentation of Buddhist, Hindu, Jewish, and Greek religion, respectively:

> 1824—Buddhism, Hinduism, Judaism, Greek Religion
> 1827—Buddhism, Hinduism, Greek Religion, Judaism
> 1831—Hinduism, Buddhism, Judaism, Greek Religion

And yet it remains true that Hinduism and Buddhism are always on the nature side of the spiritual divide, while the Jewish and Greek religions are always on the freedom side. The reason for this is the relative constancy of the conceptual framework which Hegel uses, not simply to place the history of religions in serial order, but to inquire of each moment what its meaning is.[7] Accordingly, this essay will focus on continuity rather than change in Hegel's treatment of Hinduism.

In the 1821 lectures Hegel gives a prominence to the triad Being, Essence, Concept which it does not get in subsequent lectures. But it may be as misleading as illuminating to suggest that he abandoned it (DR, 86) and that in later lectures "it is not the dialectic of being, essence, and concept, but rather that of immediacy, rupture, and reconciliation" that Hegel employs (DR, 74). For the latter is but a helpful commentary on the former, and, for that matter, on a number of closely related triads, including the two mentioned at the beginning of this essay and the following:

Identity, Difference, Ground[8]
Abstract Universal, Concrete Particular, Concrete Universal
Unity, Plurality, Totality

Hegel moves back and forth among these triads as if they were essentially interchangeable. While they do not tell him just where to fit Hinduism into his scheme, they decisively shape the questions he asks and the consequent critique he develops.

The metaphysical critique comes first. In the first three lecture series Hinduism appears as part of the story of natural or immediate religion. It involves "the natural unity of the spiritual and the natural" (DR, 234). Because this unity of spirit and nature, God and world, infinite and finite is immediate it is an entirely "undisturbed, untroubled unity" (DR, 238). At the heart of romanticism is a longing for the paradise in which unity was given and did not have to be achieved. But in Hegel's way of thinking, the first, whether speaking logically or historically, is "the lowest level, the most imperfect and thus the first . . . " (DR, 238). Hence the polemic against the tendency of Schelling and Schlegel, among others, to idealize the state of nature and its natural or immediate religion (DR, 239–49 and 521–30).[9]

For freedom is "the unity of human beings with their own nature . . . with freedom and spirituality" and "human freedom thus defined, is no natural, unmediated unity" (DR, 244). The latter is rather the mode of existence appropriate to plants and animals, children, sleepwalkers and simple folk, those whose innocence has not yet experienced and overcome the "infinite gulf, the rupture of the inner being" which is theologically expressed in the concept of sin (DR, 239–47). Hodgson's description of this immediacy as a "cheap identity of finite and infinite" (DR, 70) expresses Hegel's view perfectly, for what we have here is identity without difference, or, in other words, the moments of the concept in isolation from each other.

The specifically Hindu form of this identity without difference is Brahman as the one all-encompassing substance. As "universal substance" Brahman embodies the "first element in the concept"— "the eternal rest of self-containment, this essence that has its being within itself . . . As the universal, this substance is likewise the power that has being in itself" (DR, 325).

This is all to the good, but it falls short of conceptual adequacy. For, as Hegel expressed it so eloquently in the *Phenomenology*, "everything depends on grasping the True, not only as *Substance,* but equally as *Subject.*" For the "living Substance is being which is in truth *Subject,* or, what is the same, is in truth actual only in so far as it is the movement of positing itself, or is the mediation of its self-othering with itself . . . Only this self-*restoring* sameness, or this reflection in otherness within itself—not an *original* or *immediate* unity as such—is the True" (PS, 10).

But in natural or immediate religion in general substance does not become subject (DR, 235, 269; cf. HP 1:144–45). Brahman is a good example of this deficiency, especially in contrast with the gods of the Greeks and the God of the Jews, in whom the difference between spirit and nature, God and world is explicit.[10] The gods of Olympus were first and foremost the ones who subjugated the Titans, thereby sublimating and subordinating the natural to the spiritual. Of course, in Hodgson's summary, "Zeus is [still] the natural firmament generally, but also the father of gods and humans and especially the political god, the god of the state" (DR, 68–69; cf. 52).

The difference between nature and spirit is, if anything, more sharply highlighted in the Jewish understanding of the creation of the world *ex nihilo* (DR, 19, 49–50, 70). Because "nature is divested of divinity" and God is fully distinct from the world, "there is no cheap identity of finite and infinite" here (DR, 70). By contrast with Brahman who is *das Eine,* this creator God is *der Eine,* a personal God who is subject as well as substance (DR, 19; cf. BG, 185–86). Both the Jewish God and Brahman can be described as "the One, the universal, a completely nonsensible substantiality," as "pure, self-identical substantiality." But they differ in that "the Hindu God . . . is just the One, just neuter, not a personal One. . . . On the other hand the God of Judaism is defined as the personal One . . . This is a quite essential difference . . . Brahman is only the in-itself; it does not exist as being-for-self." In contrast to "the personal One, who is *subject,*" Brahman is "what is abstract (not subjectivity) . . . " (DR, 337–40).

Hegel seems unacquainted with the upanishadic formula for Brahman so dear to Shankara, "one only, without a second." But he clearly understands Brahman to be identity without difference. Because it is substance without subjectivity, the whole which lets its parts or moments fall outside it, it is "dry and barren" (HP, 1:146). Brahman is understood as pure being in which all Particularity is dissolved (BG, 190). Or, in the language of the *Philosophy of Right,* it is the pure Universality which is abstracted from all Particularity. As such it is beyond all differences, most basically that between subject and object. "But the necessity and thus the power of difference (*Macht des Unterschiedes*)[11] is so great that even at this highest pinnacle [of abstract unity] it inevitably breaks out [*rekurrieren muss*]" (BG, 185).

But difference does not merely break out. It also breaks loose. At one moment difference disappears into the immediate oneness of the all-devouring substance, taking with it everything concrete, determinate, and particular. At the next moment it reappears as a world of finitude quite independent of that substance (DR, 325, 581). "In this disintegration of the Universal and the Concrete, both are spiritless,—the former an empty unity, the latter an unfree manifold" (BG, 158). The finite has significance, but only "outside the infinite, not within it" (DR, 352). The infinite substance is like "a universal space that has not yet organized what fills it, namely the particularization that has proceeded from it, has not yet idealized this and subordinated it to itself" (DR, 585).

The polytheism that in this way stands over against Brahman is as spiritless as Brahman itself (DR, 267). On the other hand, the gods as subjective self-consciousness are "entangled in natural determinacy." Accordingly, it is some "singular aspect of nature (this visible sky, this sun or moon, a river, a tree, this beast or human being, and so forth), an immediate natural existence of this kind, that is apprised as God in general" (DR, 250). The ape and the cow are specially sacred, even to the point that there are animal hospitals where there are none for humans (A, 336–37; PH, 158) Because of this entanglement in natural determinacy Hegel says that the personification involved in Hindu polytheism, which might appear to be a move from substance to subject, is "superficial" (DR, 607, 735; BG, 186).

On the other hand, and at the same time, the sheer plurality is "unbridled" and represents a "wild" and "unruly" lack of any systematic organization (DR, 582–85, 600). The plurality of polytheism is that of sense and understanding, not of reason (DR, 318). For this reason the independence of the various gods is not that of spirit but one characterized by contingency of purpose and caprice instead of intelligible connection and coherence (DR, 319–23, 267). The categoreal elements are there: unity/plurality, identity/difference, abstract/concrete, and so forth. But they have been "degraded" by their isolation from each other so that the "basic categories emerge in a way that is perfectly devoid of spirit." The result is a world that is "baroque" and that often has a "wild and repulsive shape" (DR, 324).

Hegel recognizes in the Hindu trinity of Brahma, Vishnu, and Shiva, a later attempt to bring some order to this chaos. Hegel here sees the "instinct of the concept" at work, and finds that the three-headed representation of the Trimurti "echoes the spiritual, but in spiritless fashion" (DR, 586, 734). In other words this attempt to introduce coherence into polytheistic pandemonium fails. The most conspicuous indication of this is the role of Shiva, symbolized by the bull and lingam and thus signifying procreation and life, but representing judgment and destruction as well. While the third moment in accordance with the concept would be the return of the whole to itself after, but including, concrete differentiation, and thus would mean reconciliation after rupture, Shiva instead represents "only the spiritless determination of coming to be and passing away," "change in general," "sheer becoming, sheer change" (DR, 734, 591–92, 328, 334).

In summary, Hindu polytheism represents, on Hegel's view, difference run amok. But underlying the irrepressible difference among the gods is the irremediable difference between their world of difference without identity and that of Brahman's identity without difference. The irreconciled difference between these two worlds shows up most dramatically for Hegel in the realm of the Hindu cultus. As we turn from his metaphysical to his cultic critique of Hinduism, we hear a final reminder of how deeply he views the problem as categoreal. Towards the end of his Humboldt review he gives a kind of summary of the logical problems he finds in Hinduism. The problem, he says in effect, is that Hinduism has only had the category of substance to work with. They've gone about as far as you can go without richer conceptual tools (BG, 190–91).

With the cultus the human side of the religious equation is brought into view. It is defined as "all that pertains to the relationship of the subjective, of the subject, the existent self-consciousness, to this God" (DR, 316; cf. 328). Sometimes "this God" means Brahman, and the cultus is defined as "the relation of human beings to Brahman" (DR, 595). On other occasions it is just the opposite. "The cultus is not a cultus of Brahman; there is only a relatedness to particular divinities—and they, being forsaken by the unity, are unrestrictedly natural beings" (DR, 348).

In fact, Hegel's view is that there are two different types of cultus appropriate to Hinduism, just as there are two different ways of spelling out what is meant by "this God." Just as the concept of the divine oscillates between Brahman, in which all concrete determination and particularity vanishes, and the polytheism in which they gain their independence of the primal unity, so there is, so to speak, an abstract cultus of vanishing worldliness and a concrete cultus of independent worldliness. "With this Duality—abstract unity on the one side and the abstract isolation of the world of sense on the other side—exactly corresponds the double form of *cultus,* in the relation of the human subjectivity to God. The one side of this cultic duality consists in the abstraction of pure self-elevation—the abrogation of real self-consciousness; a negativity which is consequently manifested, on the one hand, in the attainment of torpid unconsciousness—on the other hand in suicide and the extinction of all that is worth calling life, by self-inflicted tortures. The other side of worship consists in a wild tumult of excess; when all sense of individuality has vanished from consciousness by immersion in the merely natural . . . In all the pagodas, therefore, prostitutes and dancing girls are kept, whom the Brahmins instruct most carefully in dancing, in beautiful postures and attractive gestures, and who have to comply with the wishes of all comers at a fixed price" (PH, 157).

Just as Hegel can find no real union between Brahman and the gods, so he finds that even the *Bhagavad-Gita* can maintain the cults of faith and of works, of inwardness and of outwardness respectively, "only as opposition, as ultimate contradiction without reconciliation" (BG, 181). On the one hand is the elite cult of Yoga practices of concentration and meditation in search of union with Brahman. On the other hand is the more popular cult of prayers and sacrifices directed toward an earthly paradise of sensual pleasures (BG, 175, 180–81).

Hegel has relatively little to say about the latter cultus, the popular religion of altars and temples. Since the gods to whom prayers and sacrifices are offered are "unrestrictedly natural beings," we find ourselves once again "entangled in natural determinacy" (DR, 348, 250). This naturalism which has not yet been raised to spirit shows itself in two ways. One is the external legalism of religious duty, defined ritualistically (DR, 349). Since the realm of ritual duty tends to extend to the whole of life and not just to the altar and temple, Hegel's discussion of this feature of Hinduism tends to belong more properly to his political critique than to his cultic critique. The other form which ritual naturalism takes is the one already alluded to, the "wild debauchery" the drunken orgies, sexual promiscuity, and all kinds of ugliness" (DR, 349–50; cf. 735).

Hegel has much more to say about Yoga and its techniques of concentration and meditation, which has just been referred to as the cult of vanishing worldliness. He finds it, compared with the infinite variety of Indian mythology, to be the heart and soul (*das Innerste, die Grundvorstellung*) of Indian religion (BG, 145). In the setting of his Humboldt review it represents the two highest stages (out of four) of spiritual perfection (*Vollendung*).[12] The first two con-

sist of doing good works (1) without regard to the fruit of one's action, and (2) in place of self-interest as a motive, doing them for the
sake of Krishna. Hegel dismisses these moments quite quickly, primarily for reasons that belong to his political rather than his cultic
critique of Hinduism. From the ethical point of view "action means
nothing more than to bring some purpose or other to realization.
One acts that something may come of it, that some result may occur" (BG, 152). Further, if one asks what acts are to be done as duties for duty's sake or out of devotion to Krishna, no answer is
contained in these imperatives. All content comes from the caste
system, which remains entangled in natural determinations (BG,
152–55).

It is only with the altered consciousness of the third and
fourth stages that the cultus rises above nature, but, typically for
Hinduism, in Hegel's view, it can do so only by turning utterly
against nature. Thus one here rises above works and action of every
sort, even those of "*Gottesdienst*", whether they be defined as the
prayers and sacrifices of the cultus of temple and altar or as the
acts whose essence is their inward motivation, negatively indifferent to the fruit of action or positively for the sake of Krishna (BG,
156). It is thus only at this stage that Hegel finds the Hindu ana-
logue to the biblical thought, "Sacrifice and burnt offering please
you not; what delights you is only a pure heart" (BG, 181, Hegel's
paraphrase of Psalm 40:60–8 and 51:16–17).

What distinguishes the third from the fourth stage of perfection is that the former involves great effort and only temporary rising above all concreteness to unity with Brahman in all of its
indeterminacy. It can be called "assiduous devotion",[13] while at the
fourth stage the strenuousness is left behind in an effortless and
more or less permanent state of trance.

Most of the time Hegel ignores the difference. It is the project
itself, whether easily and entirely fulfilled or only partly and with
great effort, that concerns him, and he has no sympathy for it. In
one passage he describes it as *geistlos,* commenting on this epithet,
as it were, with three others: *gedankenlos, sinnlos,* and *lebenslos*
(BG, 158–59). He emphasizes the fact that Hindus themselves insist that they do not worship Brahman. This means (1) that the experience of I and We in terms of which spirit is defined in the
Phenomenology (PS, 110–11) is missing, just because the personal
character of God characteristic of Jewish religion is excluded (DR,
336–39); it means (2) that renunciation does not have a penitential
character in that it involves no sense of grief over a broken relationship of love (A, 547–48; cf. DR, 343 and BG, 158); and finally, it

means (3) that the believing soul, who stands essentially outside all personal relationships, need not be a personal self at all. Hence, "I neither am, nor is anything mine, nor do I exist." In other words, "finally personality and self-consciousness disappear for the Indian." Self-knowledge is "without personality" (HP 1:140). As in the Buddhist nirvana, blessedness is found in the "annihilation of personality" (BG, 183).

Since Brahman itself is wholly indeterminate, union with Brahman involves a "flight from every content as from a restriction" (PR, ¶5). Hence Hegel speaks of flight, escape, withdrawal, and retreat. The ego seeks to make itself totally abstract by abstracting from all determinacy. Hegel often itemizes that from which Yoga is the systematic escape: "all consciousness and willing, all passions and needs" (DR, 595); "all emotion and all volition" (PH, 149); "all attention to external objects, the activity of the senses . . . all inner sentiments . . . wish . . . hope . . . fear . . . inclinations and passions . . . all images, ideas, and all determinate thoughts" (BG, 151); "all sensations, all needs and ideas of external things. . . . all outer and inner determinacy, all content of sentiment and of spirit in its affirmative, specific existence" (BG, 181–83). Hegel finds the aimed at or resultant self to be immobile and lifeless. It is indifferent to the point of emptiness, absorbed to the point of annihilation. The only *Vereinigung* it knows is that of *Vertiefung* and *Versenkung* (BG, 148–51). Because it seeks the sheer immediacy of "objectless" and "unsituated" thought, it ends up devoid of any content or truth (BG, 144, 181–84, 161). This total assault on all that makes up life and spirit is a fitting expression of failure to distinguish spirit from nature in such a way as to give human life a distinctive worth (DR, 602).

We have seen that Hegel's philosophy of religion involves a strong correlation of theory and practice and that in his eyes the metaphysical inadequacies of Hindu theory result in cultic practices which either remain immersed in nature or which rise above it, but only through the thoroughgoing negation of nature and denial of difference. In neither case do such practices express a genuinely spiritual notion of personhood. But Hegel is never willing to isolate the individual from society nor the sacred from the secular. Hence the question of practice becomes the question of social practice in general, and the cultic critique becomes the political critique as inevitably as the metaphysical critique became the cultic critique.

It is here that Hegel's view of Hinduism as a religion of unfreedom comes most fully to the fore. He sees the Orient in general as embodying a *Sittlichkeit* (though the word does not have its full and proper meaning here) where substance prevails to the exclusion of true subjectivity. Its laws are experienced as "external force" and as the expression of an "entirely foreign" will (*durchaus fremd*). Government operates by the "prerogative of compulsion (*Zwangsrecht*)" (PH, 111–12).

Correspondingly, Hindu society is one of external legalism in at least two ways. On the one hand the governing will that is *durchaus fremd* to those who are ruled is that of the prince, who is obeyed out of fear and force (PH, 165). On the other hand the external source of law is a set of sacred traditions which tend to ritualize the whole of life by means of rules which define duties without corresponding rights and which have no grounding in insight or conscience. Hegel often repeats his offense in the story of King Nala, against whom the jealous gods were able to get their revenge when he stood on ground where he had urinated, thereby breaking the law and bringing certain punishment on himself (PH, 151–52; A, 214–15; DR, 603).

A second dimension of Hegel's political critique of Hinduism relates to the issue of sectarian violence. He often notes that devotees of Vishnu (*Vaishnavas*) and of Shiva (*Saivas*) not only tend to get into bloody conflict at various religious festivals but often allow matters to develop into full-scale war (DR, 334, 593 and n. 226, 734). Related to this is the feudal warfare associated with petty dynastic struggles, which Hegel sees as the natural result of the Hindu world view (PH, 165–66). Without detailed comment, Hegel presents these tendencies to violence as fundamental defects in the Hindu spirit, the natural political fruit of its metaphysics and cultus.

But by far the primary point of Hegel's political critique concerns the caste system. Especially here he finds the social system of classical Hinduism so deeply mired in nature as to be incapable of freedom. Here is a brief sketch of his brief against this "barbarism" which "in our eyes at least" is "absolute injustice" (A, 212).

1) Within the social organism it is right and just that there should be differences of role. But that these should be based on the accident of birth instead of "aptitude, talent, skill, and education" (A, 208–209) and thus wholly subordinated to nature is equivalent to serfdom and the political form *par excellence* of substance without subjectivity (PHI, 136; DR, 206; PH, 144–45; BG, 154).[14]

2) The special privileges of the Brahmins, who are viewed more as gods than as men, produces a theocratic aristocracy incompatible with political freedom. For example, their exemption from taxes, their autonomy *vis-à-vis* the king, and the impossibility of including them in a system of jury trials make a free society under law impossible (PHI, 200; PH, 113, 152–55; BG, 174).

3) In the absence of freedom as the principle of duty, the content of right behavior must be derived from legalistic, ceremonial traditions. The caste system plays the major role here, and more than anything else, duty consists in maintaining caste distinctions (BG, 137–40, 152–53). Thus the caste system plays a major role in Hegel's first critique (above) of Hindu "*Sittlichkeit*." In this setting such terms as action, character, and duty may be used, but they have a meaning quite different from what "we" mean by them (BG, 155, 172–74).

What especially strikes Hegel about these matters is not simply the presence of a social system of unfreedom, but the fact that the Hindu elevation of the mind from the finite to the infinite occurs without generating a challenge or protest against it (PHI, 200; BG, 154). Hindu religion and Hindu society seem themselves to stand in a relation of identity without difference.

Critical reflection on Hegel's reading of Hinduism no doubt seems long overdue. Within the limits of the present setting, I will focus on the nature of Hegel's bias against Hinduism in order to emphasize its political character. It is important to remember that we learn at least as much about Hegel as we do about Hinduism from his discussion and that ultimately the question is about neither of them but about ourselves and our own being-in-the world. In the present state of hermeneutical self-understanding we would do well not to expect Hegel to be free of all prejudice, but to seek to understand his a prioris in order to understand our own the better.[15]

Hegel's sources were limited, in comparison to what is available today. Further, many of them embodied a colonial, English anti-Indian bias which, for Hegel, was reinforced by his distaste for romantic idealizations of the Orient (DR, 6, 40). Today Hegel would have more texts, better translations, more historical background, less colonial bias, and virtually no romanticism to worry about. But he would still reach the same basic conclusions about Hinduism. We can best understand this by discovering the degree to which his basic prejudice is a political one.

Consider first of all Hegel's claim that in Hinduism the moments fall apart. He refers to the gulf he finds between Brahman, vanishing worldliness, and identity without difference, on the one hand, and the gods, independent worldliness, and difference without identity, on the other. Apparently he is not aware that these strands of Hindu tradition are of quite distinct historical lineage. But he is fully aware that typologically they represent two very different modes of religious life.[16] Why should he not permit Hindu culture this pluralism? Just because the result does not fit neatly into his conceptual scheme? There is an undeniable logical imperialism in Hegel's critique, but it is not just that, at least not as the 'logical' is usually understood. The moments of the concept are the moments of freedom, he believes, and when they fall apart in our experience, freedom disappears from our lives. Hegel's prejudice is not "merely" conceptual/logical but in the broadest sense political. The real question is whether there is a concept of freedom that can be held up as the criterion for all humanity and, if so, how well Hegel has expressed it.

We can get at the same point this way. Given what we know about Hegel, his sources, and his times, it is not surprising that he views Hinduism through overwhelmingly unsympathetic eyes, seldom given to charity, generosity, or humility. What is surprising is the degree to which, in agreement with Marx and the liberation theologians, Hegel gives priority to the question, What kind of social order does this religion legitimize? His treatment of Hinduism invites the suggestion that the ultimate test for any religion is neither theological, nor ritual, but political. This is what makes it possible for him to say that "we ought not to speak of religion at all in general terms and that we really need a power to protect us from it in some of its forms and to espouse against them the rights of reason and self-consciousness" (PR, ¶270). In classical Hinduism Hegel finds such a religion, a web of superstition, annihilation (*Vernichtung*), and slavery, in which "a man who is quite reduced in body and spirit finds his existence altogether stupid and intolerable, and is driven to the creation of a dream-world and a delirious bliss in opium" (PH, 167). That religion may be the foundation of the state by being the opium of the people is a crucial thesis of Hegel's philosophy of religion.

This way of seeing the matter raises another kind of question. For unlike Marx and the liberation theologians, Hegel doesn't apply this type of critique with much rigor to his own religion and society. He is like those who deplore the role of religion in sustaining apartheid in South Africa but are blind to the role of religion in supporting the (admittedly less obvious) racism and classism of the Western democracies. Unlike the reader and the author of this essay, he is sensitive to the ideological rationalizations of others but not to those which sustain the world in which he flourishes. Does he have a right to accentuate the negative and irrational aspects of "their" culture while accentuating the positive and rational aspects of "ours"? Is this the secret to his conclusion that "we" are the fulfillment of history?

If Hegel were with us and we could push him on this question, I suspect that ultimately his attempts to defend himself would fail. But part of that defense, at least as I envisage it, is at least worthy of our reflection. We could probably get him to recognize that in South Africa and in the Western democracies there are social structures incompatible with genuine freedom and there are Christian (even Protestant)[17] theories and practices which legitimize them. He himself points to the unsolved problem of poverty as the scandal of capitalist civil society (which Christendom accepts and often even baptizes) (PR, ¶¶241–46). But he would argue that within the Christian tradition such theories and practices are deviant. They stand at odds with the heart of the tradition, whereas in the case of classical Hinduism the unfreedom of society seems to flow from the very heart of the religious traditions.

Suppose for the moment that we are inclined to agree with Hegel to some significant degree. Just to that degree we have joined in the transcendental deduction of something very like Kierkegaard's attack upon Christendom. We are saying that against its own true character, Christianity has become a bulwark of a society it should be seeking fundamentally to change. Hegel's philosophy is not notorious for its critique of modern, Western society and of the role of Christianity in it. But it has this critical potential within it. All that would seem to be required is that it not exempt its own (and our) society from the criteria by which it evaluates Hindu society.

9 HEGEL AND THE REFORMATION

We have recently passed the sesquicentennial of Hegel's death and the fifth centenary of Luther's birth. The meaning of the relation of these two giants of the Western tradition is a question posed, of course, not by the accidental juxtaposition of dates, but by the self-confessed Protestantism of Hegel's mature thought. It makes sense to ask, with Karl Barth, "Why did Hegel not become for the Protestant world something similar to what Thomas Aquinas was for Roman Catholicism?"[1] One way to seek a deeper understanding of Hegel's thought and of its claims upon us today would be to seek to answer that question.

But the question poses a prior task, I believe, for those of us who seek to come to grips with Hegel. It is the task of understanding the essentially Protestant nature of his thought, of understanding how something very like becoming a Protestant Aquinas lies at the heart of the Hegelian project. For, while Hegel is by no means the first to whom the ever-problematic concept 'Christian philosopher' can be applied, however problematically, he is the first to lay claim to the even more troublesome title of 'Protestant philosopher'. While a great deal of discussion has been generated from the very first about the relation of Hegel's philosophy to the Christian faith in general, far less attention has been paid to that philosophy's professed Protestantism and its understanding of the Reformation's role in spirit's path to freedom. These are not two separate questions. The Protestant character of Hegel's own philosophy of spirit and his view of the world-historical import of the Reformation are two sides of the same coin. For his philosophy is essentially historical, the attempt to comprehend his own time in thought.

In this context, of course, Protestant means Lutheran. Speaking of the view that "the active subjective Spirit is that which comprehends the divine, and in its comprehension of it it is itself the divine Spirit," Hegel says, "We Lutherans—I am a Lutheran and will remain the same—have only this original faith."[2] Luther would surely be surprised to be associated with this conflation of the

149

human and divine spirits, but we are well reminded that "when Hegel claims to be a Lutheran Christian, one can certainly question whether his position really deserves this description, but not that he truly thought so himself."[3]

It was not always so. It is the Hegel of Heidelberg and Berlin, but not of Tübingen, Berne, Frankfurt, or even Jena who thinks of himself as a Protestant philosopher. In his so-called early theological writings, Hegel is hostile to the Christian religion as such.[4] Instead of being a folk religion that celebrates life, firing the imagination without offending enlightened reason, both Protestant and Catholic forms of the faith are corrupted by positivity and dualism. In some passages he takes special aim at Catholicism.[5] More frequently his target is the Protestantism by which he was more closely surrounded.[6] But both are seriously marred by the positivity that results in denial of civil rights to dissenters,[7] and it is over both branches of Christendom that he pronounces his sad verdict at the end of "The Spirit of Christianity and its Fate." "In all the forms of the Christian religion which have been developed in the advancing fate of the ages, there lies this fundamental characteristic of opposition in the divine which is supposed to be present in consciousness only, never in life. . . . And it is its fate that church and state, worship and life, piety and virtue, spiritual and worldly action, can never dissolve into one.[8]

The Jena period culminates in the *Phenomenology* and its affirmation of Christianity as the revealed religion that underlies absolute knowing. But while we now have a Christian philosopher on our hands, in some sense, we can scarcely be said to have a Protestant philosopher. In *Faith and Knowledge* Hegel described the critical finitism and subjectivism of Kant, Jacobi, Fichte, and Schleiermacher, whose overcoming is the central task of true philosophy, as an expression of Protestantism.[9] And in a fragment from about the same time, preserved only in Rosenkranz's account, we hear of a new religion to be generated by philosophy to replace both Catholic and Protestant forms of religion.[10] The eschatological culmination described and celebrated in the *Phenomenology* is not only postbourgeois, but also post-Protestant.[11] These conclusions are surprising only if the *Phenomenology* is read against the background of Hegel's subsequent, rather than antecedent, writings.

We meet the truly Protestant Hegel only in the *Encyclopedia* and in the great lecture series on philosophy, religion, and history. The earliest Hegel only hesitatingly acknowledges that Luther is a national hero (for lack of any others), and immediately goes on to ask, referring to the Reformation, "Apart from the usual annual readings of the Augsburg Confession in some Protestant churches (readings usually wearisome to every hearer) and apart from the dull sermon which follows these, what is the festival which celebrates the memory of this event?"[12] The later Hegel has an entirely different view of the Augsburg Confession and the Reformation it symbolizes. On the three hundredth birthday of the Augsburg Confession, in 1830, Hegel was called upon as Rector of the University of Berlin to give a speech in honor of the occasion. He began it with praise for the princes and mayors, that is, the lay political leaders who ratified the Confession, for the "immortal deed," the "memorable work" by which "they have obtained this priceless freedom for us all," namely the freedom of the laity from blind obedience to the clergy in matters of faith. In this ecumenical age we would prefer that Hegel's new pro-Protestant posture be unaccompanied by strident anti-Catholic rhetoric of the sort familiar to us from the pen of Luther himself. But on this point, at least, Hegel represents a kind of repristination of Lutheranism.[13]

Whenever Hegel talks about the Reformation—and he does so in a variety of settings—and regardless of whether his tone is affirmative or polemical, he clusters his remarks around two points. The first is the dispute over the meaning of the Eucharist, and the second is the Protestant replacement of the monastic vows of poverty, chastity, and obedience with the affirmation of the realm Hegel calls *Sittlichkeit*, participation in the familial, economic, and political institutions of modern society. As we shall see, the theme of the priesthood of every believer, with which Hegel begins his address on the Augsburg Confession, is intimately connected with the first of these two focuses. I turn now to each of them in turn.

Hegel's Ambiguity in Defining
the Protestant Principle

The general schema of world history as the progress of the consciousness of freedom from one to some to all is familiar enough. While the Greeks and Romans knew that some (citizens) were free, they thought that others (slaves) were not entitled to be. It was with Christianity that the freedom of all was first recognized—in principle, it must be added, since slavery did not by any means disappear immediately. But this Christian principle first comes to real fruition in real life with the Reformation. "The *Germanic* nations within Christendom were the first to realize that man as man is free, and that freedom of the spirit is his very essence."[14] The Reformation derives its world-historical import from this single fact. "This is the essence of the Reformation: man is the inner intention to be free."[15]

But if freedom is to be more than a *Stichwort*, it must be defined more precisely. The point of departure for getting specific is regularly the difference between the Catholic and Lutheran understandings of the Eucharist, which Hegel takes to be the continental divide between Catholic and Protestant experience. "Luther therefore could not do otherwise than refuse to yield an iota in regard to that doctrine of the Eucharist in which the whole question is concentrated."[16]

If Hegel finds that everything objectionable about Catholicism flows from its theology of the Eucharist, the fatal flaw of that doctrine can be expressed in a single term, externality (*Äusserlichkeit*). The term has much the same meaning as 'positivity' in the early theological writings. Three aspects of its meaning need to be noted.

1) The host itself, as God presented to religious adoration, is an external thing.[17] What the church offers as "the specific and definite embodiment of Deity which it recognizes" is something "sensuous," something "external in a coarse material form," so that we have the immediacy of "sensuous subjectivity not yet transfigured from the sensible to the spiritual."[18] To put the point as crudely as possible (Is Hegel quoting Luther himself here?), in the Catholic church "the Host is honoured even as an external thing; thus if a mouse eats of the Host, both it and its excrements are reverenced."[19]

2) If it be replied that the Host is not just any old bread and wine, but elements that have been consecrated and thus transfigured from the sensible to the spiritual, Hegel replies that this only brings to light another dimension of externality, that of the clergy who consecrate to the laity who partake. Because "the True is represented as something fixed and external. . . . which has a definite existence outside of the subject, it can come to be in the power of others; the Church is in possession of it as it is of all the means of grace."[20]

3) The status of the believer corresponds to this double externality of the sacred, "which is the basis of the whole Catholic religion. There arises from this a slavishness of knowledge and action . . . the subject is in this respect something passive and receptive which does not know what is true, right, and good,

but has to accept it merely from others."[21] Both in doctrine and in behavior this posture of receptivity means that "obedience" is valued more than "insight."[22]

By contrast, on the Lutheran view, consecration takes place by faith alone. On this view, "the movement starts from something external which is an ordinary common thing, but the act of communion takes place and the inner feeling of the presence of God arises to the extent to which, and in so far as, the externality is eaten not simply in a corporal fashion, but in spirit and faith. It is only in spirit and in faith that we have the present God. The sensible presence is in itself nothing, nor does consecration make the host into an object worthy of adoration, but, on the contrary, the object exists in faith only. . . . This is no transubstantiation—or rather, it is a transubstantiation through which what is external is transformed [aufgehoben], and is directly connected with the faith of the subject."[23] The immediate consequence of this is that the role of the clergy in the sacrament is dramatically subordinated. For Lutherans the host is valid "only in faith and in the actual partaking. This is its consecration in the faith and the spirituality of each one himself. The minister does nothing in particular; he does not consecrate the host, the others are only the recipients."[24]

Hegel is emphatic about the sweeping scope of the issue at hand. It is not a matter merely of how the sacrament is to be understood, but of how an entire life-world is to be shaped. So he says of the Lutheran view, "Diese Entfernung der Äusserlichkeit rekonstruiert alle Lehren. . . ."[25] For this reason it is important to Hegel to formulate the meaning of Luther's rejection of externality in a positive and general way. And here arises Hegel's ambiguity in defining the Protestant principle. On the one hand he formulates it as the Principle of Subjectivity, while on the other it becomes the Principle of Autonomy.

The ambiguity appears as early as "The Positivity of the Christian Religion," that is, before Hegel is a self-confessed Lutheran thinker. At first the emphasis is on the personal, inward involvement of the believer. "Thus the faith of every individual Protestant must be his faith because it is his, not because it is the church's."[26] While this involves a reinterpreting of ecclesiastical authority, it does not involve its entire demise. "All the rights which the church has over him rest solely on the fact that its faith is also his faith." But soon he notes with approval that "great men have claimed that the fundamental meaning of 'Protestant' is a man or a church which has not bound itself to certain unalterable standards of faith but which protests against all authority in matters of belief. . . . "[27]

Hegel's mature formulations of the Subjectivity Principle would have pleased even Kierkegaard. "In the Lutheran Church the subjective feeling and the conviction of the individual is regarded as equally necessary with the objective side of Truth. Truth with Lutherans is not a finished and completed thing; the subject himself must be imbued with Truth, surrendering his particular being in exchange for the substantial Truth, and making that Truth his own. Thus subjective Spirit gains emancipation in the Truth, abnegates its particularity and comes to itself in realizing the truth of its being." To be sure we don't read this praise of subjectivity as subjectivism, Hegel immediately adds, "If Subjectivity be placed in feeling only, without that objective side, we have the stand-point of the merely Natural Will."[28]

In another formulation of the same theme, Lutheran faith sees the believer as standing "in a relation to God which involves his personal existence: that is, his piety and the hope of his salvation and the like all demand that his heart, his subjectivity, should be present in them. His feelings, his faith, the inmost certainty of himself, in short, all that belongs to him is laid claim to, and this alone can truly come under consideration: man must himself repent from his heart and experience contrition; his own heart must be filled with the Holy Ghost. Thus here the principle of subjectivity, of pure relation to me personally, i.e., freedom, is recognized, and not merely so, but it is clearly demanded that in religious worship this alone should be considered. The highest confirmation of the principle is that it alone has value in the eyes of God, that faith and the subjection of the individual heart are alone essential: in this way this principle of Christian freedom is first presented and brought to a true consciousness." Here, again, the reminder of the importance of objectivity is not long delayed. "Truth is what it is in *my* mind; and, on the other hand, my spirit is only then in its proper attitude to truth when truth is within it, when the spirit and its content are related thus. One cannot be isolated from the other."[29]

Needless to say, Hegel does not waver from this commitment to the objectivity of truth. But alongside those formulations of the Protestant principle that confer upon each individual the responsibility for judging what is true and right and making it a self-transforming personal possession, we find formulations that go beyond this in making the individual's reason the criterion or standard by which the judgment is to be made, making Protestantism

indeed to be the faith "which protests against all authority. . . . "
Thus the claim "that man's salvation is his own affair" does not only
mean that it requires "no mediation of priests having the so-called
means of grace within their hands." It also means that "on the side
of knowledge man turned back *into himself* from the beyond of authority; and reason was recognized as the absolutely universal, and
hence as divine."[30]

The same motifs recur whenever Hegel formulates the Protestant principle as the Principle of Autonomy:

> Thus ultimately, in the Protestant conscience the principles of
> the religious and of the ethical conscience come to be one and
> the same: *the free spirit learning to see itself in its reasonable-*
> *ness and truth.*[31]

> But there lived in the German world an entirely new Spirit,
> through which the world was to be regenerated—namely free
> Spirit, which rests on its own self, *the absolute self-will [Eigen-*
> *sinn] of subjectivity.*[32]

> It is a great obstinancy [*Eigensinn*], an obstinancy which does
> honor to mankind, to refuse to recognize in conviction any-
> thing not ratified by thought. This obstinancy is the charac-
> teristic of our epoch, besides being the principle peculiar to
> Protestantism. What Luther initiated as faith in feeling and
> the witness of the spirit, is precisely what spirit, since become
> more mature, has striven to apprehend in the concept . . . [33]

Perhaps the most striking formulation of all is the one which
treats Luther and Descartes as two sides of the same coin.

> After Neo-Platonism . . . it is not until Descartes is arrived at
> that we really enter upon a philosophy which is, properly
> speaking, independent, which knows that it comes forth from
> reason as independent. . . . In this new period the universal
> principle by means of which everything in the world is regu-
> lated, is the thought that proceeds from itself; it is a certain
> inwardness, which is above all evidenced in respect to Chris-
> tianity, and which is the Protestant principle in accordance
> with which thought has come to the consciousness of the world
> at large as that to which every man has a claim. Thus because
> the independently existent thought, this culminating point of

inwardness, is now set forth and firmly grasped, the dead externality of authority is set aside and regarded as out of place.[34]

In his Gifford Lectures, William Temple makes the same as similation:

> This strong assertion of the individual as the source of medium of the authority to which he must bow found its spiritual expression when Martin Luther, standing alone for the truth as he knew it before the Diet of Worms, declared *Hier steh'ich: ich kann nichts anders.* It found its intellectual expression in the course of meditation with which Rene Descartes occupied his leisure in that stove which is the birthplace of modern philosophy.[35]

The good Archbishop and the great philosopher should have known better. For the sake of intellectual honesty they should have paid more attention to how surprised Luther would have been to find himself thus linked with Descartes, especially as Hegel interprets the Cartesian principle. It is hard to imagine anyone less Cartesian than Luther at the Diet of Worms. His defiant response can well be taken as grounded in the Principle of Subjectivity, refusing to turn over his conscience to the authority of the church. But it is entirely antithetical to the Principle of Autonomy. For, the reason he refuses to move from where he stands and claims that he cannot do otherwise is, he says, "I am *bound* by the texts of the Bible, *my conscience is captive* to the Word of God. . . ."[36] For Luther, liberty of conscience is anything but the protest against all authority. It is freedom from human authority in order to be subject to divine authority as expressed in the teachings of Scripture. That is something very different from all Hegel's formulations of the Protestant principle (as what I have called the Principle of Autonomy).

The difference can be expressed in this way. For Luther, the principle *sola fide* is intimately connected with two other principles, *sola scriptura* and *sola gratia.* According to the former, the individual is dependent upon divine authority in the cognitive realm. According to the latter, the individual is dependent upon divine help in the existential realm. But for Hegel, dependence and receptivity are marks of that externality which is the denial of freedom. So he breaks the link between *sola fide* and the other two principles; he then reduces its meaning to make it synonymous with the priesthood of every believer and, finally, expands this principle to make it into the Cartesian-Enlightenment principle of human autonomy. Hegel's account of the Reformation ends up as a paean to Reason, whereas Luther is more apt to speak of reason with the same spicy rhetoric he applies to the Pope.[37]

There seem to me to be three problems arising out of Hegel's ambiguous definition of the Protestant principle. First, there is the issue of intellectual honesty or hermeneutical humility. What Hegel celebrates as the Principle of Autonomy is a viewpoint, even a life-world, significantly at odds with the self-understanding of Luther. Hegel is, of course, under no obligation to treat the self-understanding of a rebellious sixteenth-century monk as normative for his own life and thought. But however pressing the need to bridge the gap between sacred and secular in modern culture, there can be no justification for presenting the Enlightenment Principle of Autonomy as if it were the principle of the Reformation. The differences are too deep to be papered over so easily.[38] That fusion of horizons which involves both understanding and an openness to the claims of what is historically distant is not well served by obliterating the distance at the outset. To use an Hegelian metaphor, that would be an attempt to achieve the hermeneutical goal like a shot from a pistol.

The second problem concerns the Principle of Subjectivity. By failing to distinguish it clearly from the Principle of Autonomy and by giving such prominence to the latter, Hegel gives short shrift to his own Principle of Subjectivity, both in terms of its content and in terms of its importance. In doing so he cheats both himself and us. He lays himself open to the Kierkegaardian charge that in his fear of subjectivism he has allowed subjectivity to be swallowed up in objectivity, though this does not correspond to his deepest intentions. It is clearly his view that philosophy concerns itself with the kind of truth that should transform our personal existence and that we are not merely to make the truth our own, as if we owned it, but that in doing so we are to "surrender" and "abnegate" our particular, natural selfhood in the realization that the truth owns us and has a rightful claim over our whole life.[39]

In a day when philosophy has been so largely given over to gamesmanship and intramural nitpicking (and the "analytic" tradition by no means has a monopoly on this), the Principle of Subjectivity and the deeply spiritual conception of philosophy it presupposes need to be unambiguously championed by all those who, by remaining faithful to them, can rightfully claim to be intellectual heirs of Socrates. There are those of our contemporaries who, for reasons of temperament, simply cannot hear the point from the pen of Kierkegaard, or who, preferring in bad faith not to get the point, find him all too easy to dismiss because of his emotional intensity or apparently unsystematic procedure. Hegel's challenge to contemporary philosophy to be *systematic* stands strong. It would have been matched with an even more important challenge (in partnership with Kierkegaard) to contemporary philosophy to be *serious*, if Hegel had not allowed his own Principle of Subjectivity to be so largely preempted by his preoccupation with autonomy.

The third problem concerns the Principle of Autonomy itself. In one of the passages in which Hegel takes note of the differences between the Reformation and the Enlightenment, rather than conflating them, he expresses the Principle of Autonomy this way, "But in Thought, Self moves within the limits of its own sphere. . . . This is utter and absolute Freedom, for the pure Ego, like pure light, is with itself alone."[40] But it is Hegel, ironically, who has exposed the paradox of absolute freedom better than most. In two familiar chapters of the *Phenomenology*, he first inserts his knife into the pretensions of absolute freedom, and then twists it. In "The law of the heart and the frenzy of self-conceit," he offers a critique no less powerful for being somewhat patronizing. But, in "Absolute Freedom and Terror," he does a devastatingly destructive job on the devastatingly destructive results of trying to make Absolute Freedom a reality rather than just a slogan. If, as Hegel tells us, Autonomy is Absolute Freedom and Absolute Freedom is what he portrays it to be in the *Phenomenology*, then modernity, in so far as it grounds itself on the Principle of Autonomy, can be nothing but the road to hell and holocaust. In our own time, Camus has suggested that this is precisely the case, applying as it were the analysis of the *Phenomenology* to post-Hegelian experience.[41] What we have inherited from Hegel and our own history is perhaps less an ambiguity than a dilemma, that the Principle of Autonomy is hard to deny, but even harder to live with. Unfortunately, Hegel seems to have been unaware of the sharpness with which his own writing poses this dilemma.

Hegel's Ambition in Developing the Protestant Principle

It would surely not be a way out of the problem posed above, to suggest that Hegel praises Autonomy as Absolute Freedom in the realm of theory, but criticizes it in the realm of practice. For the second major motif of Hegel's appreciation of the Reformation is its worldliness, its belief that "the present world was again present to man as worthy of the interests of mind."[42] At issue is not only whether the *Jenseits* is the source and norm of all that is spiritually valuable; it is also a question of whether the only proper locus of spiritual enjoyment and fulfillment is the *Jenseits* of the past, of the future, or of private inwardness.[43]

Hegel saw Protestantism as the affirmation of the public present, and the central expression of this is the turning away from the monastic vows of chastity, poverty, and obedience.

> From the Beyond man was thus called [by the Reformation] into the presence of spirit, as earth and her bodily objects, human virtues and morality, the individual heart and conscience, began to have some value to him. In the church, if marriage was not held to be immoral, self-restraint and celibacy were considered higher, but now marriage came to be looked on as a divine institution. Then poverty was esteemed better than possession, and to live on alms was considered higher than to support oneself honestly by the work of one's hands; now, however, it becomes known that poverty is not the most moral life, for this last consists in living by one's work and taking pleasure in the fruits thereof. The blind obedience by which human freedom was suppressed, was the third vow taken by the monks, as against which freedom, like marriage and property, was now also recognized as divine.[44]

This theme is as fundamental as the doctrine of the Eucharist, and it would be fair to say that, whereas most Protestant interpretations of the Reformation see the issue of justification by faith alone as the central issue, Hegel views it as an ellipse whose two foci are the consecration of the Host by faith alone and the repudiation of the three monastic vows along with the life-world they symbolize.

On this latter point Hegel tends to remind us more consistently of the gap between the Reformation, where the worldliness of freedom is first proclaimed, and the eighteenth-century developments in which this promise comes to fulfillment. As early as *Faith and Knowledge* he writes, speaking of the Enlightenment, "The beautiful subjectivity of Protestantism is transformed into empirical subjectivity; the poetry of Protestant grief that scorns all reconciliation with empirical existence is transformed into the prose of satisfaction with the finite and of good conscience about it."[45] But it is not the Enlightenment as such which "completed the

Reformation that Luther began."[46] It was necessary to go beyond "the abstract metaphysic of Descartes" and the "tranquil theory" of Kantian moral philosophy to give "practical effect" to Enlightenment ideas. This the French did in their Revolution.[47]

What the Reformation, along with its development in the Enlightenment and French Revolution, means for the sphere of public practice is that:

> the principle of freedom has forced its way into secular life; and since secular life so constructed is itself in conformity with the concept, reason, truth, eternal truth, it is a freedom which has become concrete, the rational will. . . . The true reconciliation whereby the Divine realises itself in the region of reality is found in the moral and legal life in the state; this is the true disciplining of secular life.[48]

It is precisely this reconciliation of sacred and secular flowing from the Reformation whose absence from both Catholic and Protestant forms of religious life Hegel found to be their Achilles heel, in his early theological writings. Instead of that "atheism of the ethical world" [*Altheismus der sittlichen Welt*] of which he speaks in the preface to the *Philosophy of Right*, Protestant modernity affirms that "the principles of the religious and of the ethical [*sittlichen*] conscience come to be one and the same. . . . The ethical life [*Sittlichkeit*] of the state and the religious spirituality of the state are thus reciprocal guarantees of strength."[49]

This reconciliation is by no means to be identified with the peaceful coexistence of a church and state hostile or indifferent to one another but agreeing to live and let live. It is an interpenetration in which religion is the foundation [*Grundlage*], but only the foundation, of the state. It is an essence that must pass over into existence "on earth, unfolding itself to be the actual shape and organization of a world."[50] The crucial middle term here is *Sittlichkeit*, that network of public (that is, nonsectarian) social institutions which is nevertheless to be neither explained nor legitimated in utilitarian or functional terms but only as the outward embodiment of moral values. For Hegel nothing is more basic than that this ethical life "is the state retracted into its inner heart and substance, while the state is the organization and actualization of ethical life; and that religion is the very substance of ethical life itself and [thus] of the state. At this rate, the state rests on ethical conviction [*Gesinnung*], which in turn rests on the religious."[51]

Whatever the ambiguity involved in the Principle of Autonomy as part of Hegel's interpretation of modernity, it is clear that his view of a Protestant society "is by no means a one-sided secularization of what was formerly sacred."[52] It is, rather, a challenge to that unholy conspiracy, described so forcefully in later times by Martin Buber (in *The Prophetic Faith*), between the priest who buys the king's support by keeping religion out of politics, and the king who buys religious legitimation for his secular policies by lending the authority and resources of the throne to such piety. As Hegel understands it, Protestantism calls religion from the isolation of inwardness or otherworldliness to worldly involvement; and it calls society from secular self-sufficiency to a serious search for its ethical and religious foundations. For there can be no revolution without a reformation.[53] Neither an apolitical religion nor an atheistic and amoral politics is acceptable.

That this dual challenge defines no easy task becomes clearer when we note two modes of religion's active involvement in public life that it is meant to exclude, theocracy and civil religion. Hegel is explicit about the nontheocratic nature of his intentions. It is inappropriate for the church to dictate public policy to the state, simply because the rights and duties of public life belong to each human being as such, and a sectarian state would of necessity violate this principle. For Hegel, the concept of a Christian or Jewish or Islamic state is a contradiction in terms.[54]

It is perhaps even more important to stress, since Hegel is less overt about it (but unambiguous, I believe), that Protestantism is not to be understood as civil religion. I mean this term in its primary contemporary usage, according to which it is more or less indistinguishable from God-and-country patriotism. Far from being apolitical, this kind of religion is very much involved in public affairs, but only as the uncritical conveyor of divine blessing upon the present (or recent past) division of power and privilege. It is quite simply what Marx calls ideology.

Hegel's Marxist critics have tended to argue that both Hegel's philosophy itself and the relation of religion to society as he presents it have an ideological character, serving as the rationalizations of social practices that do not conform with the ideals of liberty and justice for all, even in Hegel's own best formulation of those ideals. But this is not the case for the simple reason that Hegel views modernity as having received from Protestantism *a task that remains uncompleted.* Speaking of the Reformation, and the principle of spirit's freedom, he writes, "Time from then until now has and has had no other work to do than to bring the world into conformity with this principle, so that the potential reconciliation and truth also receive the form of objectivity."[55] To underscore the present and unfinished nature of this task, Hegel immediately proceeds in the imperative and subjunctive moods. "Law, property, ethical life, government, constitution, etc., must [*müssen*] be conformed to general principles, in order that they may conform with the concept of free will and be rational." Even when speaking of the French Revolution, he writes, "Anaxagoras had been the first to say that *nous* governs the world; but not until now had man advanced to the recognition of the principle that thought ought [*solle*] to govern spiritual reality. This was accordingly a glorious dawn. . . . Emotions of a lofty character stirred in men's minds at that time; a spiritual enthusiasm thrilled through the world, as if the reconciliation between the Divine and the secular was now first accomplished."[56] In short, while the principle of freedom and rationality is for Hegel and his contemporaries a matter of historical heritage, freedom is still to be won and the world is not yet rational. It may well be true that the Kingdom of God and the ethical [*sittliche*] world are "one idea"; but from the perspective of time there is only the struggle to bring this unity to pass.[57]

Hegel is not prepared to derive a revolutionary praxis from these imperatives in the manner of the French, American, or Marxist revolutionaries. He does not believe the ought is a mere mental figment with no power of its own to affect reality; nor does he believe individuals or political parties can take over the task of steering history without inviting catastrophe.[58] But these passages, along with the notably gloomy endings to the *Philosophy of Religion* and the *Philosophy of History*, indicate quite clearly that Hegel did not take the task of bringing the social world into harmony with the religious idea to be in any sense completed.[59]

The point of these remarks is not to defend Hegel against his critics. There are more important tasks than defending the dead. It is for us the living, rather, to be dedicated here to the unfinished work which he has struggled so mightily to define. As Gadamer puts it, "There is no question of Hegel discipleship, but of interiorizing the challenge that he represents." For Gadamer, this means that Hegel's notorious identification of the real with the rational "articulates a task for each individual rather than legitimation for the inactivity of us all."[60]

It is the magnitude of this task that leads me to speak of Hegel's ambition in developing the Protestant principle. For the Protestant project, as we might refer to this aspect of Hegel's thought, is a project every bit as ambitious as that of nuclear disarmament. It has been on the agenda for quite a bit longer than the disarmament project, but is just as far from completion. It can be most simply defined as providing a religious and moral but nonsectarian foundation for social life, making reality rather than nostalgia or utopia out of Hegel's concept of *Sittlichkeit*.

In our own day we have reason to be disturbed by the rise of popular movements that combine a theocratic approach to a variety of moral issues under the general heading of the family with the loud blessings of civil religion on the essentially secular military and economic postures of a nation which wants to maintain a monopoly of power and wealth. We have just as much reason, I believe, to be dismayed by the secularized society to which these movements are a response. This society not only identifies the good with power, pleasure, and wealth, but in doing so adopts a wholly instrumentalized concept of reason, reducing morality to the single maxim that the end justifies the means.

Hegel's ambitious interpretation of the Reformation puts before us the relatively easy task of saying no to these alternatives and the extraordinarily difficult task of finding an alternative.

Hegel had already seen for himself that the Enlightenment dream of a religion and morality based on a reason free of historical conditioning, and thus of all positivity, was an exercise in abstract thinking and self-deception. His own concept of an historically grounded reason that transcends the finitude of its perspective by being the reflection of the Kingdom of God on earth presupposes a realized eschatology. That is, it makes sense only to the degree that the kingdom has come and provides only the most general guidance to those for whom the identity of reality with rationality remains primarily a task.

But this means only that Hegel no more provides us with recipes for completing the task than he promises us rest in a world already completed. It is perhaps the greatness of his interpretation of the Reformation that, instead of either of these, he so clearly defines the perennial task from which it would be as foolish for us to rest as it would be to trust in recipes.

10 HEGEL, THE OLD SECULARISM, AND THE NEW THEOCRACY*

Arthur Danto began his presidential address to the Eastern Division of the American Philosophical Association last December with the observation that one normally comes to such occasions inexperienced and thus in something of a quandary about how to begin. Under such circumstances, he surmised, one could do worse than begin by quoting Hegel. If in no other respect, I am at least Danto's equal in inexperience, and, given both the setting of this address and the spirit of one-upmanship which pervades American philosophy as the spirit of thoroughness once pervaded German philosophy, I propose to begin with *two* quotations from Hegel. First, "religion is the foundation of the state." Then, "the state is the foundation of religion."[1]

Hegel makes both of these statements repeatedly, sometimes in just these words, using the crucial term *Grundlage*, sometimes in a variety of clearly equivalent locutions. Sometimes the latter statement is subsumed in the claim that ethical life (*Sittlichkeit*) or the spirit of a people (*Volksgeist*) is the foundation of religion, while at other times precisely the state is picked out as playing this role.

---

*This essay was originally presented as the presidential address of the 1984 meeting of the Hegel Society of America. It has, as the Preface notes, more of a journalistic character than the other essays, and in certain respects it is more closely linked to the time of its writing than the others. As I write this note in March of 1991, both the Cold War and the Gulf War seem to be behind us. But the world does not seem a more stable or a more humane place. I do not think the analysis offered here is dated in substance. Most fundamentally, the question whether there is an alternative to what I here call the Old Secularism and the New Theocracy, so far from being resolved, is hardly even discussed. It might not be going to far to describe public life as predominantly a pastiche that draws from both without noticing the incoherence that results.

Hegel can do this without conflict inasmuch as the state is the culmination of ethical life just as ethical life is itself the culmination of objective spirit.

Each of these statements is of interest in its own right. That interest is increased by the tension of their co-assertions. But neither by themselves nor in their dialectical unity am I interested in these statements *an-und-für-sich*, but rather *für uns*. That is to say that I am less interested in giving a critical exposition of Hegel's views because they are there, so to speak, than in asking what light they throw on our contemporary situation, about which, accordingly, something needs to be said.

The two features of our world most worthy of note here might be called the old secularism and the new theocracy. By calling the old secularism "old" I mean simply to indicate that the forces and tendencies in question have been effectively at work among us for longer than those of the (consequently) "new" theocracy. By calling them "secular" I mean to suggest that the movement of these forces and tendencies is toward the absolutizing of pre-ethical goods.* Aristotle once summarized the goods I have in mind quite nicely as pleasure, wealth, and honor.[2] By pleasure Aristotle seems to have had in mind especially the sensual pleasures of food, drink, and sex. So we can call the tendency to absolutize these pleasures sensualism, just as materialism is the obvious name for the absolutizing of wealth. By honor Aristotle seems to have meant what we call status or prestige. The cult of this goddess has no common name (a fact worth noting, but not being fooled by). I fear we shall have to speak of statusism, hoping that this linguistic grotesquery will not inspire others.

Each of these "isms" involves two distinct but functionally inseparable processes. The first is that escalation of expectations in

---

*This is not, of course, the standard definition of secularism. But it is not difficult to observe that with the decrease in the influence of religious ideas and institutions comes an increase in the tendency to absolutize pre-ethical goods in the manner subsequently specified. It is as if to a significant degree society acted on the principle, "if God is dead everything is permitted." To observe this empirical phenomenon is neither to validate the inference in question nor to deny the presence of those who repudiate it, who seek to preserve at least significant portions of traditional morality apart from the metaphysical support to be found in theological ideas and from the sociological support to be found in communal religious practice. Far from being a challenge to standard definitions, mine is only meant to call attention to an important observable feature of the secularization process.

which what can be hoped for from each of these goods rises to the place where it begins to make sense to identify its possession with happiness, the answer to the question of the meaning of human existence. Individually or in combination they come to define the good life. Although the "old" secularism is at least as old as Aristotle, perhaps we hear its secularity best when we contrast the meaning of the phrase "the good life" on Aristotle's lips with its meaning in a phrase like "the good life at Malibu." It is the latter rather than the former which is promised to us by the politicians and the advertisers, if only we leave the driving to them.

The flip side of this escalating of expectations is the autonomy of these goods from moral constraints. If it is in them that happiness, the good life, and the meaning of human existence are to be found, then the placing of ethico-religious restrictions on their pursuit and enjoyment must be, from the perspective of the old secularism, either old-fashioned, kill-joy puritanism or naïve, adolescent idealism, neither of which can win its case in the Supreme Court of Realism. Thus the sexual revolution which plays such a key role in modern sensualism has consisted almost entirely in deactivating earlier moral constraints on the pursuit of sexual pleasure. There are those who note, with a sense of irony, that the moral constraints are regularly replaced by technical limits, so that the less it comes to be that we *ought* not to have all the sexual pleasure we would like to, the more we find that we *cannot* have all the sexual pleasure we would like to in spite of all the manuals. Be that as it may, the point for emphasis here is the growing disappearance of moral constraints.

While the sexual revolution has received the most public attention, the same movement toward insulating pre-ethical goods from ethical criticism is found in other realms as well. The consumption of food and drink is by no means free from constraints today, as is clear in our preoccupation with cholesterol and calories. Anything that threatens my health or sex appeal may need to be sacrificed. But if one tries to move from this narcissism to a genuinely ethical question, by, for example, raising the question of the relation of our consumption patterns to global justice and world hunger, one immediately faces the most ultimate of all refutations the old secularism has to offer—boring. Preachers may talk about such issues (at their peril), but those who really make things happen, the politicians and the advertisers, will find other things to talk about. (The really smart preachers, and educators, who understand the importance of being effective, will catch on quickly to what it is we want to hear. Religion and liberal education will offer themselves—sell their souls—as handmaidens of secular success.)

Perhaps the most succinct expression of the autonomy motif in the old secularism comes from the economic sphere. When one of the most powerful bankers in the world was asked by church groups to discontinue making loans to the government of South Africa, providing both respectability and capital to its morally reprehensible system of apartheid, he did not debate the morality of apartheid. He only noted that his bank had but two criteria for investment, legality and profitability. His only concern with the moral issue was to make clear its irrelevance to the pursuit of profit.[3]

If we turn from the matter to the form of the old secularism, we find that it pursues its pre-ethical goods both individually and collectively. Whether one speaks of narcissism, the cult of the self, or simply individualism, the posture is as familiar as its slogans, "looking out for number One," and "each one for him- or herself and the devil take the hindermost." Of course, in an age which no longer believes in the devil, the latter must be demythologized. It now appears in a number of new translations, among which are "each one for him- or herself, and perhaps a little will trickle down to the hindermost," and "each one for him- or herself, and herpes for the unlucky."

If individualism and collectivism are opposites, this does not mean, as the propaganda of the understanding would suggest, that they are alternatives. They are rather dialectical opposites, inseparable from each other. So we should not be surprised to find that the self whose interest (read: immediate desire) is absolutized in the old secularism is the corporate self as well as the individual self. While corporate or collective selves come in many sizes, it is the national self which is of particular importance here. It does not play a particularly important role in the pursuit of pleasure, but it is central to the pursuit of wealth and status.

In the case of wealth the nation's role is a real one, for the level of my affluence is not determined just by personal effort and by my place in the national economy but also by the health of the national economy and by the share of the world's resources over which it presides. In short, you can understand as much about my economic situation by knowing that I am an American as you can by learning about my own personal talents and efforts.

In the case of status the nation's role is a symbolic one, for the benefit of belonging is not tangible, as previously, but psychological. I participate vicariously in national victories and bask in a glory I may have done nothing to earn. We have ritualized this same phenomenon on a smaller scale in competitive sports, and perhaps no clearer insight into the essence of nationalism can be gained than by watching thousands of fans who have been nothing but spectators standing with upraised index fingers and screaming "we're Number One!"

In speaking about the old secularism it has been natural to speak of goddess and cult, of ritual and sacrifice. Is this language accidental, or should we ironically find the old secularism to be itself a kind of established religion? The latter is, I think, quite clearly the case. The escalating importance of pleasure, wealth, and status to positions of centrality in the human enterprise and the corresponding absolutizing of them, along with the individual and collective selves who seek to possess them, mean that for the old secularism these things above all else are sacred. They are ultimate as the goals to be pursued, the criteria of all value, and the selves to be served.

The religion in question is polytheistic, to be sure. Sensualism, materialism, statusism, individualism, and nationalism are not so much the names of denominational differences in serving the same God, analogous to Methodism, Presbyterianism, Catholicism, etc. They are rather the names of different cults in which various members of the pantheon, e.g., Zeus, Athena, Apollo, Hermes, etc., are worshiped.

Perhaps the religious character of the old secularism is nowhere clearer than in its nuclear nationalism. Consider what we are prepared to do on behalf of the nation, or at least on behalf of what its leaders declare to be the national interest. We are prepared to incinerate millions of innocent men, women, and children, simply because they happen to belong to another people. Though Russians have been substituted for Jews, it is appropriate that this slaughter is still referred to as a holocaust. But the word holocaust is rich enough to do more than link the "Final Solution" with the nightmare of nuclear exchange. Originally the term referred to a burnt sacrifice offered in worship to a god. If we ask who is the god to whom human life on this unprecedented scale, along with human civilization and the earth's biosphere, are to be sacrificed, the answer is clear: the nation.

The morality that goes with this religion is simple. The end justifies the means, any means. In this context the abandonment of chemical weapons or the disavowal of a nuclear first strike are plainly not moral imperatives but tactical stupidities. When practiced by others this morality is sometimes called "Bolshevik morality," but it is plainly the morality adopted by the West in its effort to keep the world safe from communism. It is the morality of the Mafia, but also of law-and-order respectability in the service (and worship) of the nations.

Now a wide variety of ethico-religious traditions would agree, in spite of important differences between them, that this religion is idolatry and this morality the heart of immorality. So it is not surprising that we should find ethico-religious protests against the old secularism. Sometimes these protests have the flavor of the political left, but when they do they tend to have little effect (in North America, that is—in Latin America the situation is just the opposite). This protest tends to reside in religious hierarchies and bureaucracies and to separate religious leaders from their people more than uniting them in a challenge to the reigning secularism.

But in recent years the story has been quite different when the ethico-religious critique of "secular humanism" has had the flavor of the political right. Through a combination of charismatic television personalities and massive, computerized, direct-mail fund raising, a movement has arisen which has shaken the complacency of the old secularism rather considerably. The movement as a whole is most often designated by the name of one of its constituent organizations, the Moral Majority. This designation by reference to morality rather than religion corresponds to the earlier definition of the old secularism as the absolutizing of pre-ethical goods. The battleground is the ethical, though in the final analysis the combatants are, like Moses and Pharaoh, David and Goliath, representatives of different gods.

In calling this protest from the right the new theocracy I am not unaware of the differences between its posture and the dictionary definition. This movement does not advocate an established state church, nor, more importantly, does it propose government by clergy. That is to say that it does not suggest that religious officials should hold government office by virtue of their ecclesiastical office.

But the spirit of theocracy is present. While religious leaders do not claim the right to government office, they do claim the right to political authority and influence on the grounds of the religious authority they claim to embody. Furthermore, the religious authority to which they appeal and which they would make the foundations of the political order is epistemologically sectarian. A point of view is epistemologically sectarian, regardless of whether it is shared by a minority or majority, if the criteria by which it seeks justification are privately owned, either by being secret, as in the case of an oracle, or by being public without being universal. This latter condition exists when the criteria of justification can be expected to make sense or ring true only to those already socialized into a distinctive subcommunity of the larger community whose life is to be governed by those criteria. Thus, for example, the dictatorship of the proletariat would be another example of a politics which rests on an epistemologically sectarian basis.

During the Vietnam and civil rights era an ethico-religious protest against the old secularism from the left made itself felt briefly. The impact of the new theocracy may be as brief, but then again, it may not be. Prophecy would be foolish. In any case, the present situation is anything but attractive. The old secularism and the new theocracy may be dialectical opposites, but their dialectic is not that of the Idea, where difference is *aufgehoben* (preserved and transcended) in organic harmony. It is rather the dialectic of finite things whose internal incoherence carries the seeds of their own destruction. The fragmentation of our society is at least as serious as during the earlier protest period just mentioned.

Nor is it easy to hope for harmony and reintegration by the victory of one party over the other, for each is seriously flawed. It is far from clear how any politics which rests on an epistemologically sectarian basis can be compatible with the principles of a free society. So it is not surprising that the new theocracy's concept of freedom is simply unacceptable, a fact best illustrated by its designation of those who imposed Somoza's reign of terror on Nicaragua and who now seek to reinstate themselves in power as "freedom fighters." Whatever we may think about the Sandinistas, this is a use of language which reminds us that we are living in 1984. And on the home front it looks as if the new theocracy is prepared to give back any number of hard-fought victories for toleration and freedom of conscience.

The old secularism, child of the Enlightenment that it is, has sought to avoid epistemological sectarianism. Instead of trying to base politics on a particular world-view among others, it has appealed to the universal. There is nothing sectarian about the desire for pleasure, wealth, and honor, nor about the willingness to place self-interest (of either the personal or corporate self) above the interests of other selves. The problem is that the old secularism appeals to our lowest common denominator, rather than to what is best in us. As a result its view of freedom is also unacceptable, for it is freedom without responsibility, freedom, for example, to pursue profits in South Africa without responsibility for the human victims of that pursuit.

Furthermore, the old secularism cannot easily defend itself against the charge of idolatry. No nation is worthy of the sacrifices we are prepared to offer as a holocaust to ours. Nor are pleasure, wealth, and status worthy of being treated as the content of true happiness and the meaning of human existence. If Kierkegaard is right in seeing at the heart of the comical the confusion of the finite and relative for the infinite and absolute, then the old secularism must be the laughing stock of our time. But this is the unity of the tragic and the comic, for what could be more tragic than to make human existence into a joke?

It is on this point of idolatry that we ought to find the new theocracy most appealing. But it looks as if the majority can be enlisted only in the cause of a very selective morality. For while the new theocracy is prepared on a number of fronts to challenge the old secularism's attitudes toward sex as idolatrous, it is more inclined to reinforce than to challenge the other idolatries. It accepts without reservation its alleged enemy's definition of success in terms of wealth and status. It accepts without challenge the secularist identification of freedom with individualism and the dialectically corresponding nationalism in its military dress uniform. But it does not suffice to say positively that it accepts or negatively that it does not challenge most of the old secularism's world-view. It seeks to enshrine all this under the sacred canopy of divine approval. Thus, God wants us to be rich, personally and nationally, and God wants us to have a bigger military budget, for we are the shining city set on a hill to save the world from the evil empire. Apart from a few issues like school prayer and abortion, the new theocracy looks just like the old secularism in its Sunday go-to-meetin' clothes.

It would be foolish, of course, to read Hegel as if he were a contemporary journalist commenting on these circumstances. Yet his views about the relation of religion and the state are by no means irrelevant to them, and, just because he is operating at the level of basic principles, he may help us to get closer to the heart of the matter than the best of journalists. From the Hegelian perspective on religion and the state, both the old secularism and the new theocracy will have to be abandoned. They turn out to be opposed to each other not as contradictories, one of which must be true, but as contraries, both of which may be, and in this case are, false. If these are the operative alternatives which our society offers us, this only shows how irrational is our world, both in its reality and in its self-understanding.

At first glance it might appear that Hegel and the new theocracy are allies of principle. His claim that religion is the foundation of the state could be taken as support for its position on issues like abortion, and his claim that the state is the foundation of religion could be taken as support for its position on school prayer. But this would be a superficial reading. In fact, Hegel's views imply a three-fold critique of the new theocracy. This is not surprising in view of his strong commitment to the separation of church and state.

Since it is the genius of Hegel's view, and also the source of its greatest difficulty, that it affirms both the separation of church and state and the inseparability of religion and state, it is important to be clear that Hegel has no qualms about holding these views simultaneously. It is tempting to attribute the separation motif to the early Berlin years surrounding the *Philosophy of Right* and the inseparability motif to the later Berlin years. If the two were incompatible such an expedient would be necessary, keeping Hegel coherent by having him correct himself. But Hegel himself surely thought that, far from being incompatible, the two motifs were indispensable to each others' proper interpretation, and he affirms them both throughout the Berlin years. In doing so he is but recapitulating the position of his "early theological writings," where the separation motif in "The Positivity of Christianity" is sandwiched in between the inseparability motif in the "Tübingen Fragment" and "The Spirit of Christianity and its Fate."[4] The Hegelian critique of the new theocracy arises from the dialectical union of these motifs in the claim that religion is the foundation of the state.

Hegel is as eager to tell us what this formula does not mean as to tell us what it does mean. High on the list of what it does not mean is theocracy, either literally or in spirit. Whether in the form of tribal patriarchy, oriental despotism, feudal absolutism, Cromwellian radicalism, or romantic nostalgia for one of these earlier theocracies, Hegel consistently repudiates the attempt to wed religious and political leadership. The first problem with theocracy is the epistemologically sectarian basis on which it rests. The state's *raison d'être* is freedom, the union of the universal and the subjective will which is recognized as such. Because the recognition is as important as the union, blind obedience cannot be the principle of true patriotism. Hence the principles upon which the social order is based must be in principle accessible to all. Like Descartes at the beginning of the *Discourse on Method*, Hegel is convinced that reason is the epistemological common denominator.

This means, on the one hand, that religion is the foundation of the state only when interpreted in the light of reason, a fact which explains the frequency with which Hegel identifies *philosophy* with worldly wisdom when discussing the religious foundation of the state. The translation of religion from *Vorstellung* (prephilosophical idea) to *Begriff* (philosophical concept), which lies at the very heart of Hegelian methodology and metaphysics, also lies at the heart of his politics.

On the other hand, to put it negatively, religion has no political authority when it appeals to faith or feeling, authority, and tradition as its foundation. Neither the intensity of its subjective certitude nor the sincerity of its piety can legitimate its claims to steer the ship of state, for all of these are quite compatible with both shallowness and immorality. As Jesus might have put it, not all who say, "Lord, Lord," are doing the work of the kingdom. We might make the point more concretely by noting that all the religious devotion in the world on the part of practitioners and defenders of slavery and apartheid cannot make these racist social institutions just.

The point, of course, is not that theocracy is inherently racist, but rather that its epistemological sectarianism is an open invitation to the ideology of oppression, that is, to the religious legitimation of the imposition of the particular interests of one group upon another. Even if, by accident, this does not happen at the level of social πρᾶξις (praxis), it has always already happened at the level of theory and of "truth" insofar as the foundations remain epistemologically sectarian. Society as a whole is subjected to rules which can be expected to make sense only to those socialized into one of its subcultures.

The second reason why Hegel refuses to give a theocratic interpretation to his claim that religion is the foundation of the state is ontological. The spirit of theocracy often expresses itself as a kind of technology for social change and control which rests upon mistakenly mechanistic models of human society. These models involve spatial metaphors of externality and temporal metaphors of sequentiality, so Hegel goes out of his way to disown any interpretation which suggests that, when society is not going as it should, religion can be brought in from outside or after the fact to improve things, as if it were an antibiotic which, when properly administered, would cure the diseases of the body politic. Far less is it a rudder whose control directly steers the ship of state. Yet it is almost always in such terms that the new theocracy thinks, viewing religion as a means to political ends.

These models, however, are incompatible with the organic character of Hegel's social ontology. On his view there is no distinction between dependent and independent variables. Within the organic whole, rather, there is reciprocity and interdependence. There is no such thing as unilateral, unidirectional change. Through the life of any people a prevailing spirit already runs (its *Volksgeist*), expressing itself in the various dimensions (*Mächte, Momente,*

Sphären, Seiten, Produkten, Formen, Gestaltungen) of that life.*
There is thus already a unity of spirit permeating the religious and
political aspects of a people's life together.

Sometimes Hegel expresses the same basic organicism in a
slightly different way. The state in the narrowly political sense,
which Hegel also calls the external state, and the actual (*wirkliche*)
state is animated (*beseelt*) by the spirit of a people. The relation is
that of body to soul. In this frame of mind Hegel tends to identify
religion with the *Volksgeist* rather than treating it as one expression thereof, along with others such as the political. Then he speaks
of the relation of religion to the state as that of *Wesen* to *Dasein*, of
das Innere to *das Aüssere*, of *Wissen* to *Wirklichkeit*, and of *Substan-
tialität* to *Entwicklung* and *Verwirklichung*.†

Whether the picture is of a single *Volksgeist* particularizing itself in a variety of manifestations or of a political body animated by
a religious soul, the result is the same. Nostalgia for a past form of
theocracy is doubly inappropriate. As the union of church and state
it is to be avoided as an impingement on both religious and political
freedom, and as the union of religion and state it is always already
a reality, but not of the sort which lends itself to the projects of social engineering which are so characteristic of the new theocracy.
The different moments of a people's life stand *"in der engsten
Verbindung," "in innigsten Zusammenhang," "in unzertrennlicher
Einheit"* with each other and must be seen *"als notwendig übergehend"* into one another.‡ Under such circumstances, as Edmund
Burke insisted, social change can only be holistic, and thus both
slow and all but impossible to manage. The notion of engineering
comes from the attempt to assert human control over inorganic nature, and the concept of management comes from the project of di-
recting social entities which are constructed so as to be controllable

---

* In speaking of the powers, moments, spheres, sides, products, forms, and
shapes of the spirit of a people Hegel is obviously not concerned for a fixed,
technical vocabulary.

† The movement is from essence to existence, from inner to outer, from
knowledge to actuality, and from substantiality to unfolding and
realization.

‡ These phrases are virtually synonymous. Since the moments are in closest
association, in innermost connection, and in inseparable unity, they must
be seen as necessarily passing over into one another.

through mechanistic devices analogous to steering wheels, throttles, thermostats, and so forth. Perhaps the very idea of social engineering and of managing a society only makes sense when a society is already dead or dying. Or perhaps, beyond that, the project in question, which has its secular as well as its theocratic versions, has the power to kill a society, to turn it from a living organism into a dead machine, a body without a soul.

Hegel's organic social ontology has a corollary, mostly unnoticed by him, but worthy of mention for its bearing on the project of the new theocracy. In noting the organic inseparability of religion and state as a categoreal feature, an existential, so to speak, of social *Dasein*, Hegel regularly emphasizes that a free state and a slavish religion cannot coexist. (Hegel is not reluctant to identify such religions, which include nature religion, the religions of India, Judaism, Islam, and Roman Catholicism. We shall have to return to this point.) For the moment we need but notice that for Hegel, who uses Protestant language to express a general point, it is foolish to try to have a revolution without a reformation.

Suppose, *mirabile dictu*, that a political order based on reason and freedom were established in the midst of a religion based on spiritual bondage. We only kid ourselves, Hegel says, if we think those responsible for embodying such a political order will act according to its letter or spirit rather than according to the spirit of their religion. The latter will rather serve as a kind of inertial force to render the fine principles of the political order empty, abstract, and superficial.

Hegel here speaks as an historical idealist, taking note of the effect of absolute spirit on objective spirit. But his holism requires him (more than he notices) to be just as much an historical materialist, taking seriously the impact of objective spirit on absolute spirit. Thus it is also foolish to try to have a religious reformation (revival, in the language of the new theocracy) without a political and economic revolution.

Suppose, *mirabile dictu*, that a religious transformation were to occur in the midst of a political life opposed to it. Do we not kid ourselves if we think the powers of political and economic life will immediately realign themselves rather than serving as inertial forces to keep the new religious principles at the level of rhetoric rather than operational reality? Suppose, for example, that we became convinced as a nation of the religiously based pro-life position on abortion. Can we expect this conviction to be anything but a formal profession in a society whose political order is based on the principle that the task of government is to provide us with personal affluence and otherwise to stay out of our lives? Even if laws were passed to eliminate or severely restrict abortion, would they be effective? Our experience with prohibition suggests that Hegelian theory is right in answering these questions in the negative. From the Hegelian perspective it would appear that the new theocracy, lacking a holistic ontology and methodology, has given insufficient attention to what society as a whole would have to be like for its fondest dreams to be fulfilled anywhere but on paper.

We turn now to the Hegelian critique of the old secularism's secularism. This will constitute, incidentally, a third critique of the new theocracy, along with the epistemological and ontological critique just mentioned. We have noted that the new theocracy is only selectively critical of the primacy given to pre-ethical goods by the old secularism. Wherever it remains uncritical of this tendency, Hegel's critique of its sworn enemy turns against it as well, the price it pays for its inconsistency.

Not surprisingly, Hegel is opposed to all views which treat the relation between religion and the state as an external one, religion being primarily a private matter. On one such view it is the passive or active enemy of the state, passively undermining it by teaching attitudes of superior indifference to its merely worldly enterprise or actively undermining it by inculcating hostility toward the state as an oppressor of the faithful. Neither Hegel nor the old secularism have any enthusiasm for this view.

Not quite as external is the view that religion provides a legitimating function for the state by making obedience to the state a religious obligation. Both Hegel and the old secularism appreciate this view, but in different versions. The old secularism's version leaves its secularism unchallenged while providing the halo of sanctity which religious legitimation suggests. This is the official religion of the old secularism, which it seeks to encourage both in the civil religion which hovers around the fringes of political life and in the churchly religion which hovers around the fringes of everyday life in general. It will seem paradoxical that the old secularism should have an official religion only if we fail to notice that this kind of religion provides only support and never challenge to its projects.

Hegel's appreciation of this view is limited to contexts where religion has a bearing on the content of the state's life. The bonds of social life need to be sacred bonds and not the bonds of calculating self-interest. But only projects which have an ethico-religious substance beyond calculating self-interest are worthy of such legitimation. The state which deserves the support of religion cannot be the liberal state which defines itself in terms of the right of individual and nation to the pursuit of happiness, defined in terms of pre-ethical goods, limited only by the right of other individuals and nations to the same secular self-interest. The problem with the liberal theory and practice of the state is not just that it misunderstands freedom, thinking of the state as a limitation of freedom for the sake of security, while it has not yet even achieved the true notion of freedom. Beyond that it buys the claim, sometimes made by religion, that religion has a rightful monopoly on spiritual values, leaving political and economic life to be the amoral technology of pursuing happiness, amoral because both the ends and the means of achieving them are immune from ethical evaluation. All questions are technological. None are moral.

In Hegel's eyes this dualism of sacred and secular, which fixes a great gulf between the realm of private piety and churchly worship where ethico-religious values are to be taken seriously and the realm of everyday public life from which they have been, so to speak, excommunicated, rests on a total misunderstanding of both religion and the state. Religion is the knowledge of what is highest and absolute, namely God. But it is a *Wissen* to be seen *als notwendig übergehend* into *Wirklichkeit*. It is a *Wesen* seeking *Dasein* in the whole life of a people, an Aristotelian soul whose τελος (*telos*) is to animate the body politic, not a Platonic soul seeking separation from all that is worldly. "*Das Wahre . . . ist der ungeheure Überschritt des Innern in das Äussere, der Einbildung der Vernunft in die Realität. . . .* (The genuine truth . . . is the prodigious transfer of the inner into the outer, the building of reason into the real world. . . .)[5]

Correspondingly, the state is to be not the instrumentalism of the secular life but its *Aufhebung*. The universal principle of truth which is known in religion is to permeate all the particular realms of national life, lest they be, in separation from the truth, barren, cursed like the fig tree without figs, appearance without reality.

This critique of the secularity of the old secularism is also the critique of its idolatry. The *Aufhebung* of secular life in the Hegelian state, whose foundation is religion, is the systematic de-absolutizing of pre-ethical goods and their subordination to and incorporation into a life determined by ethico-religious values. Hegelianism is not a puritanical asceticism which turns against sensual pleasure, wealth, and status as something intrinsically evil. Nor is it an abstract and rigid universalism which denies any legitimate role to the particularity of individual and nation. But it is the prophetic protest against the idolatry which absolutizes any of these by isolating it from the ethical context in which alone it can be its true self.

You will forgive me, nay, thank me, if I restrict myself to but one of the five idolatries of the old secularism for purposes of illustration. Individualism suggests itself as by far the most frequently denounced form of idolatry, and nationalism suggests itself for just the opposite reason. That there are in Hegel's mature (Berlin) thought the elements, not very aggressively developed, to be sure, of a critique of nationalism is a point that ought not to be overlooked in elaborating his views of religion and the state. But I shall choose the sexual form of sensualism as my example, because it makes the point so lucidly and so simply.

Hegel talks a good deal about sex while developing the theme of marriage in the *Philosophy of Right* (¶¶ 158–169). But his comments are at first puzzling. Sometimes he seems to suggest a negative relation between sex and marriage, according to which marriage pulls sex down from its haughty claim, puts it in its place, and reduces it to but a moment in something else. But at other times the relation is positive, with marriage elevating sex from the realm of nature to that of spirit.

The dialectical union of these oppositional motifs is found in the formula which summarizes Hegel's position. Sex is the external embodiment of the ethical bond (*das äusserliche Dasein der sittlichen Verbindung*). If we emphasize the *externality* of the embodiment, we have the Hegelian basis for putting sex in its place. It is the *Dasein*, not the *Wesen*, the body and not the soul. Cut off from that which gives it human, spiritual meaning, the ethical bond of marriage, it is, at best, mere nature. Dogs also copulate. But it is worse that that, for when that which is spirit by nature chooses to remain at the level of mere nature, we no longer have mere nature but spirit corrupted. This corruption stems from the idolatry of treating sex as *die Sache selbst* (the thing itself) instead of as the embodiment or manifestation of something else.

If we shift the emphasis, however, to focus on sex as the *embodiment*, however external, of the ethical bond, we have the basis for Hegel's positive view of the elevation of sex to spiritual significance. We can even speak of a sacramental view of sex, for if a sacrament is an outward and visible sign of an inward and invisible grace, sex, for Hegel, is an outward and tangible expression of an inward and spiritual covenant. This is the *Aufhebung* of sex as a pre-ethical good, physical and emotional pleasure, into an ethical good, personal love and commitment in marriage. The sensual

moment, pleasure, is not abolished but transformed. By being reduced to a moment it is elevated to authentically human significance. By giving up its claim to be divine it becomes something
sacred.

There is something profoundly religious about this idea of finding life through death, of self-realization through self-sacrifice. It is
foreign to the old secularism, which never dreams of that sanctify-
ing of economic life which occurs in the *Aufhebung* of *homo economicus* by which the production and distribution of goods and
services become, not an end in themselves, *die Sache selbst*, but the
external embodiment of the ethical bond of a people committed to
the other peoples of the earth in that same spirit. It is the perennial
attraction of communism (granted in its Hegelian heritage) that,
unlike the old secularism, it is capable of dreaming of such an economic life, just as it is the perennial tragedy of communism that it
remains unable to fulfill that dream.

Hegel's vision of *Sittlichkeit* as the ethico-religious *Aufhebung*
of pre-ethical goods into their truly human form is powerful and
beautiful. His critique of the old secularism and the new theocracy
is strong enough to shake our confidence in whichever one may have
seemed attractive to us previously or perhaps to help us understand
why neither has seemed viable to us. But the question remains
whether his vision can lead us beyond his critique, whether he can
point the way beyond dissatisfaction with the old secularism and
the new theocracy to a viable new experience of religion and the
state.

The problem, which needs to be mentioned in closing, is Hegel's insistence that political freedom is not compatible with just
any religion whatever. He mentions a number of non-Christian religions as being inadequate foundations for a state in accord with
the Idea. But most frequently the Roman Catholic version of the
Christian religion is used to illustrate this point. Hegel is as reso-
lutely Protestant as he is Christian, not only in his metaphysics but
just as centrally in his politics. Of course this does not mean he
wants a theocracy with Protestant clergy running the state. But he
is firmly convinced that the spirit of Protestantism needs to permeate national life. This spirit Hegel defines as the transcendence of
the authoritarian and other-worldy aspects he finds in Roman Catholicism. It is worth noting that many who call themselves Protestant participate in a religious life which Hegel sees as Catholic,
while many who call themselves Catholic exhibit what Hegel thinks
of as the Protestant spirit. But this is of little help. For the religion
which he finds to be the only acceptable basis of a rational state,

even if it does not correspond to external denominational boundaries, is a particular, historically specific form of the religious life, present in some religious communities but absent from others. This is fully in keeping with Hegel's repudiation of the Enlightenment's view of reason as pure and unsituated and with his corresponding insistence on sticking to what is historically concrete. But how is it compatible with the earlier critique of epistemological sectarianism? Does not the Protestantism of Hegel's politics free it from secularity at the cost of sectarianism?

Perhaps it does. Perhaps, in spite of all his efforts to the contrary, Hegel remains within the hermeneutical circle of his own historical particularity in a way incompatible with his own requirements for rationality and freedom. But Hegel himself surely does not think so, though he can hardly have failed to notice how Protestant, and thus apparently sectarian at least, he remains. If he is able to avoid epistemological sectarianism it can only be through the transformation of religious truth into its philosophical form. He is fully aware of this, which accounts for the already mentioned frequency with which he speaks of philosophy as the worldly wisdom which gives the state its religious foundation. This means that the whole project summarized by the notion of translating *Vorstellung* into *Begriff* is every bit as much a political issue as it is a metaphysical and epistemological issue. It also means that we will not have gotten to the heart of the issue so long as discussion is restricted to the relation of images and pictures to so-called pure thought. For at issue is not simply the question of which cognitive faculty is involved in apprehending the highest truth, but also whether this apprehension is privately owned or not. I have little doubt that placing the question of the relation of religion to philosophy in the context of the question of the relation of religion to the state will significantly change the discussion of the former issue. But, happily, that can await another day.

11 HEGEL'S THEORY OF RELIGIOUS KNOWLEDGE

Just as Augustine's proof of the existence of God has been described as "neither an argument nor a series of arguments, but a complete metaphysics plus an ethics and a mysticism which crowns it,"[1] so Hegel's *Lectures on the Proofs of the Existence of God* are a microcosm of his systematic thought. Delivered in the summer semester of 1829, just two years before his death, and apparently intended for publication, they represent a mature statement of themes Hegel had worked on since Bern, Frankfurt, and Jena. Although they are by no means self-sufficient, due to Hegel's tendency to summarize at times what he had worked out in detail elsewhere and to the fact that only the cosmological argument gets discussed, they remain, properly supplemented, the best guide to a systematic statement of his theory of religious knowledge.

For Hegel such a theory concerns two questions, corresponding to the distinction between natural and revealed theology: Can we know God? and Can reason relate constructively to the positive (historically particular) elements of religion?[2] Since his university education at the Tübingen Seminary was in the atmosphere of conflict between Enlightenment rationalism and orthodox supernaturalism, it is not surprising that he was concerned with "The Positivity of the Christian Religion."[3] In the earliest section of this essay he sketches a theology of reason drawn from Lessing, Rousseau, and Kant. He then speculates on how this religion, which he attributes to Jesus, became the positive religion about Jesus which orthodoxy upholds. But he soon came to view both parties to this dispute as one-sided and sterile,[4] and he went on to develop a mediating position. By the time he published the *Phenomenology,* about ten years later, he not only had solved the problem theoretically to his permanent satisfaction, but had provided concrete speculative reinterpretations of the doctrines of the trinity, the incarnation, the atonement, reconciliation, the church, and the Holy Spirit.

183

The *Lectures on the Proofs of the Existence of God,* however, are devoted to the prior question, Can we know God? Its significance also relates directly to the theological situation of the time. In the first place, Enlightenment deism, whose view of reason as criticism allowed only a negative relation to the positivity of Christianity, had so limited the content of what reason could affirm that deism and materialism became indistinguishable. To be sure, it was intended that there should be a difference between "Supreme Being" and "matter," but if asked to specify the respect in which they differ, they more and more reveal themselves, like "Being" and "Nothing" at the beginning of Hegel's Logic, to be the same.[5]

In the second place, even the truncated knowledge of God which deism certified came under fire in the Humean-Kantian critique of the traditional proofs. Not only did it become "a sin against the good society of the philosophers of our time to continue to mention those proofs," but even the theologians came to view them as "a barren desert of arid understanding" and "rotten props" for belief in God.[6] Thus Hegel regularly complains that both philosophy and religion have made it a dogma that man cannot know God. When he tries to take God as the starting point in order that "we may discuss the relation in which He stands to the human spirit," he is met with the assumption that "we do not know God; that even in believing in Him we do not know what He is, and therefore cannot start from Him. To take God as the starting point would be to presuppose that we know how to state and had stated, what God is in Himself as the preeminent object. The previous assumption, however, permits us to speak merely of our relation to Him, to speak of religion and not of God Himself. It does not permit a theology, a doctrine of God, though it certainly does allow a doctrine of religion. . . . We at least hear much talk . . . about religion, and therefore all the less about God Himself."[7]

Hegel sees these assumptions as leaving theology two alternatives. It can turn to history, making theology into the history of doctrine or the history of religions; or it can turn to ethical, psychological, and existential translations of religions affirmations, a phenomenon Hegel was able clearly to observe in Kant and Schleiermacher. The former alternative treats theology as descriptive anthropology, while the latter treats it as normative anthropology; but in either case, theology is reduced to anthropology. In short, Hegel foresees Feuerbach on the scene. "If, in fact, we are to understand by religion nothing more than a relation between ourselves and God, then God is left without any independent existence. God would exist in religion only. He would be something posited, something produced by us."[8] It can be argued that Hegel has his own theory of religion as projection and that his theory of the incarnation as expressing the unity of divine and human natures universally is distinguishable (again like "Being" and "Nothing") only in intention from Feuerbach's theory of the ultimacy of human species being. But at least the intention is fundamental to Hegel's project.[9] His early enthusiasm for the slogan of autonomy is considerably tempered as he sees it destroy the objective content of religion as the knowledge of God. He sees that "since the firm standpoint which the almighty age and its culture have fixed for philosophy is one of reason dependent upon sensibility, it follows that such philosophy can proceed to knowing, not God, but what one calls Man." Consequently, his own theory, in an unexpected parallel with Kierkegaard's, begins with a critique of the present age.[10]

The Possibility of Religious Knowledge

Hegel's early declaration of war on the present age describes its culture in a number of ways. It is the culmination of Prostestantism, the principle of the north, of subjectivity; it is a culture of reflection and a culture of "healthy human reason." But above all it is the fulfillment of Locke's and Hume's empiricism; it is "Lockean and Humean culture."[11] In the *Proofs* he sees it expressed in two mutually implicative forms: the one denying knowledge, by making the understanding with its finitude absolute, the other making room for faith, by seeking in immediacy what discursive knowledge cannot provide. As Hegel interprets these two sides of his day's cultural coin they parallel almost exactly what, in the language of twentieth-century logical positivism, are the elimination of metaphysics and the emotive or noncognitive interpretation of ethical and religious language. Thus his argument for the *possibility* of religious knowledge, i.e., knowledge of God, not just of religion, takes the unexpectedly contemporary form of a critique of positivism.[12] Only when this is accomplished can he proceed to an analysis of *actual* religious knowledge in his discussion of the proofs and how they should be understood.

The procedure of positivism, then as now, involves three steps: (1) analysing the structure of formal-deductive knowledge in logic and mathematics[13] and the method of its application to empirical data in the natural sciences; (2) calling attention to the fact that knowledge of this sort can never be the knowledge of God; and

(3) asserting that there is no other knowledge. Hegel methodically considers each step.

1) Kant interpreted the methodological breakthrough of the scientific revolution as the discovery that "objects must conform to our knowledge" and not the other way around. The leaders of the revolution "learned that reason has insight only into that which it produces after a plan of its own, and that it must not allow itself to be kept, as it were, in nature's leading strings, but must [constrain] nature to give answer to questions of reason's own determining."[14]

Although he doesn't mention this Kantian formula explicitly, it lies at the heart of Hegel's analysis of that knowing which positivism countenances. He interprets this knowing as "controlling knowledge" (Scheler, Tillich) and its method as the "logic of domination" (Marcuse).[15] It is guided, not by the inner life of the object, but by the interest of the subject, whose project is environmental control and whose slogan is "knowledge is power."

This is even true in mathematics. The process of knowing is determined by *our* aim, e.g., discovering whether a certain proposition is a theorem of Euclidian geometry. *We* extend the base of the triangle, and *we* construct a line parallel to the opposite side, etc. This whole activity is ours and not the object's, though the relations we discover are really there.[16]

Such a procedure may be adequate to mathematics, whose objects it exhausts only because of their original lack of content. But the empirical sciences seek to apply it to the whole of nature and spirit. The point is not that they try to proceed deductively, but rather that their inductive procedure parallels the external and subjective method of the formal sciences. Again the material is not left to itself, but abstracting consciousness, guided by the criterion of usefulness, seeks to discover laws, forces, etc., by selecting some features of its object as essential and dismissing as unessential those which do not yield useful correlations. Locke described this process as the search for nominal essences. More recently this view has come to expression in Dewey's *Logic: The Theory of Inquiry*.[17]

It is important properly to locate the point of polemic in this analysis. Many of Hegel's empiricist opponents would accept Hegel's account as both descriptive and normative for the natural sciences. Further, Hegel does not deny that this knowledge is power or that it has its proper place. In an early critique of the Enlightenment's utilitarian intellectualism, he grants that "their wares are useful if it is a matter of building a house," but in relation to human feeling, imagination, and religious needs, "their mistake is to offer stones to the child who asks for bread."[18] Consequently, he stresses the limits of this knowledge, its externality and its subjectivity.

It is external in that "it remains in its own forms, and does not reach the qualities of the object. . . . Real knowledge . . . must be immanent in the object, the proper movement of its nature."[19] This externality is that of form to matter. The knowing subject is conceived in a formal way as a set of formal calculi and categories. It confronts an object inherently unstructured, a brute fact. But the relation of these leaves knowledge itself unintelligible. Either it is the passive matter which becomes something only through the activity of the formal ego, or the object is the agent, and knowledge is its effect in the subject. But why either of these causal relations should be called knowledge, while, e.g., the sun's warming of the stone is not, who can tell?[20]

Hegel never tires of criticizing the metaphor which sees knowledge as a tool or instrument, precisely because it demands conceiving of the subject and object in such an external relation that the language and images of the master-slave dialectic become the foundations of epistemology. The essential foreignness of subject and object is presupposed from the outset. Rather, says Hegel, than thinking of the categories of thought serving us and our interest, we should think of serving them, for only then are we truly free. A hard and puzzling saying, to be sure, but one indicative of Hegel's passion on this point, "These prejudices [unless kept to their proper limits] are errors, the refutation of which throughout all departments of the spiritual and natural world is philosophy itself; or rather, since these errors bar the way, they must be renounced at the very threshold of philosophy."[21]

Essentially the same point can be put in terms of the subjectivity of this knowledge. Since the product results from a process guided by "the subjective purpose of isolating properties for our use,"[22] there is no reason to think that this product is really knowledge of the object. It consists of abstractions guided by subjective aim, and to treat these as what is essential in the object itself would be, to put Hegel's point in Whitehead's language, a fallacy of misplaced concreteness.

In summary, "this method has its own characteristics and procedure which are quite different from the characteristics and processes of the object in itself. . . . It is seen to be a movement of thought which is outside the object and different from the development of the object itself. . . . In the opposition of the process of knowledge to the object to be known lies the finiteness of knowledge."[23]

2) If it be said that this finite knowledge knows only appearances or phenomena, Hegel will immediately agree. And since it is not even an adequate knowledge of nature and finite spirit, outside the limits of technological usefulness, it is obvious that it cannot know God. It neither needs God nor allows for Him. Like La Place, it can get along without that hypothesis. "In this manner science forms a universe of knowledge to which God is not necessary. . . . Consistent connection of what is determinate belongs to the side of knowledge, which is at home in the finite . . . but can only create a system which is without absolute substantiality— without God."[24]

This comes as no surprise to those who consider the "general character of the age," for which "the more the knowledge of finite things has increased—and the increase is so great that the extension of the sciences has become almost boundless . . . —so much the more has the sphere of the knowledge of God become contracted. There was a time when all knowledge was knowledge of God. Our own age, on the contrary, has the distinction of knowing about all and everything, about an infinite number of subjects, but nothing at all of God. Formerly the mind found its supreme interest in knowing God . . . it found no rest except in thus occupying itself with God . . . Our own age has put this need, with all its toils and conflicts, to silence. We have done with all this, and got rid of it."[25]

3) In this analysis of the instrumental and finite character of what Hegel calls the understanding and we would call common sense and scientific knowledge, and in the immediate corollary that it does not and cannot know God, Hegel is basically at one with the spirit of his age and is merely articulating it. The break comes, not when he affirms that "in the opposition of the process of knowledge to the object to be known lies the finiteness of knowledge," but only when he continues, "but this opposition is not on that account to be regarded as itself infinite and absolute." Hegel keeps repeating that it would be arbitrary to take positivism's third step and deny the possibility of any other kind of knowledge. He promises "to show by facts that there exists another kind of knowledge than that which is given out as the only kind."[26]

Both Kant and Spinoza knew well enough that this latter method of knowing yields only a world of mechanism and efficient causality (*natura naturata*). But while the former, in the spirit of the times, insisted that any other mode of knowing transcended human powers, Spinoza went out and showed, however imperfectly, that beyond the finite modes there is an infinite mode of knowledge in which man can know God (*natura naturans*). This is why "thought must place itself at the standpoint of Spinozism; that is the essential beginning of all philosophizing."[27] While Hegel accepts the challenge to show constructively that such knowledge is possible by actualizing it, he simultaneously challenges positivism to show why we should assume from the start that this cannot be done. Later positivism was to face the same challenge in the discussion of the status of the verifiability criterion.

Hegel's own position is that the critique of knowledge carried out by modern philosophy, culminating in Kant, reveals, not the limits of knowledge, but the limits of the understanding, of natural science and that philosophy which restricts itself to analysis of scientific method. But if one holds to the opposite conclusion, that "thought is capable of comprehending only one thing, its incapacity to grasp the truth ... with the result that suicide is its highest vocation,"[28] what happens to whatever gets left outside the pale of knowledge, religion in particular? Lacking even the curious objectivity (public acceptance) of that knowledge which knows only appearances, it can find its home only in subjectivity. Jacobi's philosophy of faith as immediate or intuitional certainty was the form which this obvious conclusion took in Hegel's time. It represents the other side of the positivist coin.[29] Hegel's attitude toward this standpoint is the same as Kant's toward those Scottish critics of Hume whose appeal to common sense, "taking for granted whatever he doubted," was their "method of being defiant without insight."[30] He makes no attempt to hide his contempt.

"The human heart will not allow itself to be deprived of [its elevation to God.] In so far as the human heart has been checked in this matter of elevation to God by the understanding, faith has, on the one hand, appealed to it to hold fast to this elevation, and not trouble itself with the fault-finding of the understanding; but it has, on the other hand, told itself not to trouble about proof at all, in order that it may reach the surest foundation."[31] To the demand for certainty about the divine in the face of discursive thought turned critical and negative, faith presents itself as immediate knowledge, towering above the misty flats of criticism and doubt like the Cartesian *cogito* (one example of the kind of awareness Jacobi calls faith).

Hegel takes faith's profession seriously. Is it immediate? Really? Then it is devoid of content. Since all determinations are negations, the introduction of any determination involves the mediating act of thought distinguishing something from something else. Faith is the affirmation of—mere being, the emptiest of abstractions. Like sense-certainty in the *Phenomenology*, it presents itself as full of the richest content, but reveals itself as the emptiest emptiness. By its own confession it knows for certain *that* God exists, but does not know *what* He is.[32]

This certainty, purchased at the price of content, shows itself generous to a fault in relation to any determinate content. It rests on the Cartesian criterion of subjective certainty. "Only that which I know and know as certain is true; what I know as certain is true just because I know it as certain." Consequently it is hospitable to any and every content. Men have known for certain the the sun goes around the earth and that the Dalai Lama is God. With such examples Hegel gently invokes the distinction between certainty and truth.[33]

The same immediacy which first presents itself as intuitive certainty also presents itself as feeling. And the same dialectic ensues. Feeling is an abstraction receptive to all contents and "just as little as religion is true because it exists in our feelings or hearts, as because it is believed and known immediately and for certain. All religions, even the most false and unworthy, exist in our feelings. . . . There are feelings which are immoral . . . Out of the heart proceed evil thoughts, murder, adultery, backbiting, and so forth." Both modes of immediacy, intuitive certainty and feeling "reduce the divine content, be it the religious as such or the legal and moral, to a minimum, to what is most abstract. With this the determination of the content becomes arbitrary."[34]

The philosophy of faith thus turns out to be an all-out attack on the concept of truth, not only in the religious realm but also (as in contemporary positivism) in the ethical. "If immediate knowledge is to be allowed, everyone will be responsible merely to himself. Then everything is justified. This man knows this, another that, and consequently everything is sanctioned, however contrary to right and religion."[35] For just this reason there is a practical as well as a theoretical consequence. Faith is a threat to community as well as to truth, or rather a threat to community because a threat to truth. "The man who betakes himself to feeling, to immediate knowledge, to his own ideas or to his own thoughts, shuts himself up, as I have already said, in his own particularity, and breaks off any fellowship or community with others—one must leave him alone." Romanticism with its irony, its subjective yearning, its ontological anarchism, comes to life, and in the laboratory of Jacobi's alchemy the humility of finitude (Kant) is transformed into that pride in which the finite subject posits itself as absolute. Philosophically this "apotheosis of the subject" culminates in Fichte, religiously in Schleiermacher's *Speeches on Religion*.[36]

What follows this apotheosis of the subject like its shadow is the Feuerbachian critique of religion. If God is removed from the realm of knowledge and assigned to accidental subjectivity and feeling, "it may well be a subject of wonder that objectivity is ascribed to God at all. In this respect materialistic views . . . have been at least more consistent, in that they have taken spirit and thought for something material, and imagine they have traced the matter back to sensations, even taking God to be a product of feeling, and denying him objectivity. The result has in this case been atheism. God would thus be an historical product of weakness, of fear, of joy, or of interested hopes, cupidity, and lust of power. What has its root only in my feelings exists only for me. It is mine, but not its own. It has no independent existence in and for itself."[37]

It thus appears that Hegel would scarcely be a stranger to our present situation. Since he was able to see Werther and Novalis as the natural offspring of the same spirit which produced the *Critique of Pure Reason,* he might find it less puzzling than we do to find springing up in the midst of a society heady with the advances of its technological rationality not only the theoretical subjectivism of positivistic noncognitivism, but also the practical subjectivism of a neoromantic and neoanarchist pop culture. He would be saddened but not surprised to see the way in which Marxist, Freudian, and Nietzschean atheism are welcomed by theologians on behalf of mankind come of age, as if the first step toward religious renewal were to get rid of God. He would again be saddened, but not surprised to find a new Schleiermacher who, though he understands the powerful Christian message of the forgiveness of sins and beautifully portrays faith as the "courage to accept acceptance," takes his stand instead with an "absolute faith" which avoids the problems of doubt and uncertainty about the implications of that message and that faith by surrendering all content.[38] And he would be heartened to find another theologian who recognized in every absolute theism, i.e., one which affirms God *simpliciter* without specifying what he is not and thereby what he is, the open invitation to idolatry.[39] Could he awake to the present like Rip Van Winkle, he might not detect his long nap for some time, if a few names could be changed.

In the light of the disastrous theoretical and practical implications which Hegel sees in positivism, his references to "another kind of knowledge" become crucial. If one asks where he proves its reality and displays its nature, the answer would have to be that his system (Logic, Philosophy of Nature, and Philosophy of Spirit) and the *Phenomenology* (originally published as the introduction to the system) together constitute his demonstration (proving by showing). Since an exposition of these is obviously out of the question here, a brief general account will have to suffice as background to an account of how God is known in this "true" knowledge.

To begin with, the externality of knowledge to its object must be overcome. "True" knowledge differs from "untrue" knowledge as "the knowledge which does not remain outside of its object, but which, without introducing any of its own qualities, simply follows the course of the object." This calls for a new logic, one which will surpass the formalism of both deductive calculi and categorial systems drawn exclusively from mechanistic physics. The new logic must be more radically empirical than the logic of the empiricists. Rather than being an unpacking of the Cartesian or Newtonian "I think," cut off from the rest of the world, it must reflect all the forms and processes of the real, not just those of the abstract thinker. Rather than coming to the world as a master with tools for inducing nature to do its bidding, the new logic comes to the world as a lover, confident that the beloved will reveal herself to one who is patient and open. "True scientific knowledge . . . demands abandonment to the very life of the object."[40]

This new logic implies a new ontology in so far as the object to be known is no longer conceived as a brute and formless facticity but as having an inherent intelligibility which it will share with a lover. But there is an even more important demand of the new knowledge for a new ontology. It will be objected that the knower, whether master or lover, is, after all, only finite, and that his knowledge, whether more or less formal, more or less genuinely empirical, remains incorrigibly finite and imperfect, especially when the object is the infinite, God. There can be only one solution. Knowledge of God cannot be a merely human activity. God himself must be actively involved and present in the knowing process. The classical notion of supernatural divine revelation attested to by the inner witness of the Holy Spirit addresses this problem. Hegel's solution, on the other hand, takes its starting point from the Greeks, for whom the soul, as reason, is itself divine; from Lessing, for whom the witness of the Spirit is reason; and from Spinoza—"That man knows God implies, in accordance with the essential idea of community, that there is a common knowledge; that is to say, man knows God only in so far as God himself knows himself in man. This knowledge is God's self-consciousness, but it is at the same time a knowledge of God on man's part, and this knowledge of God by man is a knowledge of man by God. The spirit of man, whereby he knows God, is simply the Spirit of God Himself."[41] Again we see why one must first be a Spinozist if one is to be a(n Hegelian) philosopher.

The Structure of Religious Knowledge

It now appears that the theory of religious knowledge presupposes a theory of God, that we can come to a rational comprehension of the proofs for God's existence only on the basis of a prior knowledge of God. Hegel is entirely untroubled by the circularity involved here for he thinks that theorizing about knowing independently of and prior to actual knowing is "inherently absurd,"[42] rather like refusing to enter the water until one knows how to swim. Nor does the logic of the theological or hermeneutical circle lead him, as it has led others, to use the language of the "leap" or other symbols of cognitive and existential discontinuity. This is why his treatment of religion, both in the *Proofs* and in the *Philosophy of Religion,* constantly and overtly presupposes his entire philosophical system, especially the Logic.[43]

Why the Logic in particular? Do not the *Phenomenology* and the *Philosophy of Spirit* contain the Hegelian ontology in so far as it is a theory of God and his relation to man? They do. But the former has a preliminary and introductory character, while the latter has something of an applied character. The heart of the matter is the Logic, and it too, or rather it above all, expresses the Hegelian ontology. Our puzzlement over his insistence that his Logic is his Metaphysics or Ontology disappears when we remember that it is not so much a theory of inference as a theory of categories. It is to be compared, not with the *Prior* and *Posterior Analytics,* but with the *Metaphysics;* not with *Principia Mathematica,* but with *Process and Reality.* Like Aristotle and Whitehead, Hegel develops a categorical scheme which culminates in a doctrine of God integral to the whole. His scheme, like theirs, is revisionary and not descriptive. It is developed in critical interaction with the categorial practices of earlier science, theology, and philosophy. One could even read Hegel's Logic fruitfully through the eyes of the Whiteheadean criteria of consistency, coherence, applicability, and adequacy.

Such an ontological logic is to guide our reflection on the proofs. Religion is the elevation of the human spirit (subjective, thinking spirit) to God. In the proofs this elevation is understood, expressed, and explained. Since the question is whether this is correctly done and "in accordance with the old belief that what is substantial and true can be reached only by reflection, we effect the purification of this act of elevation . . . by explaining it in terms of thought," i.e., of Hegelian logic.[44]

As traditionally conceived, the proofs represent an either-or confrontation of theism and atheism. This is obviously incompatible with the Spinozistic features of Hegel's ontology, and he sees it as a defect due to the way in which the understanding grasps the proofs. But they are not to be merely dismissed. For example, "the so-called cosmological proof is of use solely in connection with the effort to bring into consciousness what the inner life, the pure rational element of the inner movement, is in itself . . . If this movement, when it appears in that form of the understanding in which we have seen it, is not understood as it is in and for itself, still the substantial element which forms its basis does not lose anything in consequence. It is this substantial element which penetrates the imperfection of the form and exercises its power. . . . The religious elevation of the soul to God consequently recognizes itself in that expression, imperfect as it is, and is aware of its inner and true meaning, and so protects itself against the syllogism of the understanding."[45]

Hegel is operating on what might be called the Durkheim principle. "It is an essential postulate of sociology that a human institution cannot rest upon an error and a lie, without which it could not exist. . . . One must know how to go underneath the symbol to the reality which it represents and which gives it meaning. The most barbarous and the most fantastic rites and the strangest myths translate some human need, some aspect of life, either individual or social. The reasons with which the faithful justify them may be, and generally are, erroneous; but the true reasons do not cease to exist, and it is the duty of science to discover them. In reality, then, there are no religions which are false. All are true in their own fashion."[46] If it is far from clear that Hegel's own Logic permits such a loose relation of form and content or substance, at least the thrust of the "purification" he has in mind becomes clearer. We might say that he plans to vindicate the proofs by demythologizing them.

The Cosmological Proof

After devoting nine lectures to general considerations, including the critique of positivism, Hegel devotes the last seven lectures to "purification" of the cosmological argument. Hume and Kant, in their critiques of this and the teleological argument, had launched a devastating, double-barreled assault, first questioning the legitimacy of the inferences involved, then suggesting that even if the inferences were impeccable, the result achieved was far from being the God of the religious interest which motivated the proofs. Hegel addresses himself to both considerations.

To begin with he not only grants but insists upon the fact that the cosmological argument yields an abstract and inadequate concept of God. But his "even if" argument runs as follows: even if this way of showing *that* God exists inadequately reveals *what* He is, and even if He is more than the Infinite and the Absolutely Necessary Essence, He is not less than that—indeed, He only is infinite and absolutely necessary. Besides, this is only the first form of the elevation to God, the general basis of religion. There are other proofs which employ richer categories and supply what is lacking here. The task of philosophy is not to complain about what the proof doesn't do, but to state clearly what it does.[47]

Examination of the inference or movement of thought expressed in the proof is more complex. Thought begins with the world as finite and contingent and moves to the Infinite or Absolutely Necessary Essence. The starting point is the world conceived as an aggregate of visible things, limited by one another, which can "equally well either be or not be."[48] An element of necessity is introduced into this mass of contingency with the discovery that the particulars do no behave capriciously but in accordance with laws. But these laws themselves share the same contingency as the particulars at first seemed to possess, and they remain unexplained explainers. The contingency of the world is unmitigated by natural science, by conceiving it as *natura naturata*.

The proof articulates the act in which the human spirit "raises itself above this crowd of contingent things, above the merely outward and relative necessity involved in them," i.e., denies the ultimacy of the world as portrayed by the natural sciences. "Spirit rises above contingency and external necessity, just because these thoughts are in themselves insufficient and unsatisfying. It finds satisfaction in the thought of absolute necessity, because this latter represents something at peace with itself . . . Thus all aspiration, all striving, all longing after an other have passed away, for in [the Absolutely Necessary] the other has disappeared. There is no finitude in it. It is absolutely complete in itself. It is infinite and present in itself. There is nothing outside of it."[49]

In concert with a tradition which includes Descartes and Aquinas as well as Augustine and Pascal, Hegel is presenting the question of God as the question of human happiness, the satisfaction of man's deepest and innermost longings. To see the everyday world even in the glory which science gives it as the place where the restless human spirit cannot be at home and at peace is to see it as finite and contingent. From this we do not need to infer the Infinite in the sense of some new reality. To see the world as finite is already to have made the move to the Infinite, for it is only in the light of the latter that the former reveals itself as such. "Furthermore, this elevation is essentially rooted in the nature of our spirit. It is necessary to it . . . and the setting forth of this necessity itself is nothing else than what we call proof."[50]

It will immediately be asked whether what is already present in recognizing the world as contingent is the reality of the Infinite, or only the idea. Post-Hegelian atheism (Feuerbach, Marx, Nietzsche, and Freud) argues that just because the issue at stake is human happiness the presumption is in the direction of wish-fulfilling projection, opiates, lies, and illusions. Further, the fact that the movement of thought in question is "natural" or even "necessary" to our spirit leads to no final conclusion. Humeans and Kantians are going to ask why we should assume that the natural (Hume) and necessary (Kant) movement of human thought inevitably unveils reality, that in moving beyond the sciences to dialectic we get a logic of truth and not a logic of illusion. From the side of religion itself will come, in addition, the claim that human thought is not merely finite, but also corrupted by sinfulness, making it an even less trustworthy guide to the truth than if it were merely finite.[51]

These questions evoke the contrast between human knowledge as finite or sinful and divine knowledge as void of defect. In granting that the understanding and its knowledge are finite, Hegel seemed to agree with Kant and others who employ this contrast, but the important difference between their conclusions now appears. For Hegel that knowledge is finite because of its method and inherent purpose, not because of the ontological or moral deficiencies of its possessor. But as we have already seen, Hegel is working in the context of an ontology which so relates God to man that God's infinite and perfect knowledge resides in man. Accordingly the distinction between finite and infinite knowledge is one between two modes of human knowing. From this perspective it seems entirely arbitrary to represent a knowledge adequate to grasping God as a knowledge transcending finite human powers. "A gulf is simply fixed between them."[52]

Among those for whom the contrast between human and divine knowledge is most explicit the response will be immediate. To call the distinction arbitrary is to invite repayment in kind. For Hegel, it will be said, "A bridge is simply fixed between them." Hegel's protest that his theory of knowledge has a foundation in a systematic ontology and is therefore not arbitrary will be of no help, for the finitist position itself (at least sometimes) rests on another systematic ontology, a creationist ontology for which God and man stand in an asymmetrical dependence relation, quite distinct from one another. Spinoza knew this well and began his effort to establish an ontology and epistemology similar to Hegel's with a careful attempt to dismantle the creationist ontology (*Ethics*, Bk. 1). If Hegel's purpose is to suggest that this ontology is itself arbitrary, merely a set of axioms or meaning postulates whose theorems have no necessary relation to reality, is he not inviting the same evaluation of his own ontology and Spinoza's, which even looks the part? Kierkegaard thought so when he said the Hegelian system was a great thought experiment. Once inside the basic framework things fall nicely in place, but for the existing individual who needs something to live and die by, the problem of getting in may be of overwhelming importance and difficulty. Kierkegaard thought so when he ironically used the terms "Fragments" and "Postscript" to entitle his discussions of just this problem.

Hegel, of course, does not permit himself to be drawn outside of his own ontology to discuss these questions. He is eager to get on with the task of purifying the proof under examination by giving it its proper interpretation. Since it is essentially a denial of the ultimacy of the world as seen by the understanding, it is to be expected that the understanding will misinterpret the proof, distorting its truth. It treats the proof as a causal inference, whereas, in fact, it concerns the category of substance.[53] Thus instead of seeing the move from the finitude of the world to the infinity of God as the move to Absolute Substance from its accidents and manifestations, it sees the inference as moving from one reality, the world, to another reality, its cause. This is evident in the language used by the understanding. It says, "Because contingent being exists, therefore absolutely necessary being exists." But "the contingent is in this way retained on its own account separately from the Absolutely Necessary," even when it is explained that the conditioned is the condition of the necessary only in the order of knowing. The contingent "remains standing on the one side confronting the other side, the Eternal, the Necessary in and for itself, in the form of a world above which is heaven. Still the real point is not the fact that a double world has actually been conceived, but the value which is to be attached to such a conception. This value is expressed when it is said that the one world is the world of appearance or illusion, and the other the world of truth." Corrected by Hegelian logic, the proof would look like this: "Not because the contingent is, but on the contrary, because it is non-being, merely phenomenal, because its being is not true actuality, the Absolutely Necessary is. This latter is its being and truth." Or, "The being of the contingent is not its own being, but merely the being of an other, and in a definite sense it is the being of its own other, the Absolutely Necessary."[54]

Hegel is trying to steer clear of a theistic interpretation of the proof which portrays God as creator, a being sufficient to himself and distinct from the world He freely creates. Overlooking the fact that such an ontology places the world in an asymmetrical dependence relation to God, Hegel sees it only as a kind of Manichean dualism.[55]

Over and above this theoretical deficiency relative to the Hegelian system, there is a practical problem. If finite and infinite are conceived as separate and unrelated realities, i.e., dualistically, the actions by which we relate to them are also separate and unrelated. The sacred and secular fall hopelessly apart in experience. "When spirit occupied itself with the finite it would in turn do this in an absolute way and be entirely confined to the finite as such." But a true relation to the finite is possible, whether theoretical or practical, "only in so far as the finite is not taken for itself, but is known, recognized, and its existence affirmed in terms of its relation to the Infinite." Instead of this the "religious element in the form of devotion, contrition of heart and spirit, and the giving of offerings, comes to be regarded as a matter apart with which we can occupy ourselves and then have done with; while the secular life, the sphere of finitude, exists along-side of it, and gives itself up to the pursuit of its own ends, and is left to its own interests without any influence being exercised upon it by the Infinite, the Eternal, and the True."[56]

This criticism reveals one of the most basic elements of the Hegelian project. His secondary and university education between 1780 and 1793 exposed him to the militant secularism of the Enlightenment and to the enormous gulf between it and the supposedly official Christianity of Europe. During this period his favorite reading (except Rousseau) was the Greek poets, especially Sophocles. Through this reading and his reading of Goethe and Schiller he developed a fervent admiration for Greek culture, especially its folk religion, which he saw as permeating all of life with a sense of the presence of the Divine. In romantic reaction against the cultural dualism of his own day, he plaintively concludes one of his early essays with this lament: "between these extremes which occur within the opposition between God and the world, between the divine and life, the Christian church has oscillated to and fro, but it is contrary to its essential character to find peace . . . And it is its fate that church and state, worship and life, piety and virtue, spiritual and worldly action can never dissolve into one."[57]

The task of overcoming this sacred-secular dualism is the inner, driving spirit of all of Hegel's thought. Its purpose is to provide the conceptual tools for freeing Christianity from this fate, for recovering in a post-pagan world the harmony of divine and human which paganism had enjoyed but lost. Thus, rather than saying (as above) that Hegel's practical objection to a theistic interpretation of the cosmological proof is "over and above" his theoretical objection, we should say that the latter is possible only in a systematic framework ultimately motivated by the former. The two objections are really the same. To say from a logical point of view that the categories of finite and infinite are improperly conceived is to say in an Hegelian way that from an existential point of view the dimensions of the secular and the sacred are improperly experienced.

This does not conclude Hegel's purification, however. The truth of the cosmological proof, totally missed by the understanding, is grasped by those systems which might be called pantheistic, or, as Hegel prefers, "systems of substantiality." Oriental religion, especially Hindu, the Greek view of Fate as supreme, the Eleatic doctrine of being, and the Spinozistic movement from *natura naturata* to *natura naturans*—all of these have avoided the pitfalls of the understanding and conceived the proof in its true form. By now we are prepared for this. Since the cosmological proof is not a causal argument, but one pertaining to substance, we should not be surprised to find that Spinozism is its truth.

But its truth is not the truth, and Hegel's criticism of these systems is that they do not get beyond it. Their conception of the Absolutely Necessary, while free from all suspicion of dualism, turns out to be a one-sided monism. The Stoic's renunciation and the tragic hero's repose in the face of Fate are not the satisfaction which the human heart longs for in longing for God.[58] Absolute necessity is here conceived so as to leave no hope for the individual beyond the internal freedom of acquiescence. "They start from actual existence, treat it as a nullity, and recognize the Absolute One as the truth of this existence. They start with a presupposition, they negate it in the absolute unity but they don't get out of this unity back to the presupposition . . . Everything passes into this unity as into a kind of eternal night, while this unity is not characterized as a principle which moves itself to its manifestation or produces it." The souls of the eastern poets dive into this ocean and drown in it all the necessities, the aims, the cares of this petty, circumscribed

life, and revel in the enjoyment of this freedom." "We rise above finiteness, we forget it. But yet is it not truly transcended simply because we have forgotten it,"[59]

Hegel is criticizing the Spinozism which is his own starting
point, not for its so-called pantheism, but for not getting beyond the
category of substance in describing the Absolute. The teleological
argument, for example, while it does not yet conceive of God as
Spirit, does view Him as living substance. All the categories of Hegel's Logic are attributes of God, but the richer ones are more adequate. Thus it is true that God is the Absolute Substance, but truer
that He is living, i.e., that this substance is internally purposive in
the mode of finite organisms. To reach the category of spirit we need
only to add the concept of self-consciousness to this notion of a purposive development of substance, and the ontological argument provides this further enrichment. These conceptions begin the
movement back from the Infinite to the finite starting point. With
the ideas of purposiveness and self-consciousness Hegel believes the
finite individual is restored to a place of meaning and importance
which he seemed to be losing in the movement toward the Absolute
Substance. This is why it is so crucial, from the Hegelian point of
view, to conceive substance as subject (as in the preface to the
Phenomenology).

The Ontological Proof

Though Hegel clearly intended to discuss all three of the classical
arguments in the *Proofs,* he did not complete his project. But because of the importance of the ontological argument in his thinking
and because of the contemporary revival of interest in it, it would be
inappropriate not to summarize briefly what he says elsewhere
about it.

In spite of his special fondness for "the great theologian
Anselm of Canterbury" and his proof, it is important to recognize
that it is not his contention that "all arguments must ultimately be
reduced to the ontological argument and thus share its validity as a
description of the human spirit's elevation to God."[60] Following
Kant, he distinguishes the cosmological and teleological proofs,
whose starting points are experienced reality, from the ontological
proof, whose starting point is the concept of God. But since both directions which thought can take are one-sided, both are equally
necessary. Just as the denial of the ontological proof absolutizes an
"untrue concept," so the denial of the others would be the absolutizing of an "untrue reality."[61] It is true that the two historically

prominent arguments of the former kind, even when "purified," compare unfavorably with the properly understood ontological argument, since the latter alone grasps the Absolute as Spirit. But this superiority is accidental. There are potentially any number of proofs which start from the world as experienced, and there is nothing in principle to keep them from coming to understand God as Spirit. In fact, Hegel's own *Realphilosophie* (Philosophy of Nature and Spirit) is just as much such an argument as his Logic is a complex version of the ontological proof. Since, as we have seen, Hegel does not permit any wedge to be driven between (human) thought and being, the real is rational and the rational is real. It does not matter whether one begins with the necessities of thought which express themselves in actuality, or with given reality, which shows itself to be fully intelligible, as long as neither movement of thought is left out.

With regard to the proof itself, the same two points are to be considered as before, the adequacy of the result and the legitimacy of the inference. With regard to the first the question arises why it should be the ontological argument alone, of the classical proofs properly interpreted, which yields an adequate concept of God as Spirit. The reason is simply that it begins with the concept of God. Like all the proofs, according to Hegel, this one expresses the intelligibility of a certain kind of religious experience, but since it starts with the concept of God, each version of the proof will begin with its author's answer to the question, What is worthy of worship?[62]

Just because Anselm's formula for perfection, "that than which a greater cannot be conceived" is an entirely formal one, it has lent itself to many different concepts of perfection. The ontological proof has been used to express such widely different views of God as Anselm's, Spinoza's, Hegel's, Tillich's, and Hartshorne's. This means that Hegel must purify the proof and reconstruct its true significance. Once again this purification presupposes his system, which in this case is his lengthy answer to the question, What is worthy of worship? If his version of the ontological argument articulates the Absolute as Spirit, it is because Spirit, not Anselm's transcendent creator or Spinoza's substance, is that than which a greater cannot be conceived by Hegel.

More troublesome to many than this question of whose version of the ontological proof is most adequate is the question whether any version expresses a valid inference. To infer the reality of anything from its concept is, to say the least, highly unusual.

As it turns out, this way of putting the objection is one way of answering it. Just as Anselm had to remind Gaunilo that he was talking about God and not an island, Hegel reminds Kant that it is not a hundred thalers which is at stake. "But if it is correct that concept is not the same as being, it is truer still that God is not the same as one hundred thalers or other finite things. It is the definition of finite things that with them concept and being, concept and reality, soul and body, are different and separable, and that therefore they are perishable and mortal. While it is just the abstract definition of God that with Him concept and being are unseparated and inseparable."[63] This appeal to another kind of being and knowledge simply indicates that Kant's refutation of the argument begs precisely what is at question, namely whether there is anything other than the finite things for which ontological arguments are invalid.

But can Hegel go beyond this negative rejoinder to provide some intelligibility for the strange inference from concept to reality, from the rational to the real? He uses language which seems at first only further to mystify the doubtful. The concept "particularizes itself," "posits finitude," "generates reality from within itself," etc. This language, and the whole thrust of the ontological argument for Hegel, lose at least some of their strangeness when we remember that idea or concept for Hegel does not mean what it means for Locke or Hume, but rather what substantial form or entelechy means for the Aristotelian tradition. Relative to Aristotelian language, Hegel's references to the concept of a thing as its soul are not metaphors. The concept of a thing is the dynamic inner principle which guides the process of its development. It is "the shoot, out of which the whole tree develops itself. All the specifications are contained in this, the whole nature of the tree, the kind of sap it has, and the way in which the branches grow; but in a spiritual manner, and not performed so that a microscope could reveal its boughs, its leaves in miniature. It is thus that the concept contains the whole nature of the object, and knowledge itself is nothing else than the development of the concept."[64]

It is clear that this last definition of knowledge is radically empirical rather than a priori and is akin to Aristotle's doctrine of knowledge as the immaterial reception of the forms. No speculative microscope can beat history to the draw. Only as the object develops and reveals what its concept already contains (in the sense that an acorn is already an oak and not a milk-pail) can the development of the concept come to consciousness for a subject and thus be knowledge.

It is also clear that the movement of thought or inference involved here is not from a present and known reality to the existence of an absent and previously unknown reality. It is rather a process of coming to a fuller understanding of the nature of a reality already encountered and only partially comprehended.

But Hegel intends to do more than suggest a bio-teleological model for describing the processes of nature and history when he says that the concept "particularizes itself," etc. He also means to assert with Anaxagoras that *nous* rules the world. Like Socrates, Hegel understands this to mean that the ultimate cause of the world arranges things for the best and that comprehension and justification go hand in hand. In order to make the point perfectly clear he assimilates the Anaxagorean doctrine to the religious doctrine of Providence.[65] The language Hegel invokes in defending the ontological argument is his philosophical translation of the Christian belief that the historical process is controlled and directed by an Absolute Goodness.

The clearest statement on this theme is in the *Philosophy of History*.

The only thought which philosophy brings with it to the contemplation of history is the simple conception of Reason; that Reason rules the world; and that the history of the world is thus a rational process. This conviction and insight is a hypothesis in the domain of history as such. In that of philosophy it is no hypothesis . . . On the one hand, Reason is the substance of the universe, that by which and in which all reality has its being and subsistence. On the other hand, it is the infinite power of the universe, since Reason is not so powerless as to be incapable of producing anything but a mere ideal, a mere ought having its place outside reality, who knows where . . . That this idea [Reason] is the True, the Eternal, the Absolutely Powerful; that it reveals itself in the world, and that in the world nothing else is revealed but this and its honor and glory—this is the thesis which, as we have said, has been proved in Philosophy, and is here regarded as demonstrated.[66]

These two features of Hegel's talk about the Idea particularizing itself invite the appellation historical Aristotelianism. They also invite certain questions or criticisms which can be mentioned briefly for the sake of further clarifying the issues at stake. The Aristotelian aspect, put in the context of historical processes, raises the question whether the spectre of historicism (see notes 10 and 40 above) does not hang over even the ontological argument in Hegel.

Knowledge of the divine as a developing process is relative to the state of development at which it occurs and which it expresses. This makes it possible to explain why Anselm gave a theistic and Spinoza an abstractly pantheistic interpretation to the ontological proof. But it also makes us wonder whether Hegel's own version has a kind of obsolescence systematically built in.

A different sort of problem arises from the use of the ontological argument as theodicy. Nietzsche puts it bluntly:

> The belief that one is a latecomer in the world is, anyhow, harmful and degrading; but it must appear frightful and devastating when it raises our latecomer to godhead, by a neat turn of the wheel, as the true meaning and object of all past creation, and his conscious misery is set up as the perfection of the world's history. Such a point of view . . . has put history in the place of other spiritual powers, art and religion, as the one sovereign, inasmuch as it is the 'Idea revitalizing itself'. . . . [Hegel] has implanted in a generation leavened throughout by him the worship of the 'power of history' that turns practically every moment into a sheer gaping at success, into an idolatry of the actual for which we have now discovered the characteristic phrase, 'to adapt ourselves to circumstances.' . . . If each success has come by a 'rational necessity,' and every event shows the victory of logic of the 'idea,' then—down on your knees quickly, and let every step in the ladder of success have its reverence! There are no more living mythologies, you say? Religions are at their last gasp? Look at the religion of the power of history, and the priests of the mythology of Ideas, with their scarred knees.[67]

Marx makes the same criticism in his 1843 critique of paragraphs 261–69 of Hegel's *Philosophy of Right*. With reference to Hegel's description of the relation of family, civil society, and state, Marx writes, "They are not *as such* presented as rational. But they become rational again only in that they are presented as an *apparent* mediation, in that they are left just as they are, but at the same time acquire the meaning of a determination of the Idea, a result, a product of the Idea. . . . Empirical actuality is thus understood as it is. It is also pronounced rational, but it is not rational through its own rationality but rather because the empirical fact in its empirical existence has another meaning than its own. The initial fact is not taken as such but rather as a mystical result." In short, Hegel "uncritically takes limited existences for the expression of the Idea."[68]

These criticisms are surely not the last word on the subject, and there are a number of ways in which Hegel can be defended against them. I have introduced them neither to defend them, nor to arbitrate the dispute to which they give rise. I have simply wanted to suggest that it is when Hegel approaches historical and political issues under the impact of his own thinking on the ontological argument that he gives ammunition to his critics along these lines. Recognizing this is of considerable help when one is trying to comprehend Hegel's perplexing comments on the ontological proof.

It may seem that only half of Hegel's theory of religious knowledge has been presented, since only the question of the knowledge of God has been discussed, while the question of the positive element in religion has been ignored. This would leave us with a theory of natural theology, but no theory of revealed theology. This incompleteness, however, is only apparent. It is true that we do not know precisely what Hegel will do with this or that particular doctrine of revealed theology. But we do know how he will handle every positivity, for we have seen his theory on this question at work. The three classical proofs are, before Hegel purifies them, just as positive, just as historically particular, as revealed doctrine. The ontological proof belongs to Anselm and Spinoza as much as justification by faith alone belongs to Paul and Luther. And just as Hegel purifies natural theology by reinterpreting it in the light of his own ontological logic, so he will free the essential truth of revealed theology from distortions due to the understanding. In the light of the discovery that for Hegel the cosmological argument ends in Spinozism, while the ontological argument, which Spinoza stressed, is just what leads beyond him, we should be prepared for some surprises in Hegel's purification of the various Christian doctrines. But for his general theory of religious knowledge we need go no farther.[69]

12 HEGEL, PANNENBERG, AND HERMENEUTICS

The theological sound and fury of the present century signify nothing more clearly than that theologically speaking we are still living in the nineteenth century. That century had received from the Enlightenment the task of relating the treasures of the sacred to a secular world which had attained its majority. There is little of interest in its theology which cannot be told in terms of its hermeneutics, which came increasingly to be simply the epistemic version of the sacred-secular tension. So the present tendency for hermeneutics to become *the* theological issue, even to the extent of subsuming theology under hermeneutics as one of its subdivisions, probably expresses an increasing sense of instability in the foundations on which theology has tried to build.

In spite of the renewed interest in Hegel which was well under way both in Europe and America long before the bi-centennial celebration of 1970, his contribution to the discussion of hermeneutics is largely overlooked. Perhaps the main reason for this is that he did not use the word 'hermeneutics' as Schleiermacher and others have done. This essay presents a brief description of Hegel's hermeneutical theory and practice and a comparison of this with the work of Wolfhart Pannenberg. Although he admires Hegel and confesses a deep indebtedness to him, Pannenberg may well be the most articulate anti-Hegelian since Kierkegaard.

The Problem of Interpreting the Jesus Event

In his attempt to transcend the Enlightenment by correcting it (and thus preserving rather than destroying it) Hegel exchanged its portrayal of philosophy and religion as mortal enemies for one in which philosophy's relation to religion was that of correcting (and thus preserving rather than destroying). His ever-recurring formula for this particular example of dialectic as determinate negation is the

207

familiar assertion that philosophy provides the true form, *Begriff*, for the true content which religion already possesses in a defective form, *Vorstellung*. His attempt to make good this claim (and his larger program of reuniting the sacred and the secular is entirely dependent upon it) is the form in which he takes up the hermeneutical problem which Lessing formulated definitely for modern and contemporary theology when he said:

> Accidental truths of history can never become the proof of necessary truths of reason. . . . If on historical grounds I have no objection to the statement that Christ raised to life a dead man; must I therefore accept it as true that God has a Son who is of the same essence as himself? What is the connection between my inability to raise some significant objection to the evidence of the former and my obligation to believe something against which my reason rebels?
>
> If on historical grounds I have no objection to the statement that this Christ himself rose from the dead, must I therefore accept it as true that this risen Christ was the Son of God? . . . But to jump with that historical truth to a quite different class of truths, and to demand of me that I should form all my metaphysical and moral ideas accordingly; to expect me to alter all my fundamental ideas of the nature of the Godhead because I cannot set any credible testimony against the resurrection of Christ: if that is not a μεταβασις εις αλλο γενος, then I do not know what Aristotle meant by this phrase. . . . That, then, is the ugly broad ditch which I cannot get across, however often and however earnestly I have tried to make the leap. If anyone can help me over it, let him do it, I beg him, I adjure him. He will deserve a divine reward from me.[1]

It is customary to think of Lessing's ditch in connection with apologetics rather than hermeneutics, but the two are not always separated. The question What is evidence for what? and the question What is a sign of what? can be distinguished as the questions of truth (apologetics) and meaning (hermeneutics) respectively. But where the apologetic interest is primary, as in most post-Enlightenment theology, the task of hermeneutics can easily become that of justifying an interpretation which meets certain apologetic requirements. The contemporary understanding of hermeneutics as concerning the entire epistemology of historical

understanding and not merely rules of exegesis usually means that
the question What did the author intend to say? gets taken up in
the broader question What does it mean or matter to me? The question of interpretation becomes the question of truth.[2]

In this context the question of theological method is simultaneously an apologetical and an hermeneutical question. One can
easily see this by asking whether, e.g., Bultmann's program of demythologizing and Tillich's method of correlation are answers to the
apologetic or hermeneutical question. In a similar fashion Pannenberg's history of traditions method and Hegel's appeal to the *Begriff*
(see below) tend to merge the two questions. This merger takes
place in Lessing's dicta as well, making it possible to view them
from the viewpoint of hermeneutics. After all, he is posing the question of how to interpret the Jesus event.

His posing of the question helps us to see the twofold sense in
which "history and hermeneutics" is an appropriate way of posing
the problem. The broad sense in which hermeneutics has become
central to contemporary theology involves the interpretation of
events as well as texts, and this sense is already focal in Lessing.[3]
He is not asking how to exegete the gospels in order to understand
how early Christians understood this or that. He is asking how he
(and we) are to understand the historical event which was Jesus of
Nazareth. This question of how reason should relate to the "positive" or historically particular elements of religion was the unsolved
puzzle which led the Enlightenment to see nothing but Lessing's
ditch between philosophy and positive religion. It expresses the
most obvious sense in which hermeneutics is a problem about
history.

But there is not only the question of how reason is to relate to
historical events. There is the problem of reason's own historicity.
When Lessing refers to "necessary truths of reason" he is not referring to the ability to think abstractly or to the formal principles of
deductive logic, but to a substantive metaphysic, more or less
Spinozistic. When he says that the trinitarian concept of God is one
"against which my reason rebels" we can read "against which my
Spinozism rebels." His "fundamental ideas of the nature of the God-
head" are impervious to modification mediated through historical
events. The hermeneutical problem is essentially solved for Lessing
by the fact that an a priori ontology, which includes a specific view
of God, tells him in advance what may and may not be the significance of the historical event in question. He knows a priori that
whatever it was that happened, it was not an incarnation. Reason is

complete in itself and needs nothing from history. Thus the ditch
between history and reason (history and dogma, history and
kerygma) is deepened.

But it is precisely this negative relation between reason and
history which raises the question of reason's own historicity. Lessing can be sure a priori that an incarnation has not taken place only
because Spinozism[4] has for him the status of "necessary truths of
reason." But after Kant and Hegel, after Marx and Kierkegaard, after Nietzsche and Freud, it is not as easy as it was for Lessing to
identify any world-view with eternal truth. When the historically
particular is relegated to the Platonic cave in the name of philosophical Ideas, history wreaks its vengeance by disclosing the Ideas'
historical particularity. In so far as hermeneutics involves this
problem of the historically conditioned character of the preunderstanding brought with him by the interpreter, history and hermeneutics are linked in a second way.

In seeking to separate the event (Jesus) from the mistaken interpretation given to it by religion (Incarnation) Lessing expresses
the hostility of Enlightenment philosophy to religion. Since Hegel,
however, seeks reconciliation, he does not treat the idea of the Incarnation as mere superstition and mythology to be set aside.
Rather he sees it not only as an idea pervading every religion and
the "finest feature of the Christian religion," but also as "that speculative central point," i.e., a fundamental philosophical truth. The
only problem is to understand it properly, to free its essential truth
from the defective form in which religion articulates it.[5] Hegel accomplishes this purification in the chapter on "Revealed Religion"
in the *Phenomenology.*

The unmentioned text for Hegel's exposition is Galatians 4:4,
"When the fulness of time was come, God sent forth his son." The
world-historical religious situation was the manifest failure of oriental (including near eastern) and Greek religion. The former's exaggerated sense of the divine transcendence meant that God was
never present, that religion was the perpetual yearning for an absent God. Greek religion, on the other hand, had so humanized the
gods that its original enjoyment of the divine presence had been lost
in the secularism of the classical Enlightenment which came to expression in comedy, Stoicism, scepticism, and Roman legalism.

As it finally became clear that classical humanism could not
reconcile the sacred with the secular, i.e., when the fulness of time
was come, the discredited alternatives form "an expectant and
eager throng round the birthplace of spirit as it becomes self-consciousness," i.e., as Christ is born and Christianity enters the

world as Absolute Religion. "This incarnation of the Divine Being, its having essentially and directly the shape of self-consciousness, is the simple content of Absolute Religion." Because there is no gulf between divine and human, since "the divine nature is the same as the human, and it is this unity which is intuited [in the Incarnation]," God is finally present. "That the Supreme Being is seen, heard, etc., as an existent self-consciousness—this is, in very truth, the culmination and consummation of its *Begriff*."[6]

Thus there is a twofold sense in which the Incarnation is not merely the heart of Christianity but also the key to speculative thought. It solves for the Philosophy of History the problem of the world-historical religious dilemma posed by a dualistic relation of sacred and secular; and it provides for Logic the materials for concretely realizing its fundamental *Begriff*, the concept of God. The Incarnation is the solution to the problem of "God and Secularity." But what this means more specifically depends on what is meant in affirming the unity of divine and human natures and thus the presence of God. If we are to get beyond the question of how the early Christians understood the Jesus event to the question of how we are to understand it, the question of interpreting their interpretation (Incarnation) is unavoidable.

The idea of the Incarnation is the content of Absolute Religion. But "in order that the true content may also obtain its true form for consciousness, the latter must necessarily pass to a higher plane of mental development where its intuition of the Absolute Substance is raised to the level of the *Begriff*." A close look reveals that the entire discussion is governed by a constant appeal to the *Begriff* as an omnipresent point of reference. It supplies the necessary corrective to the imperfect form (*Vorstellung*) in which religion expresses the truth.

What then is the difference between the two ways of understanding the Incarnation? Simply that religion sees as mere historical event what philosophy sees as necessity. Before we conclude that this is just Lessing all over again we must ask what Hegel means by the necessity of the *Begriff* as opposed to mere event. His answer is unambiguous, and it reflects the Kantian fusion of necessity with universality. To view the Incarnation as an event is to view the union of divine and human natures as a particular truth, the "inconceivable event" occurring uniquely in Jesus of Nazareth. To view it via the rational necessity of the *Begriff* is to see it as a universal truth affirming the divinity of human nature as such.[7]

Two conclusions may be drawn at this point. First, the relation between form and content turns out not to be as loose as Hegel's formula suggests. He complains that "since for the ordinary consciousness the truth is bound up with that form [*Vorstellung*], it imagines that if the form be altered it will lose the content and the essential reality, and it interprets that transformation as destruction."[8] But it is Hegel's own "transformation" which confirms the suspicions of ordinary consciousness. Religion says that in Jesus of Nazareth alone we find the union of the divine and human natures (and thus the presence of God), whereas philosophy says that we find this union in mankind generically or collectively. This is a difference of substance. To say that the Christian religion is Absolute Religion because it has the true content (the union of human and divine) but in a defective form (since it mislocates this union) is like calling Hitler the Absolute Moralist (because he proclaims the struggle between good and evil) who sees the truth in an imperfect form (since he mislocates this struggle by identifying it with the conflict between Aryans and Jews). Hegel's practice makes the relation between content and form look like that between an artist's materials and his creative treatment of them. But then Hegel is a Christian philosopher in the same sense that Pasternak is a Bolshevik novelist.

The second conclusion is implicit in the first. Hegel's interpretation of the Incarnation is no less radical a rejection of what is usually indicated by the concept than is Lessing's outright rejection. Hegel is perfectly candid about adhering to his *Begriff* rather than to the understanding of Jesus and his apostles. What he rejects as "mere" historical event and opposes to his *Begriff* is not a positivistic "bare" fact without meaning, but the event as understood by Jesus and the primitive community. "What this self-revealing Spirit [God] is in and for itself, is therefore not brought out by the rich content of its life being, so to say, untwined and reduced to its original and primitive strands, to the ideas, for instance, presented before the minds of the first imperfect religious community, or even to what the actual human being [Jesus] has spoken. This reversion to the primitive is based on the instinct to get at the *Begriff;* but it confuses the origin, in the sense of the immediate existence of the first historical appearance, with the simplicity of the *Begriff*." In so doing this instinct "degrades the content" into "an heirloom handed down by tradition."[9]

The *Begriff-Vorstellung* schema now appears to be a rerun of Lessing's distinction between necessary truths of reason and accidental truths of history, in so far as the latter's interpretation is determined by the former in each case, creating a master-slave relation between philosophy and religion. No doubt the reason Kierkegaard admired Lessing and despised Hegel is that Lessing acknowledged this ("my reason rebels") while Hegel purports to be giving Christian truth in its most perfect form. To pursue the parallel, however, we must ask about the *Begriff*. What serves for Hegel as Spinozism did for Lessing? The answer is simple. Hegel refers to his Logic. Like Spinozism it is a full-blown ontology which includes a definite concept of God. This ontology provides the material principles for interpreting the Jesus event. Like Lessing, Hegel comes to the New Testament history and kerygma with an ontology which already contains what they will be able to say. It is not dependent on them, but is rather the criterion of their meaning and truth. Hegel's complaint that religion holds fast to mere event evokes the counter question whether his philosophy hasn't grasped mere idea; whether, as Baur suggested from within the Hegelian framework, Hegel is a neo-Gnostic, or as we might put it, whether Hegel has only a myth.

Hegel's Hermeneutical Theory

The failure of Hegel to get beyond Lessing in more than intention is even clearer in the *Lectures on the Philosophy of Religion* where he not only interprets the Christian ideas, but systematically reflects on the hermeneutical issues involved. To begin with he sets off his procedure from those who want their theology to be based simply on the Bible and who thereby identify theology with exegesis. For Hegel such a theology does not present the content of the Scriptures but only an historical report of how people long ago thought. The gulf between biblical theology and systematic theology which has been so problematic in our own time is taken for granted by Hegel. This is because he holds that any theology which does more than quote the Bible, which seeks to think through and explain the biblical materials, does so under the direction of categories and premises which it brings with it to the text. It never occurs to him that the categories might be derived from the materials themselves or that they might be very formal ones which would not contribute substantively to the result.[10] So it is axiomatic for Hegel that the point of view of any postbiblical theology will be at variance with the biblical point of view. "The explanation of the Bible exhibits the substance or content of the Bible in the form or style of thought belonging to each particular age. The explanation which was first given was wholly different from that given now."[11]

    This historical relativism is inescapable. The only check on it which Hegel envisages is that of self-consciousness, i.e., philosophical critique of one's categories. Kant had seen the importance of this task and had begun it, if only in a limited and negative manner. Hegel's own Logic carried out the task in a comprehensive and constructive way. At this point his critique of orthodoxy turns into a critique of Enlightenment. The latter knows that theology is not identical with exegesis, but the presuppositions it brings with it to theology are the categories of finitude without the benefit of a genuine philosophical critique such as the Logic provides. Thus its much vaunted theology of reason is in fact only a theology of understanding. In Hegel's vocabulary this is a way of saying that like the religious belief which it criticizes, the Enlightenment holds whatever truth it may rightly lay claim to in a form which distorts it. Hegel is thus sharply critical of its subordination of the biblical materials to its a priori assumptions, but not because it thereby fails to take the biblical materials in their own terms. The reason is rather that these assumptions are those of the uncritical understanding. It is this arbitrariness of the assumptions which Hegel criticizes; it is their difference from Hegelian presuppositions rather than their difference from biblical presuppositions which bothers him.[12]

The point at which the consequences of the Enlightenment's uncritical employment of the categories of finitude are most conspicuous is its concept of God. "The absolute object [is] reduced to complete poverty. . . . It has, in conceiving God as the Supreme Being, made Him hollow, empty, and poor."[13] This question of the preunderstanding of the nature of God is for Hegel as for Lessing the heart of the hermeneutical issue. This comes to fullest clarity in Hegel's treatment of the witness of the Spirit.

For the reformers the witness of the Spirit was the special divine assistance (necessary because of the noetic effects of sin) whereby the Scriptures were recognized as divinely authoritative and properly understood. Hegel invokes this concept while restating Lessing's argument about the leap and the ditch. But for him, in direct opposition to the reformers, the witness of the Spirit is identical with: reason, thought, philosophy (sometimes meaning the Logic, sometimes his entire system), the Idea, the eternal and indwelling *Begriff*, the Platonic view that the truth is within man and knowledge is recollection, man's inner nature, and finally, the idea that human reason is the divine in man, the Spirit of God at work in him.

The verification of religious truth is by this witness of the Spirit and not by historical arguments concerning miracles for the same two reasons Lessing had given. Historical arguments involve a measure of uncertainty whereas faith requires certainty. But over and above this (and this is the link with the hermeneutical issue) is the question whether the historical has any relevance to the spiritual content of religious truth. Hegel sides with the Enlightenment against orthodoxy on the question of the supernatural because the latter "is faith in a content which is not divine, which is not the witness of God to Himself as Spirit in the Spirit. . . . The content of religion is the eternal nature of God, not accidental and external things of this [historical] kind."[14] Like Lessing, Hegel knows in advance and needs but to recollect what the nature of God is. Unlike Lessing, Hegel has a doctrine of the Trinity, but it quite independent of any historical knowledge about Jesus of Nazareth, his life and destiny.

What then is the preunderstanding of God which Hegel brings with him to the biblical materials as the principle of their meaning and truth? Hegel's statement in the preceding paragraph is sandwiched between two of Hegel's most striking formulations of his view of God's nature:

1) "The eye with which God sees me is the eye with which I see Him; my eye and His eye are one. . . . If God were not, I would not be; if I were not, then He would not be." 2) "We do right to speak to a child of God its Creator, and in this way the child forms an idea of God as of some Higher Being. This is grasped by consciousness in early years, but only in a limited manner, and the foundation thus laid is then further extended and broadened. The one Spirit is in fact the substantial foundation. This is the spirit of a people as it takes a definite shape in the individual periods of the history of the world. It is the national spirit. This constitutes the substantial foundation in the individual; each person is born in his own nation and belongs to the spirit of that people. This spirit . . . is the absolute foundation of faith. It is the standard which determines what is to be regarded as truth. This substantial element exists in this way independently of the individuals; it is their power in reference to them as units, and is in this relation to them their absolute authority."[15] These are the kinds of things Hegel has in mind when he speaks of the unity of the divine and human natures.

Just as Hegel's solution of the problem of the secular depends on the ultimacy of modern bourgeois Protestant culture,[16] so his solution of the closely related hermeneutical problem depends on the finality of that culture's expression in his ontology. This is for him the point at which the question of reason's encounter with the historical becomes the question of reason's own historicity. Should the Hegelian ontology turn out to be not Absolute Knowledge but only the finest and truest expression of the spirit of his age, which is by no means absolute, then Hegelian theology would consist in imposing on the biblical materials an interpretation which is not only evidently and admittedly at variance with their own self-understanding but also devoid of any independent claim to ultimacy. Theology becomes the art of using the biblical materials to express the spirit of the times.

Pannenberg's Alternative

Like Hegel, Pannenberg operates in the framework of an eschatologically oriented ontology. For both of them an ontology of reality as history is the foundation for a theology of revelation as history. What these slogans mean precisely remains to be specified, but this much at least is agreed upon. The deliberate choice of 'as' in the slogan 'revelation as history' means that the full self-disclosure of God (though not necessarily his being) coincides with history as a whole. God is only fully revealed and known at the culmination of the historical process. But while Pannenberg finds Hegel on the right track in seeking to develop these concepts, he finds him enmeshed in serious problems.

In the first place, there is the problem of doing justice to the uniqueness and finality of the revelation of God in Jesus, and thus, of Christianity itself. "If it is only in its totality that history is the revelation of God, how can a specific event within it, such as the fate of Jesus, have absolute meaning as revelation?" Or again, "if history is to be the totality of revelation, then it appears there is further progress that must be made beyond Jesus—about God's becoming manifest. . . . [Thus] even until today, the belief in the unsurpassability of Christianity appears to stand in tension to the universal historical viewpoint."[17] Pannenberg notes that from opposite sides of the fence both Strauss and Kierkegaard pressed this point against Hegel.

Hegel's own attempt to resolve this difficulty involved claiming for himself a standpoint at the end of history. This infringed upon both his finitude as a knower and the contingency and openness of the future. But Pannenberg does now allow this to drive him from the universal historical viewpoint. "We must rather ask how a conception of universal history is possible today, a conception which preserves, contrary to Hegel's view, the finitude of human experience and with it the openness of the future, as well as the right and validity of the particular. The task thus formulated may seem comparable to squaring the circle, because the totality of history could only be considered from the perspective of its conclusion, so that there would then be no more need to speak of a further future or of the finitude of human experience."[18]

The other problem is, if anything, more fundamental. Pannenberg is haunted by the ghost of Feuerbach; and he sees the positivistic or neo-Kantian dichotomy between fact and meaning (*historie* and *geschichte,* history and kerygma, history and faith) which has determined so much of post-Kantian theology as playing right into his hands. If the meaning is not there in the events to be discovered, but rather is brought to the bare events by faith, so that only for faith can they be said to have this or that meaning,[19] then the question of content is delivered over to the individual's subjectivity and its arbitrariness. God is indeed created in the image of man. If there is to be some systematic character to the theological content, this will have to be provided by some extrabiblical philosophical framework through which the biblical materials are filtered and which, to change the metaphor, provides the theological artist with the model for his creation of God.

Hegel is as sharply critical as Pannenberg of the split between fact and meaning, of the union of a positivist theory of knowledge with a subjectivist theory of value and meaning.[20] He too sees in this union a threat to the objectivity of religious knowledge, and often foresees Feuerbach most pointedly. But since for Hegelian theology the true meaning of the Jesus event has to be brought to it by an ontology which is not derived from it, has he really avoided practicing what in theory he condemns? This could be maintained only if his claim to independent finality for his ontology could be sustained, thus freeing it from the charge of arbitrariness and subjectivism which he directs against others. The two most popular contemporary defenses of these procedures are not available to Hegel.

The first of these is that the philosophical framework in question is itself "deeply immersed in" or "heavily indebted to" the Christian tradition. But even where this means more than that they were developed in the postclassical "Christian" west, in so far as they are not derived from the biblical events and the biblical witness to these events but stand as the norm of their meaning and truth, the relation remains external. It may be, for example, that Hegelian ontology has a deeper affinity with the biblical conceptions of grace and providence than the Kantian, and that in turn, Kant has a more nearly Christian concept of sin and of God. But both Kant and Hegel are quite candid about the discrepancy between what the biblical theologian or exegete comes up with and what they will affirm. The appeal is to an extrabiblical norm, and neither the persuasive definition of this norm as "Reason" nor the fact of its having been influenced by the Christian tradition can blunt the Feuerbachian charge that God is being created in the image of man.

A second response, associated particularly with Bultmann and Tillich, is that the preunderstanding which serves as hermeneutical guide does not purport to have theological answers but only guides the framing of theological questions. It is not clear that this distinction between questions and answers is very significant in any case, for if an extrabiblical framework of thought is given veto power over what questions the biblical materials may answer (for us), its control over the content is not exactly minimal. But Hegel cannot take this route either, for it presupposes a Kantian conception of reason's finitude which he seeks to overcome.[21]

In spite of these problems which Hegel has, however, Pannenberg is unwilling to abandon his basic universal historical framework. "The task of a philosophy or theology of world history dare not be sacrificed because of the failure of the Hegelian solution. . . . The Hegelian conception of history is not the only possible one, because the end of history can be understood as something which is itself only *provisionally* known. . . . Precisely this understanding of history . . . is the understanding which is presently to be gleaned from the history of Jesus in its relationship to the Israelite-Jewish tradition. Hegel was not able to see that because the eschatological character of the message of Jesus was beyond him as it was beyond the New Testament interpreters of his time."[22] But where any other basis for understanding Jesus has been sought than this "apocalyptic horizon of expectation . . . Jesus again and again has become merely the example of a Gnostic or a philosophical idea whose truth is ultimately independent of the history of Jesus. The basis of the knowledge of Jesus' significance remains bound to the original apocalyptic horizon of Jesus' history, which at the same time has also been modified by this history. If this horizon is eliminated, the basis of faith is lost; then Christology becomes mythology."[23]

These references to the apocalyptic understanding of history contain *in nuce* Pannenberg's efforts to accomplish the two tasks which he feels Hegel left undone (with disastrous effects): preserving the uniqueness and finality of the Jesus event, and avoiding the Feuerbachian challenge to objectivity. Within the apocalyptic horizon to which Pannenberg appeals a most prominent expectation was of the resurrection of the dead at the culmination of history. The resurrection of Jesus then makes it possible to understand the entire Jesus event at the "prehappening" of the end of history. " . . . in the fate of Jesus Christ the end is not only seen ahead of time, but is experienced by means of a foretaste. . . . And, only in the sense that the perfection of history has already been inaugurated in Jesus Christ is God finally and fully revealed in the fate of Jesus. With the resurrection of Jesus, the end of history has already occurred, although it does not strike us in this way."[24] This proleptic character of the Jesus event is the clue to preserving the uniqueness and finality of Jesus within the universal historical framework, to possessing that clue to the end of history which does not destroy the finitude of the knower nor the openness of the future to further developments. It is Pannenberg's answer to Strauss and Kierkegaard as well as his critique of Hegel.

The spectre of Feuerbach is not exorcised, however, simply by reference to the proleptic meaning of Jesus' life and fate. Pannenberg's response to this problem, which brings us to the heart of the hermeneutical issue, is derived only by asking how the proleptic interpretation of the Jesus event is possible, by enquiring into the hermeneutical preunderstanding at work in such a view.

Pannenberg argues that it is unnecessary to impose a foreign ontology on the biblical events. "The past reality of Jesus did not consist of brute facts in the positivist sense, to which arbitrary interpretations, one as good as another, could be added. Rather, meaning already belongs to the activity and fate of Jesus in the original context in the history of traditions within which it occurred, from the perspective of which all subsequent, explicit interpretations can be judged."[25] That context is defined by Israel's view of God and history, universalized in the apocalyptic tradition, and presupposed in that form by Jesus himself and the early Christian witnesses. As such it is an inherent ingredient both in the Jesus event itself and in the kerygma in which its meaning was first proclaimed.

The uniqueness of Israel's view of God lies "not simply in the fact that it holds fast to historical occurrences; nor in the fact that these occurrences are understood according to a particular scheme . . . but rather in the fact that history moves from God's promise to a goal . . . and that the covenant of God is consequently not an archetypal pretemporal event but a 'historical process'. . . . The presuppositions of the historical consciousness in Israel lie in its concept of God. The reality of god for Israel is not exhausted by his being the origin of the world, that is, of normal, ever self-repeating processes and events. Therefore this God can break into the course of his creation and initiate new events in it in an

unpredictable way. . . . Within the reality characterized by the constantly creative work of God, history arises because God makes
promises and fulfills these promises."[26] This God, whose being is his
rule, is the creator in such a way as to be simultaneously the "power
of the future."

Within the horizon of this biblical creationist-eschatological
ontology and its view of God, and only there, is it possible to see in
Jesus, precisely in his resurrection, the proleptic arrival of the end,
thereby doing justice to his uniqueness and finality. At the same
time it becomes possible to answer Feuerbach. The advantage of
interpreting the biblical materials within the framework of this
ontology is not that it makes the truth of traditional Christianity
automatic. There is always the possibility which Schweitzer discovered from within this very framework of seeing Jesus as an apocalyptic fanatic whose stirring and courageous, if insane, aspirations
were tragically broken on the wheel of historical fate, period. Nor is
it the advantage of this framework that it imposes a sharp either-or
between the original kerygma and Schweitzer's verdict, though it
surely does that. The advantage from the hermeneutical point of
view is that theology avoids the necessity of bringing a foreign ontology to the events, thereby abandoning interpretation to subjectivism and historical relativism. By interpreting the Jesus event in
its own terms, i.e., within the framework of the ontology within
which it occurred, which was presupposed by those who partici-
pated in it and who first announced it as an event of world-
historical significance, we get a result with which we may not feel
immediately at home and which poses an either-or which many
would prefer to avoid. But at least we can be confident that we have
not, as the price for feeling at home with Jesus, created him in our
own image as modern men come of age; and we can be assured that
we have not avoided a distasteful either-or by ruling out both of its
possibilities a priori. This, I believe, is why Pannenberg not only articulates the biblical ontology which guides his interpretation, but
also so frequently stresses that it is biblical.[27]

Pannenberg can claim that his procedure bridges the gap between the events in question and ourselves without denying it by
dissolving the past as such into some contemporary ideology. He
can claim that he takes more seriously than his contemporaries
the attempt to let the materials challenge us and make a claim
upon us, since he lets the materials themselves decide what questions it is they are answering, thereby posing the question whether
we are even asking the right questions. This means that "theology
should 'take every thought captive to obey Christ,' as the apostle de-

scribed his endeavor," and that "it is not sufficient to accommodate Christian tradition to current opinions of the time." It does not mean that we can bridge the gap by pretending we live in the first century, again denying the reality of the past as past. "Nor is it possible to return our present intellectual world to the level of the first Christian century. But perhaps Christian tradition can contribute again to a *further development* of modern thought. . . . Thus the present situation may be related to that of early Christianity in terms of that horizon which alone connects both without blurring their differences, namely the horizon of the *historical process.* . . . [This is possible] if this history can again be regarded as the work of the biblical God."[28]

This further development of modern thought under the concept of the biblical God means that for Pannenberg, in direct opposition to Hegel, modern thought is to be reinterpreted (corrected) by biblical thought and not the other way around. Kerygma (with its historical foundation) precedes ontology, whereas for Hegel ontology is prior and serves to separate the kerygmatic kernel from its husk.[29]

If we turn to the larger issue of which the hermeneutical debate is the epistemic dimension, we find that Pannenberg's hermeneutical principles have a direct bearing on the question of the sacred and the secular. He knows of that city which has so transcended the dichotomy between the two that it is called the city of God although it has no temple. For him it is "that perfect society of men which is to be realized in history by God himself."[30] Because he has not abandoned the biblical concept of God but has grounded his eschatology in it, he is able to avoid a dilemma whose horns are particularly uncomfortable. He is able to talk meaningfully about the "already" of the Kingdom of God without in any way committing himself to the ultimacy of his age or its systems. And he can speak of the "not yet" without engendering the despair which comes from equating it with "never." In short, he can appreciate all present approximations to the Kingdom of God without absolutizing the present, and he can acknowledge all deviations from the Kingdom of God without despairing over the future.

The ability to do this while at the same time speaking so cogently to the hermeneutical problems inherent in Hegel's attempt to do theology in a universal historical context represents no mean theological achievement. But if Pannenberg has been able to see more clearly into the biblical materials than Hegel, it is at least partly due to his ability to profit from both Hegel's insights and his failures.[31]

13   Hegel, Tillich, and the Secular

The times are out of joint. Technologically we are living in the twenty-first century, while in many respects we are still living in the nineteenth century intellectually. It may thus be the case that the renewed interest in Hegel is less a fad for bored intellectuals than the discovery of his contemporaneity. He is timely not because he has answers to our new problems but because he poses the old unanswered questions so forcefully and imaginatively. This is most often seen, with the help of Marxist studies, in relation to political questions. But it is no less the case in theology. No doubt the most encompassing and most problematic horizon in which theological questions are posed today is the one designated "God and Secularity." But of course this was already true of the Enlightenment, and it should come as no surprise that the issues singled out by this phrase are absolutely central, not just to Hegel's philosophy of religion, but to his philosophy as a whole. My purpose here is to describe Hegel's treatment of this problem, compare it with Tillich's contemporary encounter with the same issues, and examine briefly the dilemma on whose horns they seem to be impaled.

The Tragedy of Modern Dualism

Hegel's secondary education has been described as classical in substance and enlightened in form.[1] What the fascinating documents known as his Early Theological Writings record is the process in which he came to sense an irreconcilable tension between that form and content, between his beloved Rousseau and his beloved Sophocles. His early critique of Christianity as a positive religion, the corruption of the religion of Jesus who taught that man's worth lies entirely in his morality and that morality is grounded in self-legislating reason, shows only that he has read his Lessing, Rousseau, and Kant.

223

But this stance is soon replaced by another which judges the Enlightenment as harshly as Christianity, this time by the standard of Greek cultural beauty. Whereas the "early" young Hegel insists that religious liberty is a civil right and, like a good *Aufklärer*, calls for the total separation of church from secular state, the "late" young Hegel concludes his analysis of the spirit of Christianity bemoaning the fact that "between these extremes which occur within the opposition between God and the world, between divine and life, the Christian church as oscillated to and fro, but it is contrary to its essential character to find peace in a nonpersonal living beauty. And it is its fate that church and state, worship and life, piety and virtue, spiritual and worldly action, can never dissolve into one."[2]

This statement formulates *the* philosophical problem which occupies Hegel from the time he wrote it, around 1800, until his death in 1831. Conquering this fate of Christianity represents *the* motive of his entire philosophical project, including even the Logic. It will pay us to examine the statement carefully.

The first thing to notice is that Hegel interprets the split between sacred and secular in terms of tragedy, as his use of the term fate suggests. And he interprets tragedy in line with the famous statement of Anaximander: "It is necessary that things should pass away into that from which they are born. For things must pay one another the penalty and compensation for their injustice according to the ordinance of time." The social whole is a totality which essentially is the equilibrium of different powers, elements, or spheres. For example, the family and the state, while different, are internally related; the family as the foundation of the state, and the state as the fruition of the family. But an actual society is not a pure essence. (Hegel is not always the essentialist Tillich finds him to be). It is a living substance in which action takes place. As such it falls out of equilibrium through the one-sided affirmation of one sphere against another, and the equally one-sided reaction of the latter, as violation leads to revenge. Thus in Hegel's favorite tragedy, the *Antigone* of Sophocles, the clash between Antigone and Creon is not between post-Socratic individuals, but between the family and the state. Since the rights of both are genuine, but neither is absolute, both combatants are ultimately destroyed and the absolute right, the subjection of both partial rights to equilibrium in the whole, is restored by that justice which is fate.[3]

Following Sophocles, Hegel sees this conflict between family rights and state rights as a conflict between a divine law and a human law. Puzzling as this may seem to us, it at least helps us to see how easy it is for Hegel to apply the categories of tragedy to the later conflict between belief (supernatural Christianity) and enlightened insight (the Enlightenment's critique of belief—*Ecrasez l'infame*). Belief retains the divine content, but without insight, that is, in a form incompatible with the demands of reason's autonomy. Insight upholds this autonomy, but in such a negative and critical way that it loses all content.[4]

The sacred and the secular have taken residence in radically one-sided agents which confront one another as divine right in conflict with human right. As in *Antigone* the representative of the sacred is the first to fall, and belief loses its content under the relentless criticism of insight. But now that Creon has dispatched Antigone, the question is whether Creon can survive. "It will yet be seen whether Enlightenment can continue in its state of satisfaction." Hegel's analysis of eighteenth-century secularism follows the tragic script to the letter. Faced with the task of some positive achievement, now that the antagonist is gone, enlightened insight reveals itself to be "merely the rage and fury of destruction." In the French Revolution, its theory of "Absolute Freedom" transforms reality into "Terror." Hegel sees history confirming his argument that one-sided secularism can only destroy, and, when left to itself, destroys itself.[5]

Hegel's position is clear. Sacred and secular, like family and state, need each other. Both sign their death warrants when they seek to isolate themselves from the other, and only a tragic spectacle ensues when the problem of their relationship is solved by choosing up sides and slugging it out. But this does not get us very far. It only suggests that history is an endless cycle of violation and revenge in accordance with the cosmology of Anaximander. Is there no escape from the cycle of fate? Hegel's Sophoclean interpretation of the eighteenth century raises for his own century and ours the question of the *Oresteia*. Can Athene and the Eumenides ever live together in the same city? Can the one be honored without sacrilege to the other? Aeschylus can only hope. He concludes his trilogy by postulating a peaceful coexistence of the cults of the subterranean hearth goddesses and of Athene as the goddess of the civic domain. But he cannot show why this situation is not precisely that from which another Antigone will arise.

Can Hegel do better?

He knows that the Greek harmony in which "worship and life are not separated, . . . [and] the temporal life with all its needs— the immediate life—is itself worship" is not an absolute harmony. He knows that because of its immediate, unreflected, and natural character it is always in danger of breaking down, as with Antigone. "Over this sphere there hovers a sense of division which is not resolved, and thus through the gladness of that living unity there sounds an unresolved chord of mourning and pain. A fate, an unknown power, a coercive necessity, unknown but yet recognized, without reconciliation, to which consciousness submits only by negation of itself, broods over the heads of gods and men."[6]

Hegel also knows that the external coexistence espoused by Aeschylus and later by Thomas Aquinas is inherently unstable, that it represents an attempt to paper over a rupture which happy endings and clever formulas cannot mend.

But beyond the immediate and therefore transient harmony of Greece, and beyond the rupture which has prevailed from the time of its demise until Hegel's present, he sees a third possibility, a new harmony whose stability rests on its having overcome rather than bypassed the rupture. Because it will be a harmony of reconciliation rather than innocence it will reside in the Christian rather than the Greek community. To be sure, the church has the world standing over against it. But it represents the Kingdom of God, which is inherently universal and not only stands related to the secular world but is its truth. And since this truth is found neither in ascetic withdrawal nor a nature-grace hierarchy, it belongs to the Protestant and not to the Catholic church. Hegel's Protestant vision replaces chastity, poverty, and obedience with the divine mandates of the Reformation, family, labor, and government, or, as they appear in Hegel, family, civil society, and state.[7] The true reconciliation of sacred and secular occurs when the opposition "cancels itself in the collective ethical life [*Sittlichkeit*], and the principle of freedom has forced its way into secular life. And since secular life so constructed is itself in conformity with the concept, reason, truth, eternal truth, it is a freedom which has become concrete rational will. It is in the organization of the State that the Divine has passed into the sphere of reality. Reality is penetrated by the Divine, and the existence of the secular element is justified in and for itself, for its basis is the Divine Will, the law of right and freedom. The true reconciliation whereby the Divine realises itself in the region of reality is found in the ethical and legal life of the State. This is the true disciplining of the secular life, i.e., here the dichotomy between the holy and the moral is transcended."[8]

Hegel does not find this reconciliation actualized in the church and state of his day, and he recognized that for this reason his philosophical reconciliation is a "partial one without outward universality."[9] But one can inquire further into its theoretical foundation, the concepts on which it rests as an ideal.

The Theology of Hegel's Reconciliation

If we return to the statement of his fundamental problem, we find that Hegel's diagnosis is not limited to invoking the categories of tragedy. The second and decisive thing to notice is that the tragic dualism is consequent to a particular view of the relation between God and the world. Thus the theoretical solution to the problem of the secular hinges on a new concept of God. This is already clear in the later Early Theological Writings where the Jesus, in whose mouth the truth is put, is no longer the teacher of Kantian morality but the teacher of a new concept of God, according to which the incarnation is a general truth about the relation between man and God. Though both friends and foes misunderstood him, Jesus understood that faith presupposes man's divinity, since only a modification of God can know God. In order to avoid positing any difference between his own being and that of his followers, he declared himself against the idea of a personal God. Rather, he saw the divine as the beautiful life of human fellowship among those who live together in love. He was thus entirely opposed to the Jewish notion of the Kingdom of God, since this implies subordination to a higher power.[10]

These ideas are developed in the *Phenomenology*. There Hegel criticizes both belief and insight for their views of God. Belief views God as someone over against the believer, a supersensible world. This leads both to a negative attitude toward the actual world and to the projection of its rich contents onto a world beyond, leaving behind nothing but sorrow and the longing for an absent and faraway God. Insight accuses belief of anthropomorphism and superstition. But in place of the theism it criticizes it has only an abstract absolute, a Supreme Being which is a "great void," a "colorless empty being," and an "unknown and unknowable absolute without predicates." This deism is indistinguishable from materialistic atheism, and both lend assistance to a utilitarianism which so absolutizes usefulness that even men are subordinated to it, that is, they are used.

Thus the entire dispute between theism and atheism is exposed, on Hegel's view, as one between ideologies rendered obsolete by the historical developments culminating in the French Revolution and its Terror. Developing his earlier idea that the true divinity is found in a certain kind of human togetherness, he points to "a reciprocal recognition which is Absolute Spirit. . . . The reconciling affirmation, the 'yes' with which both egos desist from their existence in opposition, is the existence of the ego expanded into a duality. . . . It is God appearing in the midst of those who know themselves in the form of pure knowledge." Finally, the *Phenomenology* concludes with the reminder that "only 'The chalice of this realm of spirits / Foams forth to God His own Infinitude,' " that is, God's reality is not distinct from but is constituted by the realm of finite spirits.[11]

This is a permanent move on Hegel's part. It is found throughout his writings and is a prominent feature of what can be considered his last work, the *Lectures on the Proofs of the Existence of God,* given in 1829. In a reinterpretation which he says will be intelligible only to those who have carefully studied his *Logic,* he here argues that the cosmological proof belongs to the category of substance, not causality, and that it has Spinozism for its truth. To be sure, one must go beyond the philosophy of substance and learn to recognize the Absolute as living and as Spirit, but the Infinite is surely not less than Spinoza's Absolute Substance. Of course this sets aside the entire tradition of dispute about the proof which sees it as an either/or battleground between theism and atheism. Even when God is affirmed in this latter framework and "the finite is mediated through the Infinite, still the converse is not true, which is just the real point of interest."[12]

What Hegel is repudiating here is the ontological implication of the doctrine of creation in its theistic context, for which all created beings stand in an asymmetrical relation of dependence on the God who is not dependent on them. He sees this view of God's transcendence as leading to cultural "Manicheism." "Just as the finite and the Infinite are without relation to each other, so, too, the acts of spirit, its realization of its finitude and infinity, a realization of only the one or the other, have no relation to each other. Even if they happen to exist contemporaneously . . . they are merely mixed together. . . . If, accordingly, the manner in which spirit deals with the finite, and that in which it deals with the Infinite, are supposed to represent two different forms of activity, then . . . when spirit occupies itself with the finite, it would in turn do this in an absolute way, and be entirely confined to the finite as such. But we know that one can engage the finite in a true way "only in so far as the finite is not taken for itself, but is known . . . in its relation to the Infinite. . . . [The] religious element in the form of devotion, contrition of heart and spirit, and the giving of offerings, comes to be regarded as a matter apart with which we can occupy ourselves and then have done with; while the secular life, the sphere of finitude, exists alongside of it, and gives itself up to the pursuit of its own ends, and is left to its own interests without any influence being exercised upon it by the Infinite, the Eternal, and the True."[13]

The point is clear. The advantage of Spinozism over creationist theism, imperfect as the former may be, is that it provides a more adequate theoretical foundation for bridging the gulf between the sacred and the secular. By placing God and the world in a thoroughly reciprocal relation moving in the direction of identity, the possibility of a radical separation of sacred and secular is undermined. Hegel makes fully explicit for us the inner rationale of the remarkable Spinoza revival which coincided with the decline of the Enlightenment. Those who wanted to preserve the autonomy for which the Enlightenment had struggled, but only as something more substantial than the one-sided and militantly antiseptic secularism it had become, sought to restore the sacred dimension and turned to the "holy Spinoza" for guidance. Goethe, in poetry, Schleiermacher, in theology, and Hegel, in philosophy, represent the apogee of this meteoric phenomenon. In terms of comprehensiveness and perhaps of depth as well, Hegel must be judged to have carried out the project most impressively.

Tillich's Reiteration of the Hegelian Synthesis

The problem we have seen Hegel struggling with is a perennial one for theology, and we should not be too surprised to find that it was not put to rest by his achievement. In our own time it has achieved not only new attention but widespread popular interest. Theologians, if not entirely at home in such a limelight, have responded with a torrent of literature. Some have concluded that theology can make its peace with militant secularism only by joyfully accepting it as the good news and dispensing entirely with God. To others this seems less like overcoming the dichotomy than simply holding fast to one side, more oblivious than many nihilistic philosophers to the ambiguities of a totally secular world—a world in which mankind, come of age and exultant in the discovery that he is by nature free, discovers that everywhere he is in chains to forces within and systems without which dehumanize his existence. For these theologians as for Bonhoeffer, the problem of a religionless Christianity is the problem of how "to speak in a secular fashion of God," not how to have done with him. It is *God* who "gives us to know that we must live as men who manage our lives without God. The God who is with us is the God who forsakes us. . . . The God who lets us live in the world without the working hypothesis of God is the God before whom we are ever standing. Before God and with God we live without God."[14]

Of contemporary theologians who, like Hegel, have taken the problem of the secular as fundamentally a question about the nature of God, few, if any, have proceeded more carefully or systematically than Tillich. It is the thoroughness of his approach to the problem of God and secularity which merits for his work, rather than that of the recent popularizers, a comparison with Hegel. In referring to his "reiteration of the Hegelian synthesis" I only wish to highlight the striking similarities which exist, without suggesting that these exhaust the structure of Tillich's theology or even his relation to Hegel.

The *Systematic Theology* begins with an attack on the supernaturalism of Barthian and fundamentalist theology. Equally determined, if less spirited, is its sustained polemic against the secularism of positivism, historicism, and the dehumanizing domination of technical reason and controlling knowledge. In other words, Tillich, like Hegel, interprets his own situation as a confrontation between a one-sided belief (heteronomy) and a one-sided neoenlightenment (autonomy). In fact, each of the three volumes begins with some description of this situation as the definitive context of the system. Tillich sees the two sides in a perpetual and tragic cycle in which the one-sidedness of the one side generates a one-sided reaction from the other, which in turn provokes a renewal of the original. In one sense secularist autonomy always wins in a showdown with supernaturalist heteronomy, but the self-sufficient finitude of the former suffers from both a shallowness and an openness to the demonic which keeps it from surviving; and after its self-inflicted demise, the way is once again opened for the ontological and cultural dualism of a new heteronomy. The first one hundred pages of volume 3 reveal how intimate is Tillich's awareness of the ambiguities of a totally secular society.

This initial agreement with Hegel is matched by a second, for Tillich envisages another possibility which he calls theonomy. Because religion is essentially the substance or import of culture, and culture is the form of true religion, no essential conflict between them exists. They are not two eccentric spheres but two intersecting dimensions, each of which without the other is not true to itself. The harmonious, ideal relation between the two, for Tillich as for Hegel, preserves autonomy (since the recognition of its depth dimension in no way conflicts with it but only enriches it by providing its forms with unconditional import) while dispensing entirely with heteronomy.[15]

Third, and again like Hegel, Tillich is largely indifferent to the dispute between theism and atheism. Insofar as atheism or naturalism is antitheism, he agrees with its protest against what he considers an unacceptable (blasphemous, idolatrous) concept of God. Like Hegel, who liked to speak of the death of God, especially in the context of the problem of the secular, Tillich, whose sense of rhetorical restraint limits him to the formula "God is real but does not exist," sees the theologian as friendly to those critiques of Christianity, which are usually considered most devastating. On the other hand, while antitheism may be a good disinfectant, atheism is not very nutritious food, and, like Hegel, Tillich is critical of atheism for the one-dimensionality which stems from its failure to achieve a more adequate concept of the divine.

Finally, and still like Hegel, this attitude toward what others consider a crucial dispute stems from the possession of a view of God which is alleged to transcend the mutually dependent deficiencies of the classical alternatives. It is well known that for Tillich God is not a being or even the highest being but the ground of being or being itself. Preliminary answers to the question why this must be so are that as a being, even the highest, God would become just one more entity among the others, while at the same time becoming an object which we might engage in a detached way rather than as subject and the "object" of our ultimate concern. God is the "power of being in everything and above everything, the infinite power of being."[16] If he is not this power of being then he is subject to it as Zeus is to fate.

These replies do not seem immediately evident. One could respond that a being is just one more among others if it is a created being, but not if it is the creator; and that a creator is the source of the power of being in everything, but not that power itself, since his power is complete independent of that power which he brings into being out of nothing in the free act we call creation. This brings us to the heart of the matter. Tillich's case against God as a being, and thus his siding with antitheism against theism, make sense only in the context of his ontology. It is essentially a Kantian ontology (first Critique) derived transcendentally from experience, and thus an ontology of finitude. To be is to be finite; to exist is to experience the rupture of existence and essence. Relative to the categories of this ontology God would be finite even as the highest being.

Since the function of this ontology is to help us get beyond both theism and atheism, it is natural that it should replace the traditional theistic conception of creation with another. It is at this point that Hegel invokes Spinoza, whose *Ethics* begins with the dismantling of theistic creationism. Tillich's alternative, by contrast, is more nearly Platonic. Creation is the "participation" of the finite in being itself, the Platonic *parousia* of the essences in temporal existence, the actualizing of the divine life. It is not a free act, since it is identical with the divine life. Like Hegel's Spinozism this view emphasizes the divine immanence, and like Hegel, Tillich wishes to go beyond the pantheistic category of substance to envisage the divine as living spirit.[17]

It is clear that this ontology and its view of God are the theoretical foundations for Tillichean theonomy. In the absence of the creator of theism there can be no heteronomy, for the supernaturalism presupposed by heteronomy in turn regularly presupposes the God who creates *ex nihilo*. The correlation between God's original creative act and his continuing convenantal sovereignty over history as portrayed, for example, in Genesis and Isaiah, belongs to a different set of ontological assumptions. Tillich's God can be counted on not to interfere in human affairs. Just for that reason it is questionable what dimension of depth he can provide to preserve secular humanism from its own internal dialectic of self-destruction.

The Question Posed by Barth and Fackenheim

The purpose of introducing Tillich into the discussion is not to expound or criticize his thought as such. A more detailed analysis would be required to do justice to its nuances. But even this brief sketch brings to light a deep-seated congruity between his thought and Hegel's which is usually obscured by the fact that his overt references to Hegel are regularly negative. This discovery gives concrete contemporaneity to a question posed by both Karl Barth and the Jewish philospher, Emil Fackenheim, concerning the Hegelian project. For Barth the astonishing thing about Hegel is not his boldness. "The astonishing thing is that nineteenth-century man did not acknowledge that his concern in the realm of thought, his basic intellectual concern, had truly achieved ultimate recognition in Hegel's philosophy. It was astonishing that he broke out and made off in all directions, as if nothing had happened, and that he was not content with pondering Hegel's wisdom. . . . Why did Hegel not become for the Protestant world something similar to what Thomas

Aquinas was for Roman Catholicism? . . . If the eighteenth and nineteenth centuries formed a unity in such a way that the nineteenth century was the fulfillment of the eighteenth, then it was Hegel who represented this unity in philosophy as no other man did. . . . Is it not Hegel who exploited and made fruitful to the last detail Kant's great discovery of the transcendent nature of the human capacity for reason? . . . Is it not he who is above all the great systematizer and apologist for the concern of Romanticism? . . . Was not Hegel he who should come as the fulfiller of every promise, and *was it worth waiting for another after he had come?* . . . If all things do not deceive us it was precisely when it was utterly and completely ruled by Hegel that the new age best understood itself, and it was then at all events that it best knew what it wanted. . . . If it is a question of doing what the entire nineteenth century evidently wanted to do, then Hegel apparently did it as well as it could possibly be done."[18]

While it is not exactly true that the remainder of the nineteenth century proceeded "as if nothing happened," Hegel's project of reconciling sacred and secular through a speculative reinterpretation of the concept of God, which is at the heart and not at the periphery of his system, was abandoned before the ink on his last writings was dry. Its failure is conspicuous not only in that its ideal was not realized, or even increasingly approximated, but also in that it ceased even to be the guiding ideal of nineteenth-century thought and action. One sees the extent to which this is the case by thinking, for example, of Marxism politics or Ritschlian theology. "The century had denied its truest and most genuine son and since then it no longer had a good conscience or any true joyousness or any impetus."[19]

Fackenheim makes the same point. As the one who radicalized the Kantian imperative—"have courage to use your own reason"— by bringing it into touch with the existential matrix of thought, with history, and in particular with historical Christianity, Hegel is the consummation of his age. Thus "the Hegelian peace between Christian faith and philosophy is unsurpassable, and marks the end of an era: *if it fails, no similar effort can hope to succeed.*" But his pacification program has failed with such decisiveness that "were he alive today, so realistic a philosopher as Hegel would not be a Hegelian."[20]

How is this failure to be accounted for? Barth suggests that Hegel, in giving classical expression to nineteenth-century concerns, revealed their limited nature, which is to say that the Hegelian synthesis suppressed certain problems which rose up to wreak their revenge. Fackenheim says much the same thing when he explains the failure in terms of the way in which Hegelian philosophy presupposes the ultimacy of "the modern bourgeois Protestant world," which is taken as "in principle final and indestructible," as the seminal form of the Kingdom of God in which free modern rationality comes to concrete fruition.[21]

In the light of this analysis, including Barth's question, "Is it worth waiting for another after he has come?" and Fackenheim's answer, "If it fails, no similar effort can hope to succeed," how does it stand with those in our time whose Promethean defiance of history would resist the relapse into a dualistic world of theological positivism on one hand and philosophical positivism or scientism (and other equally one-sided secularisms) on the other? In particular, is not Tillich, who follows the Hegelian program's inner movement so closely, condemned by history to the status of epigone? Was he indeed born posthumously?

While Barth leaves the question standing by itself more or less rhetorically, Fackenheim, who poses it even more sharply, seeks to resist its implications. "Philosophic thought must move beyond the extremes of partisan commitments, and grope for what may be called a fragmented middle. This is not to suggest a revival of the Hegelian philosophy. But it is to suggest that philosophic thought, however rooted in existential commitments, craves a comprehensiveness which transcends them. To be sure, this craving can no longer expect, or even seek more than fragmentary satisfaction. Yet it is not doomed to total frustration, and it is unvanquishable."[22]

Though there is no reference to Tillich here, it is clear that these are the only lines along which a Tillichean type of project (and therewith any contemporary Hegelianism) could be defended against the questions posed above. Even the wording sounds like Tillich, for he too insists that the New Being and the Kingdom of God are experienced as transcending the estrangements of personal existence and the ambiguities of social life only "fragmentarily" and "by anticipation."[23] From this perspective Tillich seeks to set his program off from Hegel's. He sees the latter as the epitome of essentialist optimism, a philosophy which so concentrates on the essential and ideal dimensions that it overlooks the tragic discrepancies between existing actuality and essential ideality. Thus the acknowledgment of "existential commitments," or better, entanglements, and the claim to be seeking only a "fragmentary" realization of the ideal harmony represent a humility which purports to save the Tillichean project from the fate of Hegelian *hubris*.

The difference from Hegel is genuine. It is true that Hegel concludes his *Lectures on the Philosophy of Religion* with the admission that his own time is filled with such disruption, destruction, and discord as to shake one's assurance that the gates of hell will not prevail against the Kingdom of God. It is also true that he does not know how "the actual present-day world is to find its way out of this state of disruption." But he does not doubt that it will, and he does not abandon the confidence expressed in the *Phenomenology* that the new age is present, has already been born, and needs but to develop out of its infancy. It is as if a wiser and more experienced parent had discovered that the physical and psychological hurdles which a child must leap over en route to maturity are more formidable than the proud father had realized in the exultation of hearing "it's a boy."

But while this difference from Hegel is real, it is of doubtful advantage. Tillich is not wedded to the modern bourgeois Protestant world as the embryonic kingdom of God, and much of his finest work is a prophetic articulation of this freedom. But while he is not faced with the embarrassment of explaining how the modern world is even seminally the Kingdom of God, he faces an equal or greater embarrassment when asked when it will be actualized, when the "by anticipation" which accompanies the "fragmentarily" will be cashed in. His answer is never. The Kingdom of God, in which the harmony of sacred and secular is symbolized by the absence of a temple (Rev. 21:22) is never anything but fragmentary. In its fullness it is not only not now, but also not ever. Eschatology concerns not promise and fulfillment but time and eternity, that is, every present, but not the future. Tillich's theology is silent about the future, and he himself is pessimistic, expecting the extinction of the human race.

This does not mean that Tillich takes the Kingdom of God to be nothing but a myth, a regulative ideal, an eternal ought. No more than Hegel is he eager to lapse into the Kantian denial of God's grace as some mode of active power. He insists that the Kingdom of God is a power at work in reality and not just an abstract ideal. Why then can God never fully realize it? Apparently because Tillich's eschatology is governed by his Kantian ontology of finitude which knows no actuality which is not finite and estranged from its essence. His God in the final analysis, as the Platonic overtones of his doctrine of creation suggest, is a finite power like the Platonic demiurge, whose attempts to realize the good inevitably encounter an unsurpassable recalcitrance. It looks as if the attempt to escape the dualism of sacred and secular which Hegel calls cultural Manicheism has led Tillich into an ontological Manicheism.

This possibility leads in surprising directions. Ontological dualism has always involved flight from the world, such as the Neoplatonic and Gnostic withdrawal from the world of Roman imperialism. If, because of the (temporary) unreality of its reconciliation in the world, Hegel's "philosophy forms in this connection as sanctuary apart, and those who serve in it constitute an isolated order of priests, who must not mix with the world,"[24] is not Tillich's theonomy—heaven forbid!—even more oriented toward withdrawal?

The question can be pushed a bit further. If Hegel's time is on the verge of "infinite sorrow,"[25] is not Tillich's discovery that its condition is perpetual and inescapable the foundation of that despair over the actual which is the last step to Stoic renunciation? The same Tillich whose call to courage so inspired our imagination now robs us of all hope. But courage without hope is the essence of Stoicism. Tillich considers Stoicism to be the one serious alternative to Christianity in the modern world. It is possible he does not know the difference between them?

When is the Kingdom of God? Hegel says now. Tillich says never. Even when all the desired qualifications are added to each answer, both of them prove too embarrassing to be sustained. The one says of the essential structures of the modern world, "This is the best God can do." The other, while not wishing to say that, ends up saying, "I'm afraid He can't do any better." Both Hegel and Tillich are trying to express the meaning of the "already-but-not-yet" understanding of the Kingdom of God which is found in the New Testament, which is why the "now" and the "never" both have to be qualified. But they fail to do so and end up on the opposite horns of an awkward dilemma. Perhaps this dilemma springs from the common ground we have already observed them sharing. Perhaps their inability to make sense of the biblical concept of the Kingdom of God springs from their abandonment of the biblical concept of the God who is King.

This concept has been briefly intimated already. At its heart is an understanding of God's creative activity and thus his primordial relation to the world which makes it possible to understand his historical activity not merely as active presence in the historical process but as ultimate sovereignty over it. It is a concept which does not always express itself in apocalyptic form, but which can do so without difficulty, and which does so in Jesus' proclamation of the Kingdom. To say this is to recognize that the essence of apocalyptic thinking is not sensational imagery but a distinctive conception of divine intervention in the historical process.

To speak of intervention is to flirt with the specter of heteronomy. It was precisely to flee this that Hegel and Tillich wedded themselves to ontologies which precluded an apocalyptic understanding of the divine kingship. The theology which can lead us beyond their dilemma will be a theology of hope whose ontology is derived from the biblical concept of divine sovereignty which encompasses apocalyptic thinking.[26] It will be a theology more concerned to understand the biblical motifs of promise and fulfillment than to make its peace with the Enlightenment and its demand for autonomy.

This different stance of theology toward the Enlightenment will not be the simple denial of Kant's imperative definition of enlightenment—"have courage to use your own reason." Rather it will stem from having learned, perhaps from Tillich, that there is more than one dimension to courage, epistemically as well as existentially; that in addition to the courage to be as oneself, there is the courage to be as a part and the courage to accept acceptance. If the Kantian conception of enlightenment is one-dimensional in capturing only the first of these modes of courage, the theology of which I speak will seek to cultivate three-dimensional courage. The courage to use one's own reason will intersect with the courage to participate in a tradition (which includes apocalyptic thinking) over which one is not sovereign and with the courage to accept as a gift the revelation of "what no eye has seen, nor ear heard, nor the heart of man conceived."[27]

NOTES

Notes to Chapter One

1. PR, ¶29. For *sigla* used throughout the notes, see Part I of the bibliography. Also consult the bibliography for full data on works about Hegel, cited here only by author and title.

2. EL, ¶10; WL 1:55ff.; and *Differenzschrift*, GW 4:77ff.

3. "Hegel's Critique of Kant," *The Review of Metaphysics* 26 (March 1973): 441–45. Italics are Smith's.

4. Cf. WL 2:220/583 (The number after the / is the page number in SL). "Ich aber ist diese *erstlich* reine, sich auf sich beziehende Einheit, und dies nicht unmittelbar, sondern indem es von aller Bestimmtheit und Inhalt abstrahiert und in die Freiheit der schrankenlosen *Gleichheit mit sich selbst* zurückgeht."

5. It is helpful to recall Hegel's analysis of Skepticism and of the Terror in the PhG.

6. EL, ¶¶160 and 163, my italics. Cf. WL 2:219/582.

7. Hegel uses *bei sich sein* more or less interchangeably with *bei sich bleiben*, though it obviously hasn't quite the active sense of the latter. Present translations frequently render *bei sich* as "at home."

8. My italics.

9. Especially in view of Hegel's critique of Fichte in ¶6.

10. Cf. Hegel's stress on Rousseau's distinction between *volunté général* and *volunté de tous*, EL, ¶163Z, and his analysis of the We constituted in marriage by contrast with that of contract. See ch. 3 below.

11. These phrases occur, respectively, at EL, ¶160Z; ¶163Z; WL 2: 244–45/605; 2:242/603; 2:245/605; and 2:231/592. In EL, ¶163Z, Hegel writes, "Rather the Concept is the genuine first; and things are what they are through the action of the Concept, immanent in them, and revealing itself in them. In religious language we express this by saying that God created the world out of nothing. In other words, the world and finite things have issued from the fullness of the divine thoughts and the divine decrees."

12. WL 2:236/597; 2:242/602; EL, ¶161Z; and PR, ¶1Z.

13. Cf. R. D. Laing, *The Self and Others*, part 1.

14. EL, ¶¶157–59. Cf. WL 2:214–19/578–82.

15. Cf. WL 2:218/581: "Dieser, die aus der Wechselwirkung resultier-ende Totalität, ist die Einheit der *beiden Substanzen* der Wechselwirkung, so dass sie aber nunmehr der Freiheit angehören, indem sie nicht mehr ihre Identität als ein Blindes, das heisst *Innerliches* . . . "; and WL 2:224/586: "Das Leben oder die organische Natur ist diese Stufe der Natur, auf welcher der Begriff hervortritt; aber als blinder, sich selbst nicht fassender, d.h. nicht denkender Begriff."

16. Cf. the quotation with which this chapter concludes.

17. Cf. WL 2:246/606, where Hegel uses the same notion of *übergrei-fen* which Miller here translates as "embrace." Thus, "Das Allgemeine als der Begriff ist es selbst und sein Gegenteil, was wieder es selbst als seine gesetzte Bestimmtheit ist; es greift über dasselbe über und ist in ihm bei sich."

Chapter Two

1. Michael Novak, "Human Rights: No More Small Men," from *Smith-Kline Forum for a Healthy American Society* 3:6 (September 1981), an insert in the September 21, 1981 issue of *Time* magazine.

2. Henry Shue, *Basic Rights: Subsistence, Affluence, and U.S. For-eign Policy* (Princeton: Princeton University Press, 1980), 27 and 182 n. 18. Of course liberalism has a good deal to say about the economic rights of those who already have property. It is the rights of the poor and dispos-sessed about which it is largely silent.

3. This is true not only at the national level, but also at the corpo-rate. Neocolonialism is largely the story of multinational corporations in the Third World. Often their activity has been based upon direct ownership of land and other resources. But they are discovering, like the nation-state colonial powers before them, that their interests can be served and their power maintained by means that give at least the appearance of local con-trol. Agribusiness corporations, for example, have learned that through "contract farming" and "associate producer programs," in which nationals own land used for export cropping, they can retain the benefits while re-ducing the risks of owning land directly. See Frances Moore Lappé and Jo-seph Collins, *Food First: Beyond the Myth of Scarcity* (Boston: Houghton Mifflin, 1977), ch. 34.

4. See Michael Moffit, ed., *The Crises of the International Monetary System: From Breton Woods to Arusha* (Washington, D.C.: Institute for Policy Studies, 1981).

5. Shue, *Basic Rights,* 19.

6. *Basic Rights,* 20–29.

7. From among the enormous and rapidly growing literature on neocolonialism, I mention only *Persistent Poverty,* by George Beckford; *Unequal Development,* by Samir Amin; *Global Reach,* by Richard Barnet and Ronald Müller; and *The New Gnomes,* by Howard Wachtel.

8. This oft-quoted maxim is perhaps the central thesis of the preface of PS.

9. A reminder that references to PR are to paragraph, not page numbers.

10. This occurs especially in the introduction to PR. For a detailed analysis of paragraphs 5 through 7, see ch. 1 above.

11. I have taken this formulation of historical materialism from Engels's letter to Joseph Bloch. It can be found in *Marx and Engels on Religion* (New York: Schocken, 1964), 274–75.

12. For the close link between the concepts of recognition and love in the PhG, see my *History and Truth in Hegel's Phenomenology,* 130–38. For other helpful discussions of the concept of recognition in the Jena period, see Ludwig Siep, "Der Kampf um Anerkennung," in *Hegel-Studien* 9 (1974): 155–207, and "Dialektik der Anerkennung bei Hegel," in *Hegel Jahrbuch* (1974): 388–95; Jürgen Habermas, *Theory and Practice,* 142–69; and two essays from Manfred Riedel's *Studien zu Hegels Rechtsphilosophie,* namely "Hegel's Kritik des Naturrechts," 42–74, and "Die Rezeption der Nationalökonomie," 75–99.

13. That the function of a theory is not uniquely determined by its content or intention is a central thesis of Karl Mannheim in *Ideology and Utopia.*

14. In the passage just cited, the term *transcending* renders the German *aufheben.*

15. See the passages cited in the previous paragraph from Hegel's ¶¶41Z and 45. Cf. ¶41. On the priority of spirit to life in Hegel's thinking, see the first passage cited in n. 12 above.

16. Schlomo Avineri, *Hegel's Theory of the Modern State,* 135.

17. These passages are cited by Manfred Riedel in "Nature and Freedom in Hegel's *Philosophy of Right,*" in Pelczynski, ed., *Hegel's Political*

Philosophy: Problems and Perspectives, 137 and 145–46. He also cites them, in a somewhat different context, in "Hegels Kritik des Naturrechts," 70–72.

18. John Plamenatz, "History as the Realization of Freedom," in Pelczynski, ed., *Hegel's Political Philosophy.*

19. Hegel never failed to repeat a philosophical joke of which he was fond. This one about animals had already appeared at the end of the chapter on Sense-Certainty in PS.

20. " . . . mit dem das Natürliche seiner Selbstständigkeit entrissen und in die Verfügung des Menschen gebracht wird." Joachim Ritter, "Person und Eigentum: Zu Hegels 'Grundlinien der Philosophie des Rechts', ¶34–81," in *Metaphysik und Politik,* 268–73.

21. See the section entitled "Wrong," beginning with ¶82.

22. Jürgen Habermas has noted how the transition from classical to modern political thought involves a shift from the primacy of the question of the morally good life to the primacy of the question of survival. Whereas classical politics was an extension of ethics, modern political science is a kind of technical expertise in overcoming the threats to life from one's enemies (Machiavelli) or from hunger (Thomas More). This transition, which comes to its fulfillment in Hobbes, involves the replacement of *praxis* by *poiēsis* and of *phronēsis* by *technē* and *epistēmē.* In the process, the term *good life* is redefined so that it no longer refers to virtue and freedom but to survival, security, and comfort. By giving priority to status over survival and thus to spirit over nature, Hegel gives expression to his lasting affinity for classical politics. See "The Classical Doctrine of Politics in Relation to Social Philosophy," in *Theory and Practice.* For an overview of developmental changes in Hegel's stance toward classical politics and modern, natural law political theory, see Riedel's essay, "Hegel's Kritik des Naturrechts," cited in n. 12 above.

23. I have in mind especially the writings of Avineri, Dove, Habermas, Riedel, Ritter, and Stillman as cited in nn. 12, 16, 17, 20, 22, 30, and 34. See also ch. 1 and 3.

24. It should be noted, however, that Hegel's argument provides no comfort for those contemporaries who downplay the inhumanity of the right in order to excoriate that of the left. In light of Hegelian theory the authoritarian-totalitarian dichotomy becomes a distinction without a difference.

25. See especially ¶¶45, 257–61 and ch. 3 below. Hegel's critique of an instrumentalist view of property and the state (which requires a distinction between civil society and the state of which liberalism knows nothing) is directed against both the naturalism and the individualism of liberalism. He wishes to deny both that spirit is a means to nature's ends, and that the whole is a means to the parts' ends, though he does not always clearly dis-

tinguish between the two issues. It is obviously the former point that is presently at issue. The latter will come to focus toward the end of this essay.

26. It may seem strange to speak of Hobbes as a founding father of the liberal tradition, but Habermas, for one, insists that he is "the real founder of liberalism," insofar as the rationale for his absolutist state is a liberal one. This does not remove the "antinomy" involved in the fact that it is an absolutist state that is called upon to carry out liberal hopes, resulting in "the sacrifice of the liberal content in favor of the absolute form of its sanction." The centrality of survival in Hobbesian thought is crucial to this interpretation. See "The Classical Doctrine of Politics," 63–69.

27. Novak, from pp. 3 and 4 of the insert. In fairness to Novak, it must be noted that he does not make freedom *merely* a means to wealth. In the passage just cited, freedom and wealth are reciprocally means and ends to each other. The organic nature of this relationship has Hegelian overtones, but Hegel remains suspicious of all tendencies to view freedom as a means, especially in a context like this one in which freedom is acknowledged to be an end, but emphasis falls on the claim that it enriches.

28. On the independence of function and intention, see n. 13.

29. Ritter, "Person und Eigentum," 267.

30. On the relation of the Logic to the *Philosophy of Right* see ch. 1 above, and two essays by Kenley Dove: "The Relationship of Habermas's Views to Hegel," in Don Verene, ed., *Hegel's Social and Political Thought,* 40–46, and "Logik und Recht bei Hegel," in *Neue Hefte für Philosophie* 17: 89–108. A major difference between Dove's discussion and mine is that he seeks to correlate the triad Being, Essence, and Concept to the *Philosophy of Right,* while my discussion, focusing on ¶¶5–7, involves the triad, Universality, Particularity, and Individuality.

31. It is worth noting that all three meanings that Hegel does *not* give to the priority of property rights are meanings that give expression to various aspects of classical liberal social theory.

32. That the state is based on solidarity rather than self-interest is a formulation of Avineri, *Hegel's Theory,* 134; but it applies to the family as well. They differ from each other in terms of the difference between love and patriotism as the bonding relationship. See ¶¶158, 158Z, 257, and 267–69. On the noncontractual, nonutilitarian, non-self-interest basis of both family and the state on Hegel's analysis, see ch. 3 below.

33. For a more detailed discussion of these paragraphs see ch. 1 above. Hegel had already given a detailed analysis of the Terror in ch. 6 of the PhG in a section entitled, "Absolute Freedom and Terror."

34. Peter Stillman consistently notes both the abstractness of Abstract Right and the fact that property's priority in the presentation is a

logical priority. But the connection between these points is not as explicit as it might be. See his essays, "Person, Property and Civil Society in the *Philosophy of Right,*" in Verene, ed., *Hegel's Social and Political Thought;* "Hegel's Critique of Liberal Theories of Rights," *The American Political Science Review* 68:3 (September 1974); and "Property, Freedom and Individuality in Hegel's and Marx's Political Thought," in *Property,* ed. J. Roland Pennock and John W. Chapman, *NOMOS* 22 (New York: New York University Press, 1980).

35. Had he been employing the kind of class analysis later developed by Marx, Hegel would have found nothing paradoxical here at all. Liberalism would appear simply as the bourgeoisie's overconcern for its own economic interests and its underconcern for those of the poor. That is not so much a paradox as ordinary human self-centeredness and greed.

36. The classical passages are in Locke's *Second Treatise.* See especially ¶¶3 and 123–24.

37. Ritter, "Person und Eigentum," 273ff.

38. This is of course not Hegel's language, but it is, I believe, the point he is making. Hegel's critique of contractual thought and institutions is discussed in ch. 3 below.

39. I am thinking of the kind of argument made by Schlomo Avineri in *The Social and Political Thought of Karl Marx* (Cambridge: Cambridge University Press, 1968). For an excellent summary discussion of Hegel's treatment of the problem of poverty in civil society and of the earlier development of the same motif during the Jena period, see Avineri, *Hegel's Theory of the Modern State,* 145ff.

40. See the discussion in Avineri, *Hegel's Theory,* 147–54. For commentary on the importance of Hegel's study of modern political economy, which emphasizes its positive role in Hegelian theory, see Ritter, "Die Rezeption der Nationalökonomie."

Chapter Three

1. PR, ¶75.

2. See ch. 4 of PhG. For a critique of abstract recognition, see the section entitled "Der Rechtszustand" in ch. 6.

3. *Mere Christianity,* bk. 3, ch. 6.

4. VG, 111–12.

5. See Hegel's early polemic against the notion of political authority as a kind of personal property, especially in *The German Constitution,* HPW, 149–51.

6. Rousseau makes a definite break with Hobbes and Locke on this point, but since he retains the social contract framework Hegel finds the break to be incomplete and remains ambivalent towards his thought.

7. See especially PR, ¶¶209, 217–18, and 229.

8. PR, ¶186. Hegel's reference here to necessity rather than freedom also suggests an element of compulsion, which Knox inserts into his translation. It is, of course, no uniquely Hegelian discovery that the market and those who manipulate it, whether in public or private capacities, often appear to participating individuals as external compulsion. Calling the system free enterprise cannot hide this fact except from those who do not wish to see it.

9. PR, ¶¶236, 239, and 241. On the problem of poverty see ¶¶185, 185Z, 195, and 245, along with the excellent discussion in Avineri, *Hegel's Theory*.

10. For more detailed examination of this theme see G. Heiman, "The Sources and Significance of Hegel's Corporate Doctrine," in Pelczynski, ed., *Hegel's Political Philosophy*, and A. S. Walton, "Economy, Utility and Community in Hegel's Theory of Civil Society," in Pelczynski, ed., *The State and Civil Society*. Jacques Ellul's discussion of the atomization of society resulting from the disappearance of such natural social groups as *family* and *guild* is especially interesting in relation to Hegel's views of the corporation. See *The Technological Society*, trans. by John Wilkinson (New York: Random House, 1964).

11. Hegel links the notion of need with the Understanding by calling this state the *Not-und Verstandesstaat*. Cf. PR, ¶¶187 and 189 on the Understanding.

12. Cf. PR, ¶199 and n. 8 above.

13. On Hegel's concept of freedom as self-determination see the essays by Plamanetz and Riedel in Pelczynski, ed., *Hegel's Political Philosophy*, and ch. 1 above, which focuses on ¶¶5–7 in PR.

14. Charles Taylor, *Hegel*, 376. On the notion of *Sittlichkeit* see all of ch. 14 of Taylor's book or the slightly briefer discussion in sec. 3 of ch. 2 of his *Hegel and Modern Society*. Also see sections 5C and 6A of my *History and Truth in Hegel's Phenomenology*.

15. On the transcendence of the natural, see PR, ¶¶146 and 151.

16. Cf. PR, ¶163Z on the difference between marriage and concubinage.

17. Since "natural" is contrasted with "spiritual" rather than with "unnatural" Hegel uses the term not only to refer to biological selfhood but to pre-ethical selfhood in the sense of pre-social(ized) selfhood. This is Rousseau's state of *nature*.

18. Compare PR, ¶145 with ¶¶162–63. This is the metaphor that underlies Hegel's talk about ethical substance and substantial ties.

19. On the link between universality and substantiality see the passages from PR, ¶¶258 and 260 cited below. English loses the etymological linkages which are visible and audible in German between universality (*Allgemeinheit*), community (*Gemeinschaft*), and congregation (*Gemeinde*). Since Hegel takes these linkages very seriously, true universality never signifies for him abstract similarity but always concrete participation in some actual totality.

20. It is quite clear that Hegel here uses "person" in its legal sense.

21. PR, ¶¶257 and 267–69.

22. In the so-called Frankfurt "System Fragment" of 1800 Hegel formulates the unity of identity and difference as *"die Verbindung der Verbindung und der Nichtverbindung."* *Werke* 1:422. In the *Differenzschrift* it is *"die Identitätat der Identität und der Nichtidentität."* GW 4:64.

23. Compare PR, ¶268 with the discussion of love in sec. 5B of my *History and Truth*.

24. PR, ¶¶267, 273, and 276. For a helpful discussion of what Hegel means by "the political state," see Pelczynski's "The Hegelian Conception of the State" in his *Hegel's Political Philosophy*.

25. PHI, 96.

26. *The Social Contract*, bk. 1, ch. 8.

27. The nationalism of Hegel's view of the state refuses to become the internationalism which his own logic calls for. International relations remain for him essentially contractual.

28. Thus government management of the economy as well as private economic activity is to be included in the transformation described as the sacramentalism of economic life in the remainder of this paragraph.

29. Autonomous economic life in this context means not the freedom of private interests from government regulation, but the primacy of economic goals in private and public life.

30. PR, ¶270. In his early writings Hegel was especially sensitive to the conflict between the private pursuit of wealth and the health of what he understands by the state. See *Werke* 1:205–07, 213–14, 333–35, 516–17, and GW 4:456–58. For English translations see ETW, 155–57, 164–65, 221–22; HPW, 189–90; and NL, 100–02.

31. PR, ¶¶185, 190–95, and 256.

32. See ch. 3 of John V. Taylor, *Enough is Enough* (London: SCM, 1975).

Chapter Four

1. PR, ¶138Z.

2. PR, ¶135.

3. Donagan responds to Hegel's position as stated in the section of PR entitled "Good and Conscience." An earlier discussion of the same issues is found in the sections of PS entitled "Reason as lawgiver," and "Reason as testing laws."

4. Alan Donagan, *The Theory of Morality* (Chicago: University of Chicago Press, 1977), 13.

5. Ibid., 13.

6. Ibid., 16–17.

7. Jeremiah 17:9 (RSV).

8. See Sykes and Matza, "Techniques of Neutralization: A Theory of Delinquency," in Roger Smith, ed., *Guilt, Man and Society* (Garden City: Doubleday, 1971).

9. Hegel expresses this kind of concern in his critique of Jacobi and Schleiermacher in FK, 1802.

10. Donagan, 23. Cf. Hegel in "Reason as lawgiver."

11. PR, ¶153. My italics.

12. See Soren Kierkegaard, *Fear and Trembling/Repetition,* trans. Hong and Hong (Princeton: Princeton University Press, 1983), 54–55, and *Training in Christianity,* trans. Walter Lowrie (Princeton: Princeton University Press, 1944), 88.

13. For a discussion of these themes in Kierkegaard, see "Kierkegaard's Politics" in my *Kierkegaard's Critique of Reason and Society* (Macon: Mercer University Press, 1987).

14. *Training in Christianity,* 89.

15. The sense of historicity has led to extreme versions of historicism. That makes it tempting to return to the ahistorical view of human reason shared by St. Thomas and Kant. But the social situatedness of thought is not overcome by being ignored.

16. Donagan, 54–55.

17. This is oversimplified in not distinguishing the forbidden, the obligatory, and the permitted. For the sake of logical elegance, Donagan defines all three in terms of impermissibility. See pp. 54 and 67.

18. Donagan, 66–72.

19. Ibid., 68 and 71.

20. Ibid., 66.

21. I prefer to speak of our common morality as just that. It seems to me that important questions are begged by calling it Judeo-Christian morality.

22. Donagan, 59.

23. Ibid., 58–59.

24. Ibid., 59–66.

25. See n. 3 above. A still earlier (1802–03) critique of formalism in ethics is found in NR.

26. See especially "Reason as testing laws."

27. Donagan, 66.

28. From an interview in *The Wittenberg Door* 32 (August-September 1976):14.

29. Obviously questions about culpable and inculpable ignorance arise here, though many who purchase food exported from the Third World are quite fully aware of the systems that produce it.

30. The slogan is associated, of course, with Proudhon. Part 8 of Marx's *Capital,* I, entitled "The So-Called Primitive Accumulation," deserves more attention than it has received in this context.

31. The Jubilee model can be extended to nonagrarian contexts and, like the Golden Rule and the principle of neighbor love, can be separated from its theological premises for the purposes of philosophical discussion.

32. Donagan, 13.

33. Ibid., 99–100.

34. Ibid., 95.

35. See C. B. Macpherson, *The Political Theory of Possessive Individualism* (London: Oxford University Press, 1964), ch. 5.

36. Donagan, 98.

37. Quoted in Donagan, 69.

38. Donagan, 71.

39. Ibid., 70.

40. Ibid., 71. My italics.

Chapter Five

1. In the text and the notes of this chapter will be found references of the form PhG, x/y or WL, x/y. The page number after the slash refers in each case to the Miller translation, PS and SL respectively.

2. In this respect Kant's treatment of the world is more nearly Hegelian than his treatment of either the soul or God. Hegel's rejection of logical foundationalism is found in his insistence that philosophy not succumb to the spell of Euclidian-Cartesian deductivism. See PhG, 35–41/24–29; EL, ¶¶226–32; and WL 1:207–12/212–17; 2:439–77/783–818.

3. This issue is related to but by no means identical with the question of the place of the *Phenomenology* in the system.

4. Though in the larger context of the *Phenomenology* the becoming involved here is plainly historical, in the text which immediately follows this passage Hegel describes it as a process of logical mediation. Though logical and historical becoming are not synonymous, both belong, on Hegel's view, to the development of which the absolute is the result.

5. In the light of the ultimate unity of phenomenological, logical, and ontological dimensions of dialectic, the individual finite things referred to here can be either forms of experience, categories of thought, or concrete "things" of nature or spirit, for example, rocks, camels, nations, and so forth.

6. Similar passages, which also need to be read in the light of ¶213, include the following: "But by Dialectic is meant the indwelling tendency outwards by which the one-sidedness and limitation of the predicates of understanding is seen in its true light, and shown to be the negation of them. For anything to be finite is just to suppress itself and put itself aside [*sich selbst aufzuheben*]," EL, ¶81. "But the true view of the matter is that life, as life, involves the germ of death, and that the finite, being radically self-contradictory, involves its own self-suppression [*sich aufhebt*]." EL, ¶81Z.

7. So far as Socrates is concerned, this is especially clear in the *Apology*. See Alexander Sesonske, "To Make the Weaker Argument Defeat the Stronger," *Journal of the History of Philosophy* 6 (1968): 217–31.

8. See EL, ¶¶24Z, 38–42, and 81Z. For the background to this discussion in the *Phenomenology* and the 1802 essay, "Verhältniss des

Skepticismus zur Philosophie," see my *History and Truth in Hegel's Phenomenology,* 8–14.

9. Soren Kierkegaard, *The Concept of Irony,* trans. Lee M. Capel (New York: Harper and Row, 1965), 63. Cf. 176, "Sophistry is the wild and dissolute thrashing about of egotistical thought . . . " Throughout the book Kierkegaard interprets the negative thinking of irony as seeking freedom from the ethical constraints of the social order. Sometimes this means that the individual seeks to subordinate society to personal preference, which is sophistry. But it can also mean that the individual seeks something higher than any given social order to be the worthy object of an ultimate commitment. This is true philosophy in Kierkegaard's view.

10. Richard Rorty, *Consequences of Pragmatism* (Minneapolis: University of Minnesota Press, 1982), 218–21. "Perhaps the most appropriate model for the analytic philosopher is now the *lawyer,* rather than either the scholar or the scientist. The ability to construct a good brief, or conduct a devastating cross-examination, or find relevant precedents, is pretty much the ability which analytic philosophers think of as 'distinctively philosophical'."

11. In some of its forms, of course, structuralism is an antihistoricist movement with foundationalist leanings. But Rorty puts Foucault in company with Nietzsche and Heidegger against Husserl on this issue (*Consequences,* 203–08, 226). Dreyfus and Rabinow note that this dimension of Foucault's thought is most explicit in *The Birth of the Clinic.* See their *Michel Foucault: Beyond Structuralism and Hermeneutics* (Chicago: University of Chicago Press, 1982), 12–15.

12. The term 'Cartesian empiricism' sounds strange only if we forget that Hume, the father of twentieth-century foundationalist empiricism, had Locke for a father and therefore Descartes for a grandfather. It is Wilfrid Sellars who first challenges "the myth of the given" by name and W. V. O. Quine who treats reductionism as a "dogma." See (respectively): "Empiricism and the Philosophy of Mind," in *The Foundations of Science and the Concepts of Psychology and Psychoanalysis* (Minnesota Studies in the Philosophy of Science; 1), ed. Herbert Feigl and Michael Scriven (Minneapolis: University of Minnesota Press, 1956), and "Two Dogmas of Empiricism," in *From a Logical Point of View,* 2nd ed. (1961; rpt. New York: Harper and Row, 1963). No one has expressed the pain of this for traditional empiricists as poignantly as Carl Hempel in "Problems and Changes in the Empiricist Criterion of Meaning," in *Semantics and the Philosophy of Language,* ed. Leonard Linsky (Urbana: University of Illinois Press, 1952), and "The Theoretician's Dilemma," in *Concepts, Theories, and the Mind-Body Problem* (Minnesota Studies in the Philosophy of Science; 2), ed. Feigl, Scriven, and Maxwell (Minneapolis: University of Minnesota Press, 1958).

13. For the difference between theoretical and practical holism, see Hubert L. Dreyfus, "Holism and Hermeneutics," *Review of Metaphysics* 34

(1980): 3–23. The older philosophy of science has not been abandoned nearly as completely as logical atomism and logical constructionism have been. See n. 15 below.

14. Rorty, *Consequences*, xxxvii, 185–86, 207, 167, 165.

15. The triumph of historicist holism has not been total, so this claim would be denied or seriously qualified by some contemporary thinkers. For example, see Thomas McCarthy as quoted in n. 24 of ch. 6 below. Similar attempts can be found within structuralism, and within the analytic tradition, either under the rubric of realism or as attempts within the philosophy of science to see how much of the positivist account can be saved after granting what must be granted to Kuhn, et al. But these quests for an atemporal *pou sto* are not the Hegelian remedy for the "vertigo of relativity" which comes with insight into human historicity. See n. 14 in ch. 6 below.

16. Thomas McCarthy, *Critical Theory*, 182, speaking of Gadamer.

17. This seems to be Husserl's strategy in the *Crisis* for acknowledging history and retaining the notion of philosophy as rigorous science. See n. 41 in ch. 6 below.

18. Peter Berger, *The Sacred Canopy: Elements of a Sociological Theory of Religion* (Garden City: Doubleday, 1967), 52.

19. On the relation of recognition and love and the background of this concept in Fichte and Hegel's earlier writings see n. 12 in ch. 2 above.

20. The community of reciprocal recognition emerges at the end of ch. 6, while Absolute Knowing is the theme of ch. 8. On the role of ch. 7, "Religion," see my *History and Truth*, 181–218.

21. Jacques Ellul has perhaps shown this more clearly than anyone in his analysis of social propaganda in *Propaganda*.

22. On Hegel's critique of contractual relations, see ch. 3 above.

23. On the issue of war, see Donald P. Verene, "Hegel's Account of War," in Pelczynski, *Hegel's Political Philosophy*, and Avineri, *Hegel's Theory of the Modern State*, 194–207. On the nationalism question, see Avineri, "Hegel and Nationalism," in *Hegel's Political Philosophy*, ed. Walter Kaufmann (New York: Atherton, 1970).

24. On this topic see especially O. Marquard, "Hegel und das Sollen," *Philosophisches Jahrbuch* 72 (1964): 103–19.

25. Matthew 10:39, 16:25.

26. This essay was originally presented to the Hegel Society of Great Britain in September 1984 during their annual meeting at Oxford.

Chapter Six

The following abbreviations are used in the notes to this chapter for English translations of works by Gadamer:

TM   *Truth and Method,* trans. Barden and Cumming (New York: Seabury, 1975).

PH   *Philosophical Hermeneutics,* trans. David E. Linge (Berkeley: University of California Press, 1976).

HD   *Hegel's Dialectic,* trans. P. Christopher Smith (New Haven: Yale University Press, 1976).

RAS   *Reason in the Age of Science,* trans. Frederick G. Lawrence (Cambridge: MIT Press, 1981).

1. TM, 239–40. Cf. p. 244, "The overcoming of all prejudices, this global demand of the enlightenment, will prove to be itself a prejudice."

2. TM, 245.

3. The notion of fore-sight along with the related notions of fore-having and fore-conception are part of Heidegger's analysis of understanding in *Being and Time,* ¶32. Hebermas is getting at a closely related theme when he speaks of the "transitory a priori structure" of modern science and technology. *Towards a Rational Society,* trans. Jeremy J. Shapiro (Boston: Beacon, 1970), 84. It is the historically conditioned a priori of experience that Gadamer indicates with the notion of prejudice, not the putatively universal and necessary a priori of Kant. Thus for him language becomes a "contingent absolute." See n. 20 below.

4. RAS, 53. Thus Gadamer has the intent of "learning something from Hegel," but by no means that of "renewing his perspective," RAS, 27. There is "no question of Hegel discipleship, but of interiorizing the challenge that he represents." RAS, 50.

5. On Gadamer's Kantianism, see TM, xxiv, 88–89, 245, 460–91; and PH, 130–77. The language of hermeneutics and energetics comes from Ricoeur's *Freud and Philosophy.* The debate with Habermas begins with the latter's "A Review of Gadamer's *Truth and Method,*" in *Understanding and Social Inquiry,* ed. Dallmayr and McCarthy (Notre Dame: University of Notre Dame Press, 1977). Then come Gadamer's essays in PH, "The Universality of the Hermeneutical Problem," and "On the Scope and Function of Hermeneutical Reflection." Habermas's reply is "The Hermeneutic Claim to Universality," in Josef Bleicher, *Contemporary Hermeneutics* (London: Routledge and Kegan Paul, 1980). Most of this debate is found in *Hermeneutik und Ideologiekritik* (Frankfurt: Suhrkamp, 1971), which also contains Gadamer's "Replik" to the whole debate. For helpful analysis of the debate see Thomas McCarthy, *The Critical Theory of Jürgen Habermas*

(Cambridge: MIT Press, 1981), ch. 3; Paul Ricoeur, "Ethics and Culture: Habermas and Gadamer in Dialogue," *Philosophy Today* 17 (1973): 153–65; and the relevant chapters of Bleicher.

6. Protests that Heidegger is no existentialist have their point. They are also one of the best illustrations of the Heideggerian point that revealing necessarily involves concealing.

7. Husserl, incidentally, is willing to take quite literally his own claim that "all" sciences are involved. He explicitly includes geometry, and Merleau-Ponty, agreeing, writes, "When I think the Pythagorean theorem and recognize it as true, it is clear that this truth is not for this moment only. Nevertheless later progress in knowledge will show that it is not yet a final, unconditioned evidence and that, if the Pythagorean theorem and the Euclidian system once appeared as final, unconditioned evidences, that is itself the mark of a certain cultural epoch. Later developments would not annul the Pythagorean theorem but would put it back in its place as a partial, and also an abstract, truth. Thus here also we do not have a timeless truth but rather the recovery of one time by another time." *The Primacy of Perception,* ed. James M. Edie (Evanston: Northwestern University Press, 1964), 20.

8. See n. 3 above; McCarthy, 161; and Habermas, *Knowledge and Human Interests,* trans. Jeremy J. Shapiro (Boston: Beacon, 1971), vii.

9. PH, 9.

10. Ricoeur, "Ethics and Culture," 157.

11. See the editor's introduction to PH, xliv.

12. TM, 269.

13. PH, 29 and 13. Cf. 13–16, 19, 25, 29–32, 35; TM, 345–447; and RAS, 4.

14. It is Berger and Luckman who speak of the "vertigo of relativity" in *The Social Construction of Reality* (Garden City: Doubleday, 1966), 5.

15. NL, 58.

16. See Avineri, *Hegel's Theory of the Modern State,* ch. 4.

17. SL, 26–27.

18. PR, preface.

19. PS, 3–8.

20. For these quotations, for the emergence of the question, Who is the transcendental subject?, and for a detailed analysis of the linguistic character of perception, see my *History and Truth in Hegel's Phenomenology,*

ch. 2–3. Cf. Habermas's summary of Gadamer's position, "At the level of objective spirit, language becomes a contingent absolute." Dallmayr and McCarthy, "Review of Gadamer's *Truth and Method*," 359.

21. TM, 258 and 261. Cf. TM, xvi, "My real concern was and is philosophic: not what we do or what we ought to do, but what happens to us over and above our wanting and doing."

22. PS, 110.

23. Cf. Westphal, *History and Truth*, ch. 4–8. For Gadamer's appreciation of the anti-Cartesian character of Hegel's concept of spirit, see HD, 35–36, 54–59, and 77–78.

24. According to McCarthy, Habermas is the latest to attempt this in the form of scientific social theory. "Habermas' counterposition [to Gadamer] is an attempt to mitigate the radically situational character of understanding through the introduction of theoretical elements; the theories of communication and social evolution are meant to reduce the context dependency of the basic categories and assumptions of critical theory," *Critical Theory*, 193.

25. SL, 27.

26. PS, 25–28. Cf. 32; and for Gadamer's appreciation, see HD, 16–17; and RAS, 6, where he describes philosophy down through Hegel as "a self-defense against the sciences." N. B. Whereas for Kant there is an insuperable barrier between the human subject and the thing in itself (*das Ding an sich*), for Hegel it is method that erects the barrier between the knowing subject and the thing itself (*die Sache selbst*). This is why the transition from *Verstand* to *Vernunft* can have such a different meaning for the two.

27. Cf. RAS, 41. See Hegel's account of calculative thinking as described in ch. 1 above, third paragraph from the end.

28. SL, 36.

29. SL, 826. Hegel's italics.

30. SL, 27–28. Cf. HD, 5–7, 19, 27.

31. PS, 32. My italics. Hegel goes on to speak of being "absorbed in its object" and "immersed in the material."

32. EL, ¶163Z. Cf. ¶¶166Z, 175Z, and 181Z. Hegel is most emphatic here. What is to be noted is "dass *wir* die Begriffe gar nicht bilden." Cf. RAS, 17.

33. For the argument in support of this conclusion, see ch. 1 above.

34. SL, 603. Hegel's italics.

35. *Critique of Pure Reason,* B xiii. Kant's verb *nötigen* may also be translated as "coerce" or "compel."

36. PH, 26. Cf. preface to the second edition.

37. For example, TM, xi.

38. Compare PH, 4–5 and 18–19 with TM, first part.

39. PH, 39; TM, 407; and RAS, 70–71.

40. This includes the human sciences that seek legitimacy by going Cartesian. Whether they turn to the *Port Royal Logic,* or to Hume and Mill, or to Schleiermacher and Dilthey, Gadamer wants to expose the inadequacy of their self-understanding. See TM, 19, 5, and 147–234. When he favorably quotes Heidegger's claim that the natural sciences have "strayed into the legitimate task of grasping the present-at-hand in its essential unintelligibility," he comes close to Hegel's formulations in terms of true propositions about an inferior subject matter. See TM, 230; and n. 26 above.

41. On the "unresolved Cartesianism" of both Dilthey and Husserl, see TM, 210–29. In Gadamer's view, Husserl's *Crisis* is not a joining of Heidegger, who has no wish to ground either history or philosophy as science, but rather a deflection of the anti-Cartesian thrust of Heidegger's thought by making the life-world into an object for phenomenological description rather than the subject of even philosophical reflection. See TM, 225–27; and PH, xliii–xlv.

42. TM, 311.

43. PH, 11. Statistics level themselves to propaganda because "they let facts speak and hence simulate an objectivity that in reality depends on the legitimacy of the questions asked," TM, 268. On the logic of question and answer in general, see TM, 325ff.

44. TM, 329. Cf. RAS, 47.

45. The domination motif is especially strong in RAS. See pp. 3, 14–17, 23, and 70–71.

46. TM, 277–78, 321–27, and 340–41. Some of these texts, especially the first, would be appealed to by those who see hermeneutics as uncritical acceptance of tradition. Apart from reading them in the light of other comments Gadamer makes and his own critical conversation with the philosophical tradition, what needs to be noted is the specific role these statements have in polemic against the will to power in the Cartesian tradition.

47. TM, 433.

48. TM, xxiii.

49. TM, 111. Cf. RAS, 77 and 17–18, where *theoria* is "complete self-donation."

50. TM, 422.

51. HD, 29.

52. RAS, 61–63.

53. RAS, 14–15, 30–33.

54. RAS, 39–41.

55. RAS, 14–15, 46.

56. TM, 318–20; and HD, 11–13.

57. HD, 110.

58. TM, 318; RAS, 6 and 13; HD, 79. Cf. RAS, 46, where Gadamer even speaks of Hegel's "methodological compulsion."

59. See RAS, 1.

60. On this eschatological strategy for overcoming historical relativism within history, see my *History and Truth,* ch. 2 and 8, especially sec. 2C and 8B.

61. RAS, 52.

62. TM, 318–19.

63. RAS, 40 and 59–60.

64. RAS, 37. Cf. 10.

65. 1 Cor 13:12 (NEB): "Now we see only puzzling reflections in a mirror, but then we shall see face to face. My knowledge now is partial; then it will be whole, like God's knowledge of me."

66. RAS, 36.

67. RAS, 46.

68. PH, 38. Gadamer's italics. The reference to what happens "behind my back" is meant to evoke PS, 56, where Hegel describes the scientific status of the *Phenomenology* in terms of overcoming this hiddenness, that is, of making consciousness fully transparent to itself.

69. HD, 99.

70. HD, 91. Cf. 31–33, 112; and RAS, 12.

71. HD, 93.

72. HD, 94–97; and RAS, 50. Cf. RAS, 11.

73. HD, 96. Cf. 113, where Gadamer says that if we listen to language we will hear what Hegel didn't and couldn't say.

74. HD, 116.

75. RAS, 50.

76. RAS, 53; Cf. 20, 46–47, 57–60, and 106–108.

77. Reference to the "tacit dimension" suggests that more attention needs to be given to the relation of Gadamer and Polanyi than has been given to date. For Gadamer's incorporation of the suspicion critique of Hegel, see RAS, 13, 49, 54, 58, 100–104, and 108.

Chapter Seven

1. George Schrader, "Hegel's Contribution to Phenomenology," *The Monist* 48 (1964): 18–33.

2. Quentin Lauer, "Phenomenology: Hegel and Husserl," in *Beyond Epistemology*, ed. Frederick G. Weiss.

3. Naturally the central focus will be on *Ideas I, Cartesian Meditations,* and the *Crisis,* Husserl's three major introductions to transcendental phenomenology.

4. PS, 3–4.

5. For a more detailed interpretation of this passage, see my *History and Truth in Hegel's Phenomenology,* sec. 1C. Since this occurs in the context of Hegel's attempt to distinguish his phenomenological critique of reason from that of Kant and the British empiricists, it is surprising that Husserl complains that "his system lacks a critique of reason, which is the foremost prerequisite for being scientific in philosophy." "Philosophy as Rigorous Science," in *Phenomenology and the Crisis of Philosophy,* trans. Quentin Lauer (New York: Harper and Row, 1965), 77. A detailed dialogue between Husserl and just this introduction to PS would be one very good way of thinking through the relation between the two thinkers.

6. PS, 3.

7. PS, 2–3. On the cognitive significance of tarrying or lingering (*verweilen*), see 16–17.

8. In view of the religious overtones of this language, drawn from the contemplative life, the metaphor of epistemological asceticism may be appropriate for the discipline of "world-denial" involved in Husserl's

phenomenological reduction and its disengagement not just of belief in the world but also of all worldly interests. He himself compares the epoché to "a religious conversion." *The Crisis of European Sciences and Phenomenological Philosophy,* trans. David Carr (Evanston: Northwestern University Press, 1970), 137.

9. PS, 4. Cf. *History and Truth,* 26–28.

10. PS, 6–7. On this recurring theme in Hegel's thought, see *History and Truth,* 54 n. 46. Both Kant's Copernican revolution and the French Revolution are important themes behind this one.

11. David Carr, in his translator's introduction to *Crisis,* xxxv.

12. *Phenomenology and Crisis,* 71–73, 135–42. It is worth noting that in this text from 1911 Husserl has an almost Hegelian confidence missing from the *Crisis:* "There is, perhaps, in all modern life no more powerfully, more irresistibly progressing idea than that of science. Nothing will hinder its vigorous advance," 82. Cf. the concluding paragraph of Hegel's inaugural address at Heidelberg, HP 1:xiii. It is also worth noting that Husserl begins the *Cartesian Meditations* with at least a hint of the crisis motif. Trans. Dorion Cairns (The Hague: Nijhoff, 1973), 4–5.

13. For helpful commentary on Husserl's "switching off" metaphor and the explanatory role of the world in the natural attitude, see Erazim Kohak, *Idea and Experience: Edmund Husserl's Project of Phenomenology in Ideas, I* (Chicago: University of Chicago Press, 1978), 35–40. On the difference between the epoché and the reduction, see *Crisis,* 151.

14. *Crisis,* 188–89.

15. "Verhältniss des Skepticismus zur Philosophie," GW 4:215.

16. PS, 48. On the threefold radicality of Hegel's phenomenological skepticism, see *History and Truth,* sec. 1B.

17. PS, 15, 49–51.

18. See Hegel's *Differenzschrift,* GW 4:21.

19. Gadamer suggests that the twentieth-century critique of consciousness is more radical than Hegel's critique of subjective spirit because of the rise of a hermeneutics of suspicion in Marx, Nietzsche, and Freud. Since Husserl is essentially untouched by these analysis of personal and social self-deception, it could be said that his critique of everyday experience is, like Hegel's, a nineteenth-century critique. See "The Philosophical Foundations of the Twentieth Century," in PH.

20. *History and Truth,* 5–6.

21. PS, 18. It is just for this reason that Kohak regularly stresses the nonidentity of the obvious and the evident for Husserl in *Idea and Experi-*

ence. In the *Crisis* Husserl sounds as if he has Hegel in mind when he writes, "But the great problem is precisely to understand what is here so 'obvious'," 187.

22. PS, 19, 51–52. Cf. the last paragraph of Hegel's *Antrittsrede* at Berlin, *Werke* 10:417.

23. Were I to take the time and space for further argument it would concern Hegel's affinity in PS for Husserl's eidetic reduction. Not only does the entire text have "patterns of consciousness" (*Gestalten des Bewusstseins*) for its theme; the discussion of Sense Certainty shows how the most immediate levels of sense experience are saturated with universality. We express our sense experience in a language of universals because we have already perceived the world that way. See *History and Truth*, sec. 3C.

24. PS, 17.

25. Husserl, *Meditations*, 32–37. Transcendental psychologism can also be viewed as transcendental realism. See p. 24.

26. PS, 49. The ambiguity in the adjective is probably intentional, indicating both that knowledge appears, becomes a theme for reflective thought, and that the knowledge which does thereby come under scrutiny is merely phenomenal knowledge, in a quasi-Kantian sense. It is not the genuine knowledge which reflective philosophy aspires to be.

27. PS, 54–56. Cf. Ricoeur's formulation: "an 'uninterested' impartial spectator wrenches itself away from 'interest in life'. At this point the triumph of phenomenological 'seeing' over vital and everyday 'doing' is complete." With reference to both the epistemological asceticism mentioned above (n. 8) and this splitting of the ego into observer and observed, Ricoeur is reminded of "the Platonic conversion by which the psyche, 'captivated' by reality, draws closer to the *nous* from which it came." But he is nervous, not entirely sure whether he is dealing with spiritual heroism, or perhaps, neurosis. And so he asks "what motivates such a rupture?" *Husserl: An Analysis of His Phenomenology*, trans. Ballard and Embree (Evanston: Northwestern University Press, 1967), 94. Ricoeur is discussing *Meditations*, 35. Though Hegel himself is committed to a form of world-denial and to a reflective turn in which "we" distinguish ourselves from the forms of consciousness we observe, he raises the same question. With special reference to the way his transcendental forefathers made the second of these moves, he wonders out loud whether the fear of error which leads to reflection might itself be the error to avoid. He suspects that at least sometimes "what calls itself fear of error reveals itself rather as fear of truth," PS, 47. The boundary line between sainthood and schizophrenia is not always well marked, and phenomenology's radicality seems to place it on that boundary. For an account of the "unmotivated" character of phenomenological reflection more sympathetic to Husserl, see Eugen Fink, "The Phenomenological Philosophy of Edmund Husserl and Contemporary Criticism," in

The Phenomenology of Husserl: Selected Critical Readings, ed. by R. O. El-
veton (Chicago: Quadrangle Books, 1970), 101–102. Yet Fink's own linkage
of phenomenology with the traditional question of the origin of the world
and with the aspiration to be an "absolute knowledge" of the world's "ultimate ground," "the world-transcendent knowledge of the absolute 'ground',"
suggests motivation; and he uses the term *hubris* himself. See 97–98, 103.

28. For Husserl there is a tight link between the idea of constitution
and transcendentalism. See, for example, *Ideas Pertaining to a Pure Phenomenological Philosophy: First Book,* trans. F. Kersten (The Hague:
Nijhoff, 1983), 209 and 239.

29. PS, 61.

30. PS, 66.

31. *History and Truth,* 89 n. 18.

32. *Signs,* trans. by Richard C. McCleary (Evanston: Northwestern
University Press, 1964), 110.

33. *The Conflict of Interpretations,* ed. Don Ihde (Evanston: Northwestern University Press, 1974), 191. Ricoeur frequently draws this distinction, but not, as far as I am aware, with reference to Hegel.

34. On Hegel as a critic of classical liberalism, see ch. 2–3 above.

35. I'm using these terms as Karl Mannheim uses them in *Ideology
and Utopia,* trans. L. Wirth (San Diego: Harcourt, Brace, Jovanovich,
1985).

36. Ludwig Landgrebe points out that Husserl identifies them in
Erste Philosophie, II, but distinguishes them in *Cartesian Meditations.* See
"Husserl's Departure from Cartesianism," in Landgrebe, *The Phenomenology of Edmund Husserl,* ed. Donn Welton (Ithica: Cornell University Press,
1981), 76.

37. Thus both would agree with Ricoeur's notion of a "crisis in the notion of consciousness," *Conflict of Interpretations,* 101.

38. PS, 9–14.

39. See Lauer, "Phenomenology: Hegel and Husserl," 187. Cf. 189:
"Because Husserl is more concerned with the apodictic certitude of the
knowledge he can obtain than he is with the extent of that knowledge, his
aim is to find in self-consciousness the guarantee of any knowledge, however trivial it may be. Since Hegel's aim is the attainment of knowledge
which is truly knowledge only if it is total, he cannot be satisfied with anything less than . . . a knowledge which cannot stop short of the interrelatedness of all knowing and of all that is known." Since this could only be
"absolute Spirit's absolute knowledge of itself," we can see why the sub-

stantive theses of the previous paragraph are embedded in Hegel's concept of system and why, as George Schrader puts it, it is "because Hegel's phenomenology is *ontological* that it must be *dialectical*." "Hegel's Contribution," 25.

40. My account of classical foundationalism is indebted to *Faith and Rationality: Reason and Belief in God*, ed. Plantinga and Wolterstorff (Notre Dame: University of Notre Dame Press, 1983), especially the essays by the editors. For a different kind of critique see Richard Rorty, *Consequences of Pragmatism* (Minneapolis: University of Minnesota Press, 1982).

41. Husserl, *Meditations*, 10–13. Cf. 57, where evidence means "the *self-appearance*, the *self-exhibiting*, the *self-giving*" of the intended so that the following becomes synonymous: "itself there," "immediately intuited," and "given originality." Ricoeur's summary: "Evidence . . . is the presence of the thing itself in the original . . . one would be tempted to say presence in flesh and blood, this is the self-givenness [*Selbstgegebenheit*] which Husserl calls 'originary'." *Husserl*, 101. Husserl speaks of the "*absolute nearness*" which is "*pure* givenness." *Ideas*, 153.

42. Husserl, *Ideas*, 36. In *Erste Philosophie*, II, Husserl reinforces the equivalence of apodicticity and immediacy. "At the very start . . . there must be an immediate knowledge, possibly a field, coindicated by immediate knowledge, of entirely accessible and therefore itself immediate knowledge, and these immediacies must be certain in an immediate fashion," *Husserliana*, vol. 8, ed. R. Boehm (The Hague: Nijhoff, 1959), 40. This is the meaning of the claim that "absolute justification thus presupposes absolute intuition," 367. Quoted in Landgrebe, *Six Essays*, 77–78.

43. Husserl, *Ideas*, 33, 38, 42. "The issue between Husserl and Hegel turns on whether description can be isolated from interpretation . . . " Schrader, "Hegel's Contribution," 23–24. This issue lies at the heart of the *Crisis* and motivates Husserl's attempt at an historical reduction based on the recognition that tradition is theory and that it affects not only thought but also perception. Perhaps the clearest statement of the problem is in Husserl's *Experience and Judgment*, trans. Churchill and Ameriks (Evanston: Northwestern University Press, 1973), ¶¶6–11; and in David Carr's helpful commentary, *Phenomenology and the Problem of History* (Evanston: Northwestern University Press, 1974), ch. 9, esp. 213–19.

44. PS, 11–13.

45. PS, 24–28.

46. There is a kind of holism at work in Husserl's reflection on the concepts of horizon, world, and eventually life-world. Because he begins with a *phenomenology* of perception he avoids the atomism of Hume, and because he begins with a phenomenology of *perception* he avoids the atomism of the early Wittgenstein. But his holism always remains

subordinated to his intuitionist evidentialism, however tense the relation between them becomes.

47. This sketchy summary of Hegel's critique of Sense Certainty is developed in detail in *History and Truth*, ch. 3. Hegel had already developed a critique of immediacy in the section on Jacobi in FK. He repeats this informal treatment of the matter in ¶¶61–78 of EL, with reference to Jacobi and Descartes, and in lectures 3–5 of LP. In both versions of the Logic, the opening triad, Being-Nothing-Becoming, plays the same role *vis-à-vis* all appeals to immediacy that the analysis of Sense Certainty does in PS. See Gadamer, "The Idea of Hegel's Logic" in *Hegel's Dialectic,* and Dieter Henrich, "Anfang und Methode der Logik," in *Hegel im Kontext.* One cannot overemphasize the centrality to all Hegelian thought of the critique of immediacy in any form.

48. PS, 13–14.

49. PS, 50–51.

50. For a fuller sketch of Hegel's dialectical holism and its relation to contemporary holisms, see ch. 5 above.

51. Though Leibniz is not free of foundationalist rhetoric, I think the ultimate logic of his metaphysics is holistic. The same can be said for Spinoza, with perhaps even more right, in spite of what he says about proceeding *more geometrico.* In any case the Spinoza Germany came to love during the *Goethezeit,* mediated by Herder's *Gott,* was a holistic and not a geometrizing Spinoza.

52. Husserl, *Meditations,* 7, 24.

53. See, for example, *Phenomenology and Crisis,* 76, 122, 142; and *Crisis,* 75.

54. *Meditations,* 14. I have added italics to Husserl's. For this temporal imagery of what is first or prior, also see 16, 18, 21–22, 27, and *Ideas,* 33, 38, and 42.

55. Ricoeur, *Conflict of Interpretations,* 113.

56. Husserl, *Crisis,* 389.

57. Carr, *Phenomenology and the Problem of History,* xxiii.

58. Those of a different disposition from Husserl may experience this compulsion as liberation. For an extreme example, see Rorty, *Consequences of Pragmatism.* Husserl's own efforts to avoid this verdict are the theme of Gadamer's discussion of the *Crisis.* So carefully does Husserl seek to preserve and perfect the transcendental reduction by keeping both the life-world and intersubjectivity relative to the constitutive activity of the transcendental ego, whose place is thus *not* taken by the life-world, that

Gadamer writes, "The *Crisis* attempts to give an implicit answer to *Being and Time*." See "The Phenomenological Movement" and "The Science of the Life-World," in PH. Obviously Gadamer does not find Husserl's case convincing, but his account reinforces Landgrebe's suggestion that what occurs "before the eyes of the reader" takes place "behind Husserl's back." Carr agrees that if Husserl did indeed plant the seeds of the destruction of transcendental philosophy in the *Crisis*, he himself surely did not think so. Beyond that he argues, tentatively but hopefully, that Husserl's encounter with history and the life-world does not require that verdict. *Phenomenology and the Problem of History*, xxv and ch. 9–10.

59. Landgrebe, *Six Essays*, 68–69. My italics. On the "Cartesian Way" into phenomenology, see 83 and 90, and *Crisis*, 144–54.

60. M. Merleau-Ponty, *Phenomenology of Perception*, trans. by Colin Smith (New York: Humanities Press, 1962), xiv. My italics. Still another, quite similar formulation comes from Ricoeur. In the *Crisis* and in *Experience and Judgment* "the decisive fact is the progressive abandonment, upon contact with new analyses, of the idealism of the *Cartesian Meditations*. The reduction less and less signifies a 'return to the ego' and more and more a 'return from logic to the antepredicative', to the primordial evidence of the world. The accent is placed no longer on the monadic ego; instead the accent is placed on the totality formed by the ego and the surrounding world in which it is vitally engaged. Thus, phenomenology tends toward the recognition of what is prior to all reduction and what cannot be reduced. The irreducibility of the life-world signifies that the Platonic-mathematical conversion cannot be carried out all the way." *Husserl*, 12.

61. These formulations are from Merleau-Ponty, *The Primacy of Perception*, 21 and 40.

62. Husserl, *Ideas*, 114 and 149. The differences between philosophy and geometry, 161ff., are not relevant to this point.

63. Husserl, *Crisis*, 59.

64. *Crisis*, 49ff., and appendix 6, "The Origin of Geometry," 353–78.

65. It can be said that there are three selves in Husserl, the empirical ego, the transcendental ego which comes to light as the subjective or noetic correlate of the world as phenomenon in the phenomenological reduction, and the philosophizing ego which carries out the epoché and the reduction. While Husserl is clear that rigorous science depends on a thoroughly nonworldly subjectivity, there is some ambiguity as to whether this is to be the second or third self or both. In the *Ideas*, for example, the correlation between *transcendental* ego and *transcendent* world (171 and 239) points to the second self, while the assurance that reflection can outflank life with reference to geometry (n. 54 above) points to the third. See Eugen Fink, "Husserl and Contemporary Criticism," 115ff.

66. *Crisis,* 60.

67. *Meditations,* 24, 32; *Phenomenology and Crisis,* 78–80; *Crisis,* 69, 79–88, 212, 215, 298.

68. *Crisis,* 178–80. Cf. 133, and, for Kant's entanglement in the same problem, 115–18.

69. See n. 57 above. Cf. Gadamer, *Philosophical Hermeneutics,* 160, 191–92.

70. Ricoeur, *Husserl,* 26.

71. In *Phenomenology and the Problem of History.*

72. Heidegger's *Verweisungsganzheit,* "referential totality," in *Being and Time,* 99, 91–148.

73. Husserl, *Experience and Judgment,* 41. On the "already," that is, the a priori role of the life-world, see 37, 43, 47, and *Crisis,* 110, 142.

74. *Experience and Judgment,* 30, 41.

75. Ibid., 31, 42–43.

76. Thus he anticipates the life-world of the *Crisis.*

77. *Meditations,* 76–77.

78. *Ideas,* 131.

79. *Meditations,* 55, 63.

80. *Crisis,* 135 and 147.

81. *Crisis,* 286.

82. *Crisis,* 8 and 72.

83. See Carr, *Phenomenology and the Problem of History,* 117, and *Experience and Judgment,* 47–48.

84. On the life-world as ground, see *Experience and Judgment,* 30, and *Crisis,* 130–31, 155.

85. *Crisis,* 295–96 (The Vienna Lecture) and 175.

86. *Crisis,* 111–13.

87. *Crisis,* 112–13, 122–25, 137–48.

88. *Crisis,* 123, 139–42, 173–74.

89. *Crisis,* 122, 148–52.

90. *Crisis,* 151.

91. *Crisis*, 153. Cf. 113 where the life-world is presented first as constituting subjectivity and then as a constituted meaning construct, "the construct of a universal, ultimately functioning [*letztfungierende*] subjectivity."

92. James 1:27 (NEB).

93. See Carr's account of Husserl's use of *Besinnung* to express this difference. *Phenomenology and the Problem of History,* 59–62.

94. *Experience and Judgment,* 50, 43–45. I have omitted Husserl's italics.

95. In giving his imprimatur to Eugen Fink's famous defense of phenomenology from neo-Kantian criticism, Husserl claims that his own mode of doing transcendental philosophy is unique while acknowledging that other philosophical projects can rightly call themselves transcendental. "Husserl and Contemporary Criticism," 75, 88–103. The distinguishing feature of Husserl's version is the anteworldly character of the transcendental ego. See 95–99.

96. Quentin Lauer sees Hegel as a transcendental philosopher but with a difference, as "the exercise of the epoché and the reductions has permitted Husserl to eliminate whatever is idiosyncratic to individual subjectivity and has provided him with a sort of subjectivity as such." Though Hegel is in the transcendental tradition that seeks "a subject which will find in the consciousness of itself the consciousness of all reality, [he] does not come up with *such* a 'transcendental subjectivity'," that is, a thin, pure, worldless kind. "Phenomenology: Hegel and Husserl," 188. My italics. When Lauer correctly adds that "Hegel . . . is not bothered by contingency" (196), this does not mean he does not see and address the problems it raises for a philosophy that would be scientific.

97. PS, 102. *History and Truth,* ch. 2–4.

98. See *History and Truth,* 64–65 and ch. 5. The difference, then, is not so much that Hegel moves more quickly and easily from I to We than Husserl does, but that for Hegel both I and We are naturally and culturally in the world. As Maurice Natanson puts it, "The Cartesian 'I' is the subject of the statement, 'I think'. It is an 'I' without depth . . . One slips into the 'I' as one tries on a shoe. There is no indication the 'I' can be ravaged, that the course of experience may be dark, that mood and desire are central to the ego. The 'I' . . . is apparently sexless—an epistemic neuter." *Edmund Husserl: Philosopher of Infinite Tasks* (Evanston: Northwestern University Press, 1973), 148. Hegel's departure from this Cartesianism is deliberate and conscious, Husserl's reluctant and unwitting.

99. See ch. 1.

100. Hegel, GW 4:419, 479.

101. It is just this idea which appalls Husserl in his discussion of *Weltanschauung* philosophy in *Phenomenology and Crisis*, 129ff.

102. PS, 1–2.

103. PS, 7. To emphasize the *essential* nature of the mediation involved, Hegel uses organic metaphors in this and the preceding paragraph: first bud, blossom, and fruit; then acorn and oak. Science is the crown of a spiritual world as the top of a tree.

104. PS, 14. My italics.

105. See Reinhart Klemens Mauser, *Hegel und die Ende der Geschichte: Interpretation zur Phänomenologie des Geistes* (Stuttgart: Kohlhammer, 1965).

106. PS, 487.

107. For a fuller account see *History and Truth*, secs. 2B–2D, 6C–8B, and ch. 5 above.

Chapter Eight

1. Dale M. Schlitt, "Feature Book Review: Hegel's Berlin Lectures: Determinate Religion," *The Owl of Minerva* 18 (1987): 179.

2. *Sigla* for works of Hegel are found at the beginning of the Bibliography.

3. Hegel's sustained and systematic discussions of Hinduism come in the great lecture series, unpublished during his lifetime, on the history of philosophy, the philosophy of history, and the philosophy of religion, along with his lengthy review of Humboldt's essay on the *Bhagavad-Gita*. There are numerous, but scattered references in the lectures on aesthetics.

4. For a more detailed study of this passage, see ch. 1 above.

5. For a helpful account of features of Hinduism which are central to Hegel's analysis of it and which emphasize both the element of technique and the claim of freedom, see Mircea Eliade, *Yoga: Immortality and Freedom*, trans. Willard R. Trask (Princeton: Princeton University Press, 1958). See also the selections from *The Yoga Sutras of Patanjali* in *A Sourcebook in Indian Philosophy*, ed. Sarvepalli Radhakrishnan and Charles A. Moore (Princeton: Princeton University Press, 1957).

6. For extended discussion of this theme, see ch. 9 and 10 below.

7. Walter Jaeschke has suggested that Hegel's method is typifying and typologizing, DR, 87. This is helpful, especially if we think of the way in

which Weber's ideal types are at once a priori and empirical. Paul Ricoeur puts it nicely: "The 'types' which we propose are at the same time *a priori*, permitting us to go to the encounter with experience with a key for deciphering it in our hands and to orient ourselves . . . and *a posteriori*, always subject to correction and amendment through contact with experience." *The Symbolism of Evil*, trans. Emerson Buchanan (New York: Harper and Row, 1967), 171–72. Hegel's Logic can be thought of in just this way.

8. Hegel himself identifies Identity, Difference, and Ground with Universality, Particularity, and Individuality at EL, ¶164, just as he identifies the latter with Indeterminacy, Determination, and Self-Determination at PR, ¶¶5–7.

9. That Hegel has these two in mind is clear from PHI, 132. Cf. DR, 241 n. 27.

10. If there is any point at which Hegel's treatment of world religions is "surprisingly appreciative" (see n. 1 above), it is his treatment of Judaism. In 1821 he still sounds much like his "early theological writings," but in the latter three series he is much more positive (DR, 48–49, 67–69). While he often stresses the strangeness and remoteness of oriental religion to the Western mind, especially in the lectures on aesthetics (A, 20, 272, 308–309, 978, 1058, 1095; cf. NR, 271; and BG, 134–36, 149–50), he emphasizes how easily we can be at home in the Old Testament (A, 374–75, 1058).

11. Compare with this the famous passage about the "power of the negative" in PS, 19.

12. We might speak here of spiritual 'consummation', in keeping with the translation of *die vollendete Religion* as Consummate Religion in the new Hodgson translation. But while 'consummate' makes a better adjective than 'perfect', 'perfection' makes a better noun in this context than 'consummation'.

13. Hegel criticizes Schlegel's translation of Yoga as '*devotio*' in comparison to Humboldt's translation as '*Vertiefung*', for reasons that will appear shortly. But he recognizes in the adjective Schlegel uses an important element of Yoga, one possibly best known to Western readers today from the Zen tradition.

14. Hegel seems unaware of the degree to which aptitude, talent, and skill are matters of nature, too. He does recognize the tension between this assault on position by birth and his view of monarchy, though his defense has the character of mere assertion. "The sole exception is the ruling dynasty and the peerage, for higher reasons grounded in the essential nature of the state itself. This apart, birth makes no essential difference in relation to the class which an individual can or wishes to enter," A, 209–210. Students of Hegel's political theory will also find his comments on war in the previous section of ironical interest.

15. Here I use the terms bias, prejudice, and a priori in keeping with the meaning Gadamer gives to prejudice in *Truth and Method.*

16. For an account of the typology I would use for interpreting these strands of Hindu tradition, see *God, Guilt, and Death: An Existential Phenomenology of Religion* (Bloomington: Indiana University Press, 1984), ch. 9–10.

17. See ch. 9 below.

Chapter Nine

1. Karl Barth, *Protestant Thought: From Rousseau to Ritschl,* 268.

2. HP 1:73.

3. Charles Taylor, *Hegel,* 486. For one expression of the view that one can only speak in a "very attenuated sense" of Hegel's Protestantism, see Karl Löwith, *From Hegel to Nietzsche,* 19–20. On 34 he adds, "For Luther, the content of the Christian faith was determined by revelation; through Rousseau's mediation, in the French Revolution [which Hegel treats as the fulfillment of the Reformation] the European spirit determined for itself the content of its goal."

4. The one exception is the Jesus he seeks to save from his followers, sometimes a Kantian moralist, at other times a pantheistically oriented humanist.

5. ETW, 131, 141.

6. See Westphal, *History and Truth in Hegel's Phenomenology,* 48, and the passages cited in nn. 75–78. Also see ETW, 117–23. In the fragments, "Volksreligion und Christentum," in Nohl's *Hegel's Theologische Jugendschriften,* 42, Hegel writes, "How far Luther was, for example, from the idea of worshiping God in spirit and in truth is clear from his dismal disputes with Zwingli, Oecolampadius, etc. He denied to spiritual authorities the power to rule through force and over the pocketbook, but he wanted to retain authority over people's beliefs."

7. ETW, 93, 105–107, 110, 113–14. In the drafts now known as "The German Constitution," Hegel reiterates this point, noting that sometimes practice was better than constitution. He also repudiates the corresponding principle in the Peace of Westphalia, *cuius regio eius religio,* and notes the role of the sectarian Thirty Years War in Germany's disunity. HPW, 189–92. These drafts were begun in Frankfurt and continued in Jena.

8. ETW, 301. For the difference between the "early" young Hegel, concerned for religious liberty and the separation of church from state, and the "late" young Hegel, concerned for uniting sacred and secular, see ch. 13 below.

9. FK, 57.

10. Karl Rosenkranz, *Georg Wilhelm Friedrich Hegels Leben*, 139–41.

11. I find this case entirely convincing as argued in *History and Truth*, ch. 2.

12. ETW, 146–47. He adds: "It looks as if the authorities in church and state were content that the memory of how our forefathers had a sense of this right [to make reforms in religion], how thousands could stake their lives to vindicate it, should slumber in our hearts and not be retained in any living fashion."

13. Hegel's address can be found in BS, quotations from 31 and 33. For examples of Hegel's anti-Catholic rhetoric, see 35, 49, and the following: HP 3: 389; PH, 412, 449; PM, 285.

14. PHI, 54. Hegel's italics. The German text in VG, 62, reads, "Erst die *germanischen* Nationen sind im Christendom zum Bewusstsein gekommen, dass der Mensch als Mensch frei ist . . . " I have modified Nisbet's translation, which reads, "The *Germanic* nations, with the rise of Christianity, were the first . . . " Both his "with the rise of Christianity" and Sibree's "under the influence of Christianity," PH, 18, call attention to the influence of Christianity on the Germanic nations. The thrust of Hegel's "Erst die germanischen nationen . . . im Christendom" seems to me to emphasize a different aspect of the matter, that the German nations were the first to understand the Christian meaning of human freedom.

In reference to the question of Hegel's nationalism and the subsequent "German Christian" phenomenon under the Third Reich, it is worth noting here that "German" is essentially synonymous with "Protestant," not with "German-speaking." That in the concluding section of PH, "The German World" refers to the northern, Protestant nations of Europe has been pointed out by Walter Kaufmann, in *Hegel's Political Philosophy*, 6, and by W. H. Walsh in "Principle and Prejudice in Hegel's Philosophy of History," in Pelczynski's *Hegel's Political Philosophy*, 183.

15. PH, 417. The German reads, "der Mensch is durch sich selbst bestimmt, frei zu sein." Especially against the background of Luther's doctrine of Christian calling or vocation, it seems to me necessary to read *Bestimmen zu* as intention rather than as destiny. The "durch sich selbst," which Luther would surely have had trouble with, seems to imply self-determination rather than mere essence. So I've altered Sibree's translation, which reads, "Man is in his very nature destined to be free."

270   *Notes*

16. PH, 415.

17. PM, 284. (All quotations from PM in this chapter from par. 552.)

18. PH, 412–13.

19. HP, 3:54–55.

20. LPR, 3:133.

21. LPR, 3:133. On spiritual slavery, cf. PM, 284–85. That the difference between Catholic and Protestant involves both theory and practice, theology and ethics, or even politics, is also expressed in HP, 3:147, and PH, 413–14.

22. CR, 271.

23. LPR, 3:133–34. For other formulations of this consecration by faith alone theme, see HP, 3:43, 149; PM, 284–85; and PH, 415. In both LPR and CR, Hegel also distinguishes the Lutheran view from the "Reformed" view, which he criticizes for giving up the "mystical" element in the sacrament, the real presence of Christ, by reducing the rite to a memorial. He evidently has the Zwinglian view in mind rather than the Calvinist, which retains the concept of real presence.

24. CR, 271–72.

25. PH, 415.

26. ETW, 121.

27. ETW, 128. Cf. 71, where he portrays Jesus as the opponent of all authority in matters of behavior.

28. PH, 416. Cf. 456 on the necessary balance of the subjective and objective poles.

29. HP, 3:149, 152.

30. HP, 3:147. Emphasis added. Cf. 114, where the Reformation is assimilated to the Renaissance because "its principle is simply this, that it led man back to himself . . . "; and 154, where "the basis of the Reformation is the abstract moment of mind being within self, of freedom, of coming to self; freedom signifies the life of the spirit in being turned back within itself in the particular content which appears as another."

31. PM, 291. Emphasis added.

32. PH, 343. Emphasis added. Cf. 344–45, where with reference to both theory and practice this is interpreted as the supremacy of Thought or Reason over custom and tradition.

33. PR, 12, preface.

34. HP, 3:217–18. Cf. 191, where a similar passage relates the Protestant principle to Boehme.

35. *Nature, Man, and God* (London: Macmillan, 1960), 62–63.

36. Preserved Smith, *The Life and Letters of Martin Luther* (New York: Houghton Mifflin, 1911), 118. Emphasis added.

37. See, for example, his 1535 *Lectures on Galatians.*

38. Hegel is not wholly unaware of the differences, and while he all too often treats them as nonexistent, there are places where he takes note of them. Thus he overtly sides with Descartes and the Enlightenment against the earlier view that "the command of God, externally imposed as written in the Old and New Testament" should be the norm for human behavior, and he complains that the content of the salvation whose subjective appropriation Luther championed "was taken for granted by Luther as something already given, something revealed by religion," PH, 440–42. And he acknowledges the importance of the Bible in Lutheran thought, but (1) he interprets this almost entirely in terms of the Bible as a "people's book," translated into their own language, without reference to its normative character (PH, 418; HP, 3:150; LPR, 3:81); (2) he complains about the attempt to ground theology on the kind of exegesis that seeks to make the Bible normative (HP 3:12, 151–53); and (3) he completely transforms the Lutheran teaching about the testimony of the spirit in relation to Scripture by writing, "Luther repudiated the authority of the church and set up in its stead the Bible and the testimony of the *Human* Spirit," PH, 417, emphasis added. For Luther the testimony of the Spirit refers to the need of each individual to be dependent upon God the Holy Spirit in seeking to understand what the Bible means. It is precisely the finitude and sinfulness of the human spirit that makes this necessary. On Hegel's repudiation of exegetical theology and his reinterpretation of the witness of the Spirit, see ch. 12 below. For a sympathetic and unsympathetic view of Hegel's assimilation of Protestant Faith with Enlightenment Autonomy, compare Emil Fackenheim, *The Religious Dimension in Hegel's Thought,* 11, with Löwith's *From Hegel to Nietzsche,* 20, 34.

39. For a discussion of how Hegel remains vulnerable to Kierkegaardian criticism in spite of his clear affirmation of subjectivity, see my "Abraham and Hegel," in *Kierkegaard's Fear and Trembling: Critical Appraisals,* ed. Robert L. Perkins (Tuscaloosa: University of Alabama Press, 1981), 71–72 in the context of 62–72.

40. PH, 435–39. "Aber in Denken ist das Selbst sich präsent. . . . Das ist schlechthin die absolute Freiheit, denn das reine Ich ist, wie das reine Licht, schlechthin bei sich."

41. In *The Rebel.*

42. HP 3:159. Cf. PH, 422, where Hegel speaks of the Reformation's recognition of the secular (*das Weltliche*) as capable of being an embodiment of the truth, whereas it had previously been regarded as evil only, incapable of good, which remained *ein Jenseits*.

43. LPR, 3:135.

44. HP, 3:147. For other discussion of Protestantism's turning from the three monastic vows, see LPR 1:251; 3:138–39; PM, 286–87; PH, 380–81, 422; BS, 45–49.

45. FK, 61. For other passages in which Hegel emphasizes the difference between the sixteenth and eighteenth centuries, see HP 3:148–50, 159, 398; LPR, 1:248–50; PH, 419–24.

46. HP 3:398.

47. HP 3:385; PH, 443. For sharply contrasting interpretations of Hegel and the French Revolution, see the title essay of Joachim Ritter, *Hegel and the French Revolution,* and "Hegel's Critique of the French Revolution," in Jürgen Habermas, *Theory and Practice.* Ritter's short essay, "Hegel and the Reformation," also appears in the former volume.

48. LPR 3:138. Speaking of the sixteenth century, Hegel says, "Secularity appears now as gaining a consciousness of its intrinsic worth—becomes aware of having a value of its own in human ethical life, law, personal integrity, and activity. The consciousness of independent validity is aroused through the restoration of Christian Freedom. . . . This third period of the German world extends from the Reformation to our own times. . . . Political life was now to be consciously regulated by reason." PH, 344–45. On 442 he speaks of secular life as the embodiment of the spiritual kingdom.

49. PM, 291. Cf. PH, 456, " . . . through the Protestant church the reconciliation of religion and law [*Recht*] has taken place. There is no holy, religious conscience separated from or even opposed to secular law." When Hegel expresses this, on page 423, by saying that "Reason and the Divine commands are now synonymous," it becomes clear that the Principle of Autonomy is at work in Hegel's concept of Protestant worldliness. This statement occurs in a commentary on the rejection of the monastic vow of obedience and a Rousseauean statement of political citizenship.

50. PR, ¶270.

51. PM, 283. Cf. PH, 417: "This is the sense in which we must understand the state to be based on religion. States and laws are nothing else than religion manifesting itself in the relations of the actual world." Also see BS, 51.

52. Fackenheim, *Religious Dimension,* 177.

53. PM, 287; PH, 453; BS, 39, 51.

54. See the oft-quoted passage (in PR, ¶209:) "A man counts as a man in virtue of his manhood alone, not because he is a Jew, Catholic, Protestant, German, Italian, etc."

55. PH, 416. "Die Zeit von da zu uns hat kein anderes Werk zu tun gehabt und zu tun, als dieses Prinzip in die Welt hineinzubilden . . . " Sibree's translation weakens Hegel's emphasis on the present nature of the task by reducing his two verb tenses to one, "Time . . . has had no other work." In the context of the Revolution, Ritter defines the task as "finding the legal form of freedom and . . . developing a legal order which accords with the freedom of selfhood and does it justice and enables the individual to be himself and achieve his human determination." *Hegel and the French Revolution,* 49–50.

56. PH, 447. In context, it is clear that the reservation expressed by the "as if" applies to the "accomplished" more than to the "first."

57. PH, 380.

58. For discussion of the role of imperatives in Hegel's thought, and the larger question of the relation of theory to practice, see Odo Marquand, "Hegel und das Sollen," and Michael Theunissen, *Die Verwirklichung der Vernunft.*

59. This has implications for the status of his philosophy, which presupposes the reality of the new world of spirit. The social life in which sacred and secular are unified is the existential condition for the union of thought and life which Hegel's philosophy represents. See especially Fackenheim, *Religious Dimension,* 208–20. But if the former unity is present only as the idea whose realization is still in process, Hegel's philosophy, like Luther's theology earlier, could only be, on Hegel's own principles, a preliminary and partial preview of what a fully true system would be. "The Owl of Minerva spreads its wings only with the falling of the dusk." PR, preface.

60. Gadamer, *Reason in the Age of Science,* trans. Frederick G. Lawrence (Cambridge: MIT Press, 1982), 36, 50. On 37 he adds that, since the freedom of all has come to light,

> history is not to be based upon a new principle. The principle of freedom is unimpugnable and irrevocable. It is no longer possible for anyone still to affirm the unfreedom of humanity. The principle that all are free never again can be shaken. But does this mean that on account of this, history has come to an end? Are all human beings actually free? Has not history since then been a matter of just this, that the historical conduct of man has to translate the principle of freedom to reality? Obviously this points to the unending march of world history into the openness of its future tasks and gives no becalming assurance that everything is already in order.

Chapter Ten

1. These formulas, either in just these words or in equivalent phrases, are basic to the four most extensive discussions by the mature Hegel on the relation of religion and the state. Two of these can be identified by paragraph numbers which are standard to German and English editions: PM, ¶552 and PR, ¶270. The other two come from lectures given in 1830 and 1831 respectively: VG, 110ff. and ICR, 451–60.

2. Aristotle, *Nicomachean Ethics,* 1095b 15ff.

3. "Financing Apartheid—Citibank in South Africa," an ICCR Brief published by the Interfaith Center on Corporate Responsibility, 3A.

4. The Tübingen Essay is translated as an appendix to Harris, *Hegel's Development: Toward the Sunlight 1770–1801.* The other two essays are in ETW and in *Werke* 1.

5. PR, p. 167 (¶270Z).

Chapter Eleven

1. Etienne Gilson, *The Christian Philosophy of Saint Augustine* (New York: Random House, 1967), 23.

2. LPR 1:48–52.

3. See ETW.

4. LP, 161. See also PhG, 376–413/549–98. In this chapter and the following two, page numbers after the slash in PhG references will be to the English translation by Baillie, *The Phenomenology of Mind* (New York: Macmillan, 1949).

5. PhG, 397–410/576–94. Cf. HP 3:420.

6. LP, 239 and 156. The first of these references is not from the lectures proper but from a separate discussion of Kant's critique of the proofs found among Hegel's papers and included with the lectures by the German and English editors.

7. LP, 191–92. In the light of statements like this it is clear that the problem of *religious knowledge* for Hegel is the problem of the *knowledge of God* (as well as the problem of positive religion). But there is an ambiguity here. Hegel distinguishes a religious and a philosophical form in which God is known. Were he to use the phrase "religious knowledge" he might well intend only the former. As used in the title and body of this essay, however, the phrase refers generically to the knowledge of God within which such a distinction could be made.

8. LP, 191–92.

9. In this regard Hegel's relation to Schleiermacher parallels Tillich's to Bultmann in our day. Against the failure of Schleiermacher and Bultmann to articulate a systematic theory of God and their tendency to reduce theology to normative expressions of pious self-consciousness and human existence respectively, Hegel and Tillich insist that theology must first and foremost be ontological, and only then existential. The real target, however, is Kant, who is the starting point for both Schleiermacher and (via Heidegger) for Bultmann. It was indeed Kant who insisted that we know God not as He is in Himself, but only in relation to us.

10. GW 4:323. Modernity is not always a reproach on Hegel's lips. See PhG, 24/85–86, and LPR, 1:253; 3:111. But in LPR and LP references to "the present standpoint," "the culture of the age," "our age," etc., normally carry strongly negative implications. When combined with Hegel's frequent statements that philosophy cannot transcend its age, the problem of historicism in Hegel emerges. By historicism I mean the view that reality is an historical process and that knowledge arising within it is so conditioned by its immediate horizon as never to be simply true but only true for such and such a period. If the "almighty age and its culture" are to be surpassed as limited historical perspectives, what assurance can be given that Hegel does not replace them with another, different, but equally limited point of view? Marx and Kierkegaard make this question central to their critiques of Hegel.

11. GW 4:388.

12. The deliberately anachronistic description of Hegel's opposition as positivistic is designed to underscore the deep affinities between what he saw in the prevalent temper of his times and what has since become known as positivism. Similarly, the frequent comparisons of Hegel with other thinkers is designed neither to reduce him to his sources nor to suggest that he must have been a very bright fellow (since he anticipated what some twentieth-century thinker said). Rather, it is assumed that some students of philosophy and theology who are trying to overcome the hurdles of getting into Hegel will be more familiar with some of these other thinkers than with Hegel, and that the comparisons will serve to illumine the unknown by the known.

13. Hegel is fully aware of the close link of logic to mathematics. See LP, 171–72, and WL 1:34/1:63–64; 2:333/2:342. In this chapter and the next numbers after the slash in WL references will be to the Johnson and Struthers translation, *Science of Logic* (New York: Humanities, 1929).

14. *Critique of Pure Reason,* B xvi and xiii.

15. Hegel would have applauded Tillich's description of "controlling knowledge" as knowledge which "unites subject and object for the sake of the control of the object by the subject. It transforms the object into a com-

pletely conditioned and calculable 'thing'. It deprives it of any subjective qualities. [It] looks upon its object as something which cannot return its look . . . [It] 'objectifies' not only logically (which is unavoidable) but also ontologically and ethically." *Systematic Theology* (Chicago: University of Chicago Press, 1951), 1:97.

16. PhG, 35–38/100–103.

17. LP, 167–71.

18. ETW, 171. Today one might make the same point by noting that our technological rationality is useful if it is a matter of getting to the moon, but it offers nothing but moon rocks to a world starving for food, justice, and peace.

19. LP, 163.

20. GW, 4:331. For a helpful discussion of this same issue as developed in the introductory materials to EL, see John Smith, "The Relation of Thought and Being: Some Lessons from Hegel's *Encyclopedia*," *The New Scholasticism* 38 (January 1964).

21. WL 1:13–16, 25/1:43–45, 55; PhG, 63–68/131–36.

22. LP, 168.

23. LP, 169–70.

24. LPR, 1:15.

25. LPR, 1:35–36; PhG, 14/73.

26. LP, 173.

27. HP 3:257; GW 4:342. This contrast presupposes that one either ignores or rejects Kant's repeated claim in the second Critique that we do achieve *knowledge* of God.

28. LP, 161.

29. This position can be called fideism only if it is remembered that it has absolutely nothing to do with another way of elevating faith above reason as in Augustine, Luther, Kierkegaard, Barth, and, with well-known qualifications, Aquinas. According to these thinkers, special, divine revelation in history and scripture and not reason as a universal human capacity, whether intuitive or discursive, is the final norm for the knowledge of God.

30. *Prolegomena, Werke,* Akademie Textausgabe 4:258–59.

31. LP, 232.

32. LP, 174–77.

33. LP, 178.

34. LP, 181–83; cf. LPR 1:129–30.

35. HP 3:421.

36. LP, 183–86; LPR 1:131, 188–89; GW 4:385.

37. LPR 1:51.

38. Paul Tillich, in ch. 6 of *The Courage to Be*.

39. Leslie Dewart, in ch. 2 of *The Future of Belief.*

40. LP, 189; PhG, 45/112. Among the commentators Findlay, Haym, and Fackenheim are particularly sensitive to the Hegelian empiricism. The latter two stress its connection with the problem of historicism. If the subject matter to which knowledge abandons itself is an historical subject matter, that knowledge will be relative to and valid only for the epoch which it chooses or is given as its beloved. Thus when Hegel complains that "there are no traces in Logic of the new spirit which has arisen both in learning and in life," and when he describes his own Logic as a work "pertaining to the modern world," he seems to be all but confessing that his own Logic is ideology. See WL 1:5 and 22/1:35 and 51.

41. LP, 158, 303–304. Cf. 195 and 283.

42. LP, 163.

43. A student manuscript of LP begins with the sentence, "These lectures may be viewed as a supplement to the Logic." Hegel's own manuscript reads, in the opening paragraph: "I have therefore chosen a subject which is connected with the other set of lectures which I gave on logic, and constitutes, not in substance, but in form, a kind of supplement to that set, inasmuch as it is concerned with only a particular aspect of the fundamental conceptions of logic. These lectures are therefore chiefly meant for those of my hearers who were present at the others, and to them they will be most easily intelligible," LP, 155.

44. LP, 202. Elsewhere Hegel describes the task as "reconstructing their true significance, thus restoring their fundamental ideas to their worth and dignity," WL 2:356/2:346.

45. LP, 264–65.

46. Emile Durkheim, *The Elementary Forms of the Religious Life,* trans. Joseph Ward Swain (New York: Free Press, 1965), 14–15. It was Hegel's adoption of this principle around 1800 which constituted his break with Enlightenment criticism. He called for a theology that "would derive that now discarded theology from what we now know as a need of human nature and would thus exhibit its naturalness and inevitability. An attempt to do this presupposes the belief that the convictions of many centuries, regarded as sacrosanct, true, and obligatory by the millions who lived and

died by them in those centuries, were not, at least on their subjective side, downright folly or plain immorality." ETW, 172. Cf. PhG, 391–92/569–70.

47. LP, 229 and 313.

48. LP, 267.

49. LP, 269 and 276–77. Marx and Kierkegaard both complain that Hegel talks as if thinking could replace existence; as if conceiving the ideal were identical with realizing it. Hegel explicitly denies that here, for he goes on to add: "It is not the act of rising to this necessity on the part of spirit which in itself produces satisfaction. The satisfaction has reference to the goal spirit tries to reach and is in proportion to its reaching this goal."

50. LP, 164.

51. Had he remembered his Luther or been able to foresee Kierkegaard, Hegel might have examined this latter point of view as the fourth attitude of thought toward objectivity in the introduction to EL.

52. LP, 290–92. Hegel's language here evokes the picture of Luke 16:26 (Luther's translation) in which Lazarus in Abraham's bosom and the rich man in Hades are separated by a gulf fixed between them.

53. LP, 315–17. Cf. 247–48.

54. LP, 285–90.

55. LP, 297. Tillich has said that since "pantheism" has become a "heresy label" it "should be defined before it is applied aggressively." *Systematic Theology* 1:233. Whether the usage is aggressive or otherwise, one could do worse than defining as pantheistic those systems which view classical theism as dualistic. In this sense the label fits both Hegel and Tillich.

56. LP, 298–99.

57. ETW, 301.

58. Bertrand Russell's essay, "A Free Man's Worship," is a classical modern expression both of the view of the world which is supposed to be transcended in the cosmological proof and of the inadequate way of doing so which Hegel is here criticizing.

59. LP, 318–20; LPR 1:109. Cf. PhG, 19 and 43/79 and 110.

60. Quentin Lauer, "Hegel on Proofs of God's Existence." 444. The constant reiteration of this thesis mars this otherwise helpful essay.

61. LP, 215; WL 2:356 and 229–30/2:345 and 225–26.

62. This has been made particularly clear by J. N. Findlay in the second part of his essay, "Can God's Existence Be Disproved?," *Mind* (April, 1948); and by John Smith in his emphasis on the importance for Anselm of

discovering the appropriate philosophical formula for expressing the content of his religious faith. See *Experience and God* (New York: Oxford, 1968), ch. 5. Another striking example indicates that such a preliminary reflection determines the neoclassical direction of Charles Hartshorne's version of the proof. He writes, "For reasons that I have given in various writings, I take 'true religion' to mean serving God, by which I do not mean simply admiring or 'obeying' him, or enabling him to give benefits to me and other nondivine creatures, but also, and most essentially, contributing value to God which he would otherwise lack. Even in this religions case, to 'serve' is to confer a benefit, in precisely the sense that the served will to some extent depend upon the server for that benefit. This is genuine dependence . . . In short, God with contingency but lacking dependence is not the God we can serve or, in what I think is the proper meaning, worship," "The Dipolar Conception of Deity," *The Review of Metaphysics* 21 (December 1967), 274.

63. WL 1:75/1:102. Cf. 2:355/2:345. Hegel's invoking of the distinction between abstract and concrete in God raises the question of his relation to Hartshorne's neoclassical version of the ontological argument. He sees in Hegel "a man who is and wants to be in a perpetual systematic muddle between classical theism, classical pantheism, and something like neoclassical theism, with a dose of humanistic atheism, or the self-deification of man, thrown in for good measure," *Anselm's Discovery* (LaSalle: Open Court, 1965), 235. As LP is understood in the present essay Hegel's position is considerably less muddled. He clearly wants nothing to do with either the kind of transcendence affirmed in classical theism or the finitude affirmed by neoclassical theism. His position is and wants to be a systematic mediation between classical pantheism and atheistic humanism. Hartshorne is misled, probably by Hegel's use of the abstract-concrete distinction, into sensing an affinity for neoclassical theism. But that distinction is present in Aquinas, and is no sure sign of the neoclassical. See "Temporality and Finitism in Hartshorne's Theism," *The Review of Metaphysics* 19 (March 1966): 561ff.

64. LPR, 1:61.

65. PH, 11–13; VG, 36–39.

66. PH, 9–10; VG, 28–29.

67. *The Use and Abuse of History,* trans. Collins (New York: Liberal Arts Press, 1957), 51–52.

68. *Writings of the Young Marx on Philosophy and Society.* trans. Easton and Guddat (Garden City: Doubleday, 1967), 156–57, 179.

69. Since Hegel regularly describes this purification as the raising of the content from its defective religious form (*Vorstellung*) to the adequacy of philosophical form (*Begriff*), Mure's treatment of the relation of the two is relevant here. See "Hegel: How, and How Far, is Philosophy Possible?" in

Weiss's *Beyond Epistemology.* One of Hegel's most important claims is to have provided a mode of thinking free of dependence on the imagination. It is also one of the most difficult claims to understand and evaluate.

Chapter Twelve

1. *Lessing's Theological Writings,* ed. Chadwick (Stanford: Stanford University Press, 1957), 54–55.

2. A helpful historical treatment of this conflation of apologetics and hermeneutics is found in Hans Frei's *The Eclipse of Biblical Narrative* (New Haven: Yale University Press, 1974). I am indebted to Hans Frei for helpful criticisms of an earlier version of this essay.

3. Lessing also speaks of the latter when he writes that "the written traditions must be interpreted by their inward truth," *Theological Writings,* 18.

4. Or whatever nontrinitarian ontology he has in mind. I do not mean to beg the question of his exact relation to Spinoza.

5. LPR, 1:77, 151; 3:75.

6. PhG, 525–29/755–60. See n. 4 in ch. 11.

7. Compare PhG, 530–35/762–68 with 541–43/775–78. Of the religious interpretation Hegel says, "This *Vorstellung,* which in this manner is still immediate and hence not spiritual, i.e., it knows the human form assumed by the divine as merely a particular form, not yet as a universal form—becomes spiritual for this consciousness in the process whereby God, who has assumed shape and form, surrenders again His immediate existence, and returns to his essential being."

8. LPR, 1:156.

9. PhG, 532 and 535/764 and 768.

10. The former alternative is that attempted by Pannenberg. The latter is that adopted by Hans Frei. See n. 2 above.

11. LPR, 2:342.

12. LPR, 1:28–32; 2:342–45.

13. LPR, 1:29–30. This is why Hegel's own Logic is not only a theory of categories but also a theory about God. It "shows forth God as He is in His eternal essence before the creation of nature and finite spirit." WL 1:31/ 1:60. See n. 13 in ch. 11. Similarly, at EL, ¶85, he writes, "Being itself and the special sub-categories of it which follow, i. e., the logical categories as

such, may be looked upon as definitions of the Absolute, or metaphysical definitions of God."

14. LPR, 1:219–20.

15. LPR, 1:217–18, 223. The first quotation is itself quoted from Meister Eckhardt, favorably of course. The second bears a striking resemblance to Durkheim's later analysis. See n. 46 in ch. 11.

16. See ch. 13 below.

17. Wolfhart Pannenberg, *et al., Revelation as History* (New York: Macmillan, 1968), 17–18.

18. "Hermeneutics and Universal History," *History and Hermeneutics* (New York: Harper and Row, 1967), 151.

19. In endorsing Karl Popper's verdict, "Although history has no meaning, we can give it a meaning," Ronald Gregor Smith exemplifies the union of theology and positivism which is Pannenberg's concern here. See *Secular Christianity* (New York: Harper and Row, 1966), 175–85.

20. See LP, first four lectures, and EL, ¶¶37–78.

21. Pannenberg, "Hermeneutics and Universal History," 130–32, 138–41.

22. "Hermeneutics and Universal History," 150–51.

23. *Jesus—God and Man* (Philadelphia: Westminster, 1968), 83.

24. *Revelation as History,* 139–42. Cf. 144, "While it is only the whole history that demonstrates the deity of the one God, and this result can only be given at the end of all history, there is still one particular event that has absolute meaning as the revelation of God, namely the Christ event, insofar as it anticipates the end of history."

25. *Jesus—God and Man,* 49.

26. "Redemptive Event and History," in *Essays in Old Testament Hermeneutics,* ed. Claus Westermann (Richmond: Knox, 1966), 315n and 316–17. The link between creation and eschatology makes intelligible, indeed demands, the universalizing of the concept of the Kingdom of God as the future of man and not merely the future of Israel. On this link also see the title essay of Pannenberg, *Theology and the Kingdom of God* (Philadelphia: Westminster, 1969).

27. *Theology and the Kingdom of God,* 63; "Redemptive Event and History," 315n and 324–29; "The Revelation of God in Jesus of Nazareth," in *Theology as History,* ed. Robinson and Cobb (New York: Harper and Row, 1967), 132n; and "The Crisis of the Scripture Principle in Protestant Theology," *Dialog* 2(Fall 1963): 308 and 312.

28. "The Crisis . . . ", 312.

29. Some of the church fathers liked to quote Deuteronomy 21:10–13 as a paradigm for the relation of theology to secular thought. Apparently Pannenberg would not entirely object, in spite of the freeness of the allegory.

30. *Theology and the Kingdom of God,* 76.

31. An earlier version of this essay was presented to the annual Philosophy Conference at Wheaton College (Illinois) in November 1969.

Chapter Thirteen

1. Karl Rosenkranz, *Georg Wilhelm Friedrich Hegel's Leben,* 10.

2. ETW, 104–29, 301. Actually the earliest of these writings, the fragments on folk religion, not in ETW, belong as much to the "late" as to the "early" young Hegel.

3. PhG, 317–42/462–99. See n. 4 in ch. 11. For a brief but valuable statement of Hegel's view of tragedy, see Robert Corrigan, *Tragedy: Vision and Form* (San Francisco: Chandler, 1965), 428–42.

4. Hegel's especially vigorous repudiation of his early heroes of autonomy reminds one of Whitehead's description of the Enlightenment as the age of "one-eyed reason" and his claim that "if men cannot live on bread alone, still less can they do so on disinfectants," *Science and the Modern World,* ch. 4.

5. PhG, 376–422/549–610. Hegel would not agree with Peter Gay or Ernst Cassirer, whom Gay quotes favorably as saying that the Enlightenment "joined to a degree scarcely ever achieved before, the critical with the productive function and converted the one directly into the other," *The Enlightenment: An Interpretation: The Rise of Modern Paganism* (New York: Random House, 1968), 131.

6. LPR, 1:231–32, 241.

7. See ch. 9 above.

8. LPR, 3:135–38.

9. The final paragraphs of LPR, from which this statement comes, are perhaps the most depressing anywhere in Hegel's work. These lectures were given by Hegel four times during his Berlin years, the period during which he is supposed to have been deifying the Prussian state.

10. ETW, 253–81.

11. PhG, as in n. 5 above, plus 471–72, 564/677–79, 808.

12. LP, 293–99. Cf. ch. 11 above. The movement beyond substance to living spirit is also found in PhG, 19–24/80–86.

13. See the first reference of n. 12.

14. Ronald Gregor Smith makes this point nicely, and quotes Bonhoeffer in so doing. *Secular Christianity* (New York: Harper and Row, 1966), 175–85.

15. This is not entirely unambiguous. An essential quality of a theonomous culture is "the affirmation of the autonomous forms of the creative process." But this is immediately qualified by the addition of "valid," i.e., it is the valid autonomous forms which are preserved. This is consistent with the fact that Tillichean theonomy does not preserve the autonomous forms of, for example, positivistic philosophy, but appears to it as an entirely heteronomous enemy. Since this theonomy does not leave secular culture's autonomy entirely untouched, but accepts only what is "valid," it is not clear why (since Barth would say exactly the same thing) this "theonomy" is not just an honorific title for Tillich's own particular heteronomy, just as "ortho-doxy" is frequently a synonym for "my opinion." See *Systematic Theology* (Chicago: University of Chicago Press, 1951–63), 3:251. Henceforth cited as ST.

16. ST 1:12, 172, 236.

17. ST 1:188–252.

18. Barth, *Protestant Thought,* 268–72. My italics.

19. *Protestant Thought,* 271.

20. Fackenheim, *The Religious Dimension in Hegel's Thought,* 224. My italics.

21. Ibid., 232–33.

22. Ibid., 242.

23. The suggestion that Fackenheim and Tillich stand together against Hegel concerns only the specific point in question. That there will be important differences between them is apparent from the fact that one is a Jewish, the other a Christian thinker. Since the substance of Fackenheim's pursuit of the fragmented middle is not presented, nothing in the following discussion locates him with reference to the dilemma posed by Hegel and Tillich.

24. LPR 3:149–51.

25. Ibid.

26. In continuing to speak of *"the* biblical concept" I am not overlooking the differences and developments to which biblical theology directs our attention. Rather, the suggestion is like that of Eichrodt's *Theology of the Old Testament,* that living in and through those differences and developments is a single, unifying core which can be recognized.

27. 1 Cor. 2:9 (RSV). For further discussion of these issues, see ch. 12 above, and "On Thinking of God as King," *Christian Scholar's Review* (Fall 1979): 27–34.

BIBLIOGRAPHY

I. Works by Hegel

The abbreviations given to the left are used throughout the notes and in the text of several chapters.

A   *Aesthetics: Lectures on Fine Art*, 2 vols. translated by T.M. Knox (Oxford: Clarendon, 1975).

BG   Über die unter dem Namen Bhagavad-Gita bekannte Episode des Mahabharata. Von Wilhelm von Humboldt. In *Werke*, Bd. 11.

BS   *Berliner Schriften: 1818–31*, edited by J. Hoffmeister (Hamburg: Felix Meiner, 1955).

CR   *The Christian Religion.* Translated by Peter C. Hodgson (Missoula: Scholars Press, 1979).

DR   *Determinate Religion*, vol. 2 of *Lectures on the Philosophy of Religion.* Edited by Peter Hodgson (Berkeley: University of California Press, 1987).

EL   *The Logic of Hegel*, translated from *The Encyclopedia of the Philosophical Sciences* by William Wallace, 2d ed. (Oxford: Clarendon, 1892). N.B. Citations are to paragraph numbers, not page numbers, unless otherwise indicated.

ETW   *On Christianity: Early Theological Writings.* Translated by T.M. Knox (New York: Harper, 1961).

FK   *Faith and Knowledge.* Translated by Walter Cerf and H.S. Harris (Albany: SUNY, 1977).

GW   *Gesammelte Werke*, hrsg. im Auftrag der Deutschen Forschungsgemeinschaft, (Hamburg: Felix Meiner).

HP   *Lectures on the History of Philosophy.* Translated by E. S. Haldane and Frances H. Simpson (New York: Humanities, 1955).

HPW   *Hegel's Political Writings.* Translated by T.M. Knox (Oxford: Clarendon, 1964).

HTJ   *Hegels Theologische Jugendschriften,* hrsg. von H. Nohl (Tübingen: J. B. C. Mohr, 1907).

ICR   *Introduction and the Concept of Religion,* vol.1, of *Lectures on the Philosophy of Religion.* Edited by Peter Hodgson (Berkeley: University of California Press, 1984).

LP   *Lectures on the Proofs of the Existence of God,* in vol. 3 of LPR.

LPR   *Lectures on the Philosophy of Religion.* Translated by E. B. Spiers and J. Burdon Sanderson (New York: Humanities, 1962). See DR and ICR for reference to the newer, Hodgson edition of LPR.

NL   *Natural Law.* Translated by T.M. Knox (n.p.: University of Pennsylvania Press, 1975).

PH   *The Philosophy of History.* Translated by J. Sibree (New York: Dover, 1956).

PhG   *Phänomenologie des Geistes,* hrsg. von Johannes Hoffmeister (Hamburg: Felix Meiner, 1952).

PHI   *Lectures on the Philosophy of World History: Introduction, Reason in History.* Translated by H. B. Nisbet (Cambridge: Cambridge University Press, 1975).

PM   *Philosophy of Mind.* Translated from *The Encyclopedia of the Philosophical Sciences* by William Wallace and A.V. Miller (Oxford: Clarendon, 1971).

PR   *Philosophy of Right.* Translated by T.M. Knox (Oxford: Clarendon, 1942). N. B. Citations are to paragraph numbers, not page numbers, unless otherwise indicated.

PS   *Phenomenology of Spirit.* Translated by A.V. Miller (Oxford: Clarendon, 1977).

SL   *Science of Logic.* Translated by A.V. Miller (New York: Humanities, 1969).

SuW   *Werke in zwanzig Bänden,* hrsg. von Eva Moldenhauer and Karl Markus Michel (Frankfurt: Suhrkamp, 1970–71).

VG   *Die Vernunft in der Geschichte,* hrsg. von J. Hoffmeister (Hamburg: Felix Meiner, 1955).

WL   *Wissenschaft der Logik,* hrsg. von Georg Lasson (Hamburg: Felix Meiner, 1934).

Z   *Zusatz.* The *Zusätze* to PR are given by Knox as Additions at the conclusion of the text. Those in EL and PM are found right with the paragraph to which they are assigned.

Minor changes in some of the English translations have been made without noting them.

II. Works about Hegel

Avineri, Schlomo. *Hegel's Theory of the Modern State.* Cambridge: Cambridge University Press, 1972.

Barth, Karl. *Protestant Thought: From Rousseau to Ritschl.* Translated by B. Cozens. New York: Harper and Row, 1959.

Dove, Kenley. "Logik und Recht bei Hegel." *Neue Hefte Für Philosophie,* vol. 17.

————. "The Relationship of Habermas's Views to Hegel." In Verene.

Fackenheim, Emil. *The Religious Dimension in Hegel's Thought.* Bloomington: Indiana University Press, 1967.

Fulda, H. *Das Recht der Philosophie in Hegels Philosophie des Rechts.* Frankfurt: Klostermann, 1965.

Gadamer, Hans-Georg. *Hegel's Dialectic: Five Hermeneutical Studies.* Translated by P. Christopher Smith. New Haven: Yale University Press, 1976.

Habermas, Jürgen. *Theory and Practice.* Translated by John Viertel. Boston: Beacon, 1973.

Harris, H.S. *Hegel's Development: Toward the Sunlight: 1770–1801.* Oxford: Clarendon Press, 1972.

————. *Hegel's Development: Night Thoughts (Jena 1801–1806).* Oxford: Clarendon Press, 1983.

Henrich, Dieter. *Hegel im Context.* Frankfurt: Suhrkamp, 1971.

Kaufmann, Walter, ed., *Hegel's Political Philosophy.* New York: Atherton, 1970.

Lauer, Quentin. "Phenomenology: Hegel and Husserl." In Weiss.

Löwith, Karl. *From Hegel to Nietzsche: the Revolution in Nineteenth Century Thought.* Translated by David E. Green. New York: Holt, Rinehart and Winston, 1964.

Lukacs, G. *The Young Hegel.* Translated by R. Livingston. Cambridge: MIT Press, 1976.

Maker, William, ed. *Hegel on Economics and Freedom.* Macon: Mercer University Press, 1987.

Marquand, O. "Hegel und das Sollen." *Philosophisches Jahrbuch.* 72 (1964).

Mauser, Reinhart Klemens. *Hegel und das Ende der Geschichte: Interpretation zur Phänomenologie des Geistes.* Stuttgart: Kohlhammer, 1965.

O'Malley, J. J., *et al.*, ed., *The Legacy of Hegel.* The Hague: Nijhoff, 1973.

Pelczynski, Z. A., ed., *Hegel's Political Philosophy: Problems and Perspectives.* Cambridge: Cambridge University Press, 1971.

———. *The State and Civil Society: Studies in Hegel's Political Philosophy.* Cambridge: Cambridge University Press, 1984.

Plant, Raymond. *Hegel.* Bloomington: Indiana University Press, 1973.

Riedel, Manfred. *Studien zu Hegel's Rechtsphilosophie.* Frankfurt: Suhrkamp, 1969.

Ritter, Joachim. *Hegel and the French Revolution: Essays on the Philosophy Of Right.* Translated by Richard Winfield. Cambridge: MIT Press, 1982.

———. *Metaphysik und Politik: Studien zu Aristotles und Hegel.* Frankfurt: Suhrkamp, 1969.

Rockmore, Tom. *Hegel's Circular Epistemology.* Bloomington: Indiana University Press, 1986.

Rosenkranz, Karl. *Georg Wilhelm Friedrich Hegels Leben.* Darmstadt: Wissenschaftliche Buchgesellschaft, 1963.

Schlitt, Dale. "Feature Book Review: Hegel's Berlin Lectures: Determinate Religion." *The Owl of Minerva* 18:2 (Spring 1987).

Schrader, George. "Hegel's Contribution to Phenomenology." *The Monist* 48 (1964).

Siep, Ludwig. "Der Kampf um Anerkennung." *Hegel Studien* 9 (1974).

————. "Dialektik der Anerkennung bei Hegel." *Hegel Jahrbuch* (1974).

Smith, John. "Hegel's Critique of Kant." *The Review of Metaphysics* 26 (March 1973).

————. "The Relation of Thought to Being: Some Lessons from Hegel's *Encyclopedia.*" *The New Scholasticism* 38 (January 1964).

Taylor, Charles. *Hegel.* Cambridge: Cambridge University Press, 1975.

————. *Hegel and Modern Society.* Cambridge: Cambridge University Press, 1979.

Theunissen, Michael. *Hegels Lehre vom absoluten Geist als theologisch-politischer Traktat.* Berlin: deGruyter, 1970.

————. *Die Verwirklichung der Vernunft: Zur Theorie-Praxis Discussion im Anschluss an Hegel.* Tübingen: J. C. B. Mohr, 1970.

Verene, Donald, ed. *Hegel's Social and Political Thought.* Atlantic Highlands: Humanities, 1980.

Weiss, Frederick G., ed. *Beyond Epistemology: New Studies in the Philosophy of Hegel.* The Hague: Nijhoff, 1974.

Westphal, Merold. *History and Truth in Hegel's Phenomenology.* 1979: rpt. Atlantic Highlands: Humanities, 1990.

INDEX